RECONSTRUCTING RESPONSE TO STUDENT WRITING

RECONSTRUCTING RESPONSE TO STUDENT WRITING

A National Study from across the Curriculum

DAN MELZER

UTAH STATE UNIVERSITY PRESS
Logan

© 2023 by University Press of Colorado

Published by Utah State University Press
An imprint of University Press of Colorado
1624 Market Street, Suite 226
PMB 39883
Denver, Colorado 80202–1559

 The University Press of Colorado is a proud member of
the Association of University Presses.

The University Press of Colorado is a cooperative publishing enterprise supported,
in part, by Adams State University, Colorado State University, Fort Lewis College,
Metropolitan State University of Denver, University of Alaska Fairbanks, University
of Colorado, University of Denver, University of Northern Colorado, University of
Wyoming, Utah State University, and Western Colorado University.

∞ This paper meets the requirements of the ANSI/NISO Z39.48–1992 (Permanence of
Paper).

ISBN: 978-1-64642-448-1 (hardcover)
ISBN: 978-1-64642-367-5 (paperback)
ISBN: 978-1-64642-368-2 (ebook)
https://doi.org/10.7330/9781646423682

Library of Congress Cataloging-in-Publication Data

Names: Melzer, Dan, author.
Title: Reconstructing response to student writing : a national study from across the curriculum / Dan Melzer.
Other titles: Reconstructing response to college writing
Description: Logan : Utah State University Press, [2023] | Includes bibliographical refer-
  ences and index.
Identifiers: LCCN 2023000214 (print) | LCCN 2023000215 (ebook) | ISBN 9781646423675
  (paperback) | ISBN 9781646424481 (hardcover) | ISBN 9781646423682 (ebook)
Subjects: LCSH: English language—Rhetoric—Study and teaching (Higher) | Report
  writing—Evaluation—Study and teaching (Higher) | Peer teaching. | Students—Self-
  rating of. | Group work in education. | Team learning approach in education.
Classification: LCC PE1404 .M454 2023 (print) | LCC PE1404 (ebook) | DDC
  808/.042071—dc23/eng/20230127
LC record available at https://lccn.loc.gov/2023000214
LC ebook record available at https://lccn.loc.gov/2023000215

This publication was supported, in part, by University of California, Davis.

Cover image © johnwoodcock/istock.

To the memory of my friend and mentor, Dr. Richard Straub.

CONTENTS

ACKNOWLEDGMENTS

I would like to thank two reviewers who had a major impact on the organization and development of this book, Michael Rifenburg and an anonymous reviewer. Their advice regarding my research methods, the scope and organization of each chapter, the presentation of my data and analysis, and attention to diversity and access in response had a transformative effect on the multiple drafts of this book. I would also like to thank Rachael Levay, editor at Utah State University Press, for her smart guidance and advice throughout the process. Finally, I would like to thank my colleagues at the University of California, Davis, Amy Lombardi and DJ Quinn. Their help in analyzing my data led me to new understandings and findings. In addition to these thanks for the helpful feedback I received during the process of drafting and revising the book, I would like to acknowledge the Writing Studies and TESOL scholars whose work on response and self-assessment has influenced my own research and teaching, among them Chris Anson, Kathleen Blake Yancey, David Boud, Lil Brannon, Nancy Falchikov, Dana Ferris, Lynne Goldstein, Brian Huot, Ken and Fiona Hyland, C. H. Knoblauch, and Nancy Sommers.

RECONSTRUCTING RESPONSE TO STUDENT WRITING

1

A NATIONAL STUDY OF RESPONSE TO STUDENT WRITING

When I am writing my papers I usually take into account which target audience will be reading my paper, especially if I am writing for a scholarship or a job. However in a school setting I am not too worried about my audience because the audience is one person, the teacher. Sometimes it's hard writing papers to a new teacher because in the beginning I do not know my teacher very well and it is hard to decide what kind of style of writing to use. However after the first paper I see the comments and then I can kind of get a feel to whom I am writing for.

Excerpt from a first-year writing
student's midterm reflection

The perspective on instructor response described in the student reflection above is an all too familiar one to teachers. Over the course of my college teaching career, I have certainly been guilty of designing response in the narrow, teacher-focused way this student describes. Too often as a writing teacher, I constructed response in my classes as a means to meet what must have felt to students as idiosyncratic criteria I handed down to them in a rubric that was designed in large part to justify a grade on a final draft. I always looked forward to reading my students' drafts, but I wondered if all of the response I was giving my students was worth the effort. Whether it was bringing home a pile of stapled student essays to pore over all weekend in my earliest days of teaching, or trying to find a quiet place to scroll through electronic files of student drafts to insert my supposedly helpful comments later in my career, I wondered if students were paying close attention to my feedback and applying it to future drafts, and if students were able to transfer my suggestions to the writing they were doing in their other courses. I promote language diversity in my assignments, but as a white cis male, I worried about the ways that implicit biases impacted my feedback, and I wondered how my response was received by the diverse student

https://doi.org/10.7330/9781646423682.c001

populations of the institutions where I taught. Even though I tried to get students involved in giving feedback by asking them to respond to each other's drafts, it often felt to me that students viewed peer response as a waste of time, since I was the one who would ultimately be giving them a grade. Response also felt isolated and disembodied. Whether it was returning at the end of class a set of marked-up essays early in my career or emailing students an electronic file with comments later in my career, there was little dialogue, and students were mostly passive recipients of my comments.

I began to ask myself some fundamental questions about the way I was constructing response for my students; questions that I explore in the research reported on in this book. I began to question my own dominant role in response, and I wondered what the research had to say about the role of peer response and student self-assessment. I began to rethink what the focus of response should be, and I began to explore what the alternatives were to focusing on sentences and paragraphs of a rough or final draft. I became curious about what kind of response students were getting from teachers in their other classes. What did teachers across disciplines focus on when they responded, and what were students' perspectives on the feedback they received from their college teachers? When students engaged in peer response or self-assessment, how did their feedback and self-reflections differ from teacher feedback? Were there national trends in the ways teachers across disciplines respond that could help inform my teaching and the advice I gave to teachers in writing across the curriculum (WAC) faculty development workshops?

My interest in exploring response to college writing on a national scale began with a previous large-scale research project—a study of over two thousand college writing assignments from across disciplines that was reported in the book *Assignments across the Curriculum* (2014). In *Assignments across the Curriculum,* I analyzed teachers' evaluation criteria included in their writing assignments and rubrics, but I did not look at student writing and teacher response to student writing. I found that teachers who claimed to value content and critical thinking in their assignment prompts often focused on grammatical and citation style correctness in their assessment rubrics. I found an overall obsession with correctness of form, language, and format in assignment criteria and assessment rubrics. And I found that most teachers played the role of judge, asking for regurgitation of textbook or lecture information in exams. However, I also found that it was common for teachers across disciplines to respond to drafts and to make use of peer response, especially in courses that satisfy a writing-intensive requirement. What

I did not have evidence of in the data reported in *Assignments across the Curriculum* was the extent to which teachers' responses to student writing matched the examiner role they set for themselves in their assignment prompts, or what role students played in peer response. I also did not have evidence of how students responded to the assignments and the comments they received from teachers in the form of student drafts in progress and final drafts.

Reconstructing Response to Student Writing is part 2 of an ongoing research project that aims to provide a national view of college writing in the United States, offering evidence that *Assignments across the Curriculum* lacks and providing a bird's eye view of the other side of the coin of assigning writing—responding to it. In a review of response and assessment research in higher education, Carol Evans (2013) observes that most studies of response "are small scale, single subject, opportunistic, and invited" (77). Understandably, most studies of college teachers' response to student writing focus on a single course or a small number of courses, providing depth but not necessarily breadth. Perhaps this is one reason there have been few book-length studies focused on response. Evans calls for more large-scale response and assessment research, and Writing Studies scholars have begun to answer that call. Recent large-scale studies of response involve corpuses of thousands or even tens of thousands of teacher or peer comments (I. Anson and C. Anson 2017; Dixon and Moxley 2013; Lang 2018; Wärnsby et al. 2018). These researchers analyze big data to discover patterns about teacher and peer commenting on writing that provide a valuable complement to smaller scale studies. However, by focusing solely on written comments, these large-scale studies of response understandably lack context. Recently researchers have called for a greater focus on student perspectives in studies of response (Anson 2012; Edgington 2004; Formo and Stallings 2014; Lee 2014; Zigmond 2012), and large-scale studies lack the important context of the students' perspectives on the feedback they receive from peers and the teacher. Both small- and large-scale studies usually focus on one actor in the response construct (typically the teacher or peers) and one component of response (e.g., comment types, mode of delivery, the impact of feedback on revision). For pragmatic reasons, it is understandable that response researchers would narrow their focus in this way, but this narrowing often results in researchers not being able to capture the complex social contexts of response constructs.

To date no researcher has completed a national study of response to college writing that attempts to include and synthesize the many actors that make up scenes of response, the multiple components of response constructs, and the perspective of the most important actor in response: students. In *Reconstructing Response to Student Writing*, I present the results of a corpus study that aims to provide a panoramic view of response to college writing in the United States while also providing richer contexts than prior large-scale studies of response and a consideration of the multiple factors and actors that make up response constructs. My corpus includes teacher and peer responses to over one thousand rough and final drafts of student writing as well as student reflection on response and self-assessment of their writing from first-year writing courses and courses across the college curriculum. In addition to reporting on my analysis of tens of thousands of teacher and peer comments, I consider the impact of these comments on students' drafts. Most importantly, throughout *Reconstructing Response to Student Writing* I provide students' perspectives on teacher and peer comments and students' own self-assessment of their writing. I also introduce a heuristic that takes into account the varied factors that should be considered when research-ing response and when designing response constructs. The heuristic is aligned with recent response research, which draws primarily on social-epistemic theories of literacy and learning.

CONSTRUCTIVIST RESPONSE RESEARCH

Constructivism emphasizes both the social context of learning and the learner's central role in the creation of knowledge. A constructivist approach to response takes into account the prominence of social-epistemic theories in recent response research (Anderson 1998; Askew and Lodge 2000; Crook 2022; Evans 2013; K. Hyland and F. Hyland 2019; Molloy and Boud 2014; Price and O'Donovan 2006; Siczek 2020; Villamil and de Guerrero 2020), the growing body of knowledge on student self-reflection and self-assessment (Boud 1995; Falchikov 2005; Yancey 1998b), and recent research on transfer and writing (Anson and Moore 2016; Moore and Bass 2017; Yancey et al. 2014). Constructivist response considers the entire social construct of responding: the student, teacher, class, assignment genre, discipline, and sociocultural and sociopolitical contexts. Constructivist response encourages social interaction and dialogue rather than response as a one-way transmission from teacher to student.

In a constructivist model of response, each factor of the response construct affects the others. For example, the common practice in English as a Second Language (ESL) courses of dynamic written corrective feedback improves students' ability to correct sentence-level errors, but it may also reinforce students' perceptions that good writing is merely correct writing. Assignment genre choices will ultimately affect the teacher's approach in responding, depending, for example, on whether the genre assigned has strict or flexible writing conventions. Changing the mode of response and moving peer response from face-to-face in the classroom to an online forum will affect students' orientation to peer response, depending on students' comfort with the technology, their preferences regarding face-to-face versus digital feedback, the type of technology used, and so on.

Constructivist response emphasizes the learner's central role in constructing response, including student self-assessment and peer response. In this way, the research on self-reflection and transfer is relevant to constructivist response. The Writing Studies scholarship on transfer has emphasized writing and reading assignment design (Adler-Kassner et al. 2012; Anson and Moore 2016; Beaufort 2007; Carillo 2014; Downs and Robertson 2015; Moore and Bass 2017; Wardle 2009; Yancey et al. 2014; Yancey et al. 2018; Yancey at al. 2019), but perhaps because this research has focused mostly on designing curriculum, the transfer scholarship has not delved into the role of responding in writing transfer. The Teaching for Transfer literature has had little to say about responding for transfer. International literature on response does explore the concept of *feedforward*, but this concept has tended to focus on response that can be applied by the student to the next assignment within a course, rather than response aimed at more far-reaching transfer (Carless 2006; Duncan 2007; Martini and DiBattista 2014; Orsmond and Merry 2011; Pokorny and Pickford 2010; Vardi 2012).

Influential models of response, such as Brian Huot's (2002) Theory of Response in his seminal book *(Re)Articulating Writing Assessment for Teaching and Learning*, and Lynne Goldstein's (2005) response model in *Teacher Written Commentary in Second Language Writing Classrooms*, frame response as a dialogue between teacher and student but do not put student self-assessment at the center of the response construct. Goldstein argues that the key to response "is the effectiveness of the commentary provided and the quality of the communication between teachers and students about the students' revisions" (4). Huot encourages teachers to involve students in all stages of the evaluation of their work in a process he refers to as "instructive evaluation" (69). But Huot's chapter focused on building a theory of response emphasizes the central role of the teacher as responder, even as Huot argues that the teacher must remain in dialogue with the student. Thanks in large part to the scholarship of David Boud and Nancy Falchikov, self-assessment and self-reflection

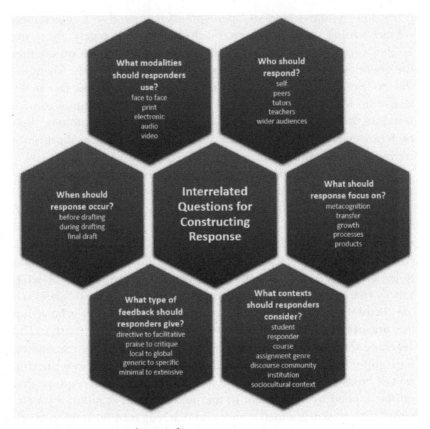

Figure 1.1. A constructivist heuristic for response.

have been more integral to recent research on response and assessment in international scholarship. Self-assessment is integrated in John Hattie and Helen Timperley's (2007) Model of Feedback to Enhance Learning, and student self-assessment is central to Charles Juwah and coauthors' (2004) Model of Formative Assessment and Feedback.

As a tool for researchers to capture the social and cognitive contexts of response and for teachers across the curriculum to design more sophisticated response constructs that invite students to play a more central role in their own learning and assessment, I introduce a constructivist response heuristic (figure 1.1). The heuristic is built around fundamental questions that researchers can ask in studying response and that teachers can ask in constructing response for their classes. The heuristic distills, organizes, and synthesizes fifty years of empirical research on response in Writing Studies and Teaching English to Speakers of Other Languages (TESOL). Additionally, the heuristic organizes my analysis of the data in my corpus. Because the heuristic is informed by constructivist educational theory and research in response that points to the value of peer response and student self-assessment, the heuristic involves a conceptual reframing of response research and shifts the focus of researching response and of designing response constructs from teachers to students. In answering the questions who should respond, what should response focus on, and what contexts should be considered when responding, the heuristic emphasizes the student: student self-assessment, students' literacy histories, and students' ability to transfer knowledge to future writing contexts. The heuristic consists of six interrelated questions researchers can consider when studying response.

The heuristic is informed by the results of my national study of response to college writing and a comprehensive review of the literature on teacher and peer response and student self-assessment, including research from Writing Studies, English as a Second Language/ English as a Foreign Language (ESL/EFL), Writing across the Curriculum (WAC), and international scholarship published in English. I discuss my approach to both my primary and secondary research in more detail in the following section.

THE RESEARCH DESIGN

Data Collection

When I set out to study response to college writing, I did not want to solicit responses directly from teachers, in the fear that they would share only what they considered to be their best comments. I also wanted richer data than just teacher comments, and I especially wanted to include student voices, which were missing from *Assignments across the Curriculum* and from much response research. At the time that I was considering a project on response, feedback to student writing was not accessible online in the same way I was easily able to collect a large corpus of writing assignments via Internet searches for my research in *Assignments across the Curriculum*. I postponed the project on response and spent the next few years collaborating with colleagues on a different project focused on a methodology for developing sustainable WAC programs. When that project was completed, I revisited my idea of a national study of response, and by this time—2018—I discovered that it was possible to collect a large corpus of response via the Internet. The key was to focus my search on ePortfolios.

Portfolio assessment is a pedagogical approach that involves students collecting their work for the class in a portfolio and the teacher typically assessing the compiled portfolio rather than individual assignments. Contents included in a portfolio of student work vary, but most portfolios include rough and final drafts of student writing and a culminating self-reflection memo/letter/essay (Calfee and Perfumo 1996; Yancey 1996, 2009; Yancey and Weiser 1997). Portfolio reflection essays have been of special interest to researchers focused on student self-assessment of their writing (Bower 2003; Emmons 2003; Yancey 1998b). ePortfolios have become popular in first-year writing courses and are becoming more common in courses across disciplines and as a tool for students to collect and reflect on their work throughout their academic career, thanks in part to the availability of robust ePortfolio platforms such as Digication and Mahara. Through Internet key term searches such as "teacher comments," "peer feedback," and "reflection essay" combined with the term "portfolio," I was able to locate student ePortfolios that collect work from individual courses as well as institutional portfolios that gather work from students' entire undergraduate careers. Most of the ePortfolios I collected include multiple artifacts of both peer and teacher feedback as well as student self-assessment in the form of process memos and portfolio reflection essays. Common platforms students used to create the ePortfolios in my corpus include Digication, WordPress, and Weebly. Because there were few ePortfolios available published in courses outside of the United States, and because I considered this study to be the second part of the work I began with a study of writing assignment in US institutions of higher education, I focused only on courses at US institutions.

Carol Rutz (2004) argues that "piles of student papers may bear thousands of fascinating teacher comments, but at least half of the story remains untold as long as student writers are not part of the conversation" (122). I was especially interested in studying how students react to response from their teachers and peers, and what I found to be extremely useful qualitative data available in the ePortfolios were the many cases in which students reflect on teacher and peer responses and on their own writing processes in process memos, introductions to portfolios and to individual web pages, midterm reflections, and final portfolio reflection essays. Most of the portfolios in my corpus contain at least some student reflection on peer and teacher comments, and a little over half of the portfolios (128) include extended portfolio reflection essays that reference peer and/or teacher feedback. Throughout *Reconstructing Response to Student Writing*, student voices are predominant.

In 2018 and 2019, I searched online for as many ePortfolios that included response as I could locate. I was able to collect 240 portfolios

Table 1.1. Overview of corpus

Total number of portfolios	240
Total number of artifacts of student writing with teacher or peer response	1,054 635 teacher responses • 442 responses to drafts in progress • 193 responses to final drafts 419 peer responses
Distribution of teacher responses	70% from first-year composition 30% from courses in the disciplines
Total number of student self-reflection essays	128
Total number of institutions	70

and formative and summative responses to 1,054 pieces of student writing (635 teacher responses and 419 peer responses) as well as 128 student self-reflection essays. The portfolios represent first-year writing courses and courses from across disciplines at 70 institutions of higher education across the United States (see appendix for a list of the institutions). The portfolios are primarily from individual courses, but a handful are undergraduate career portfolios. Seventy percent of the teacher responses are from first-year writing courses, and 30 percent are from courses across disciplines. This reflects the greater availability of ePortfolios from first-year writing courses and not any intent on my part to have a larger representation from first-year writing courses. Approximately 25 percent of the teacher responses are final drafts of student writing (n=193), with the rest being drafts in progress. The corpus includes a broad range of genres: literacy narratives, research articles, business memos and reports, film reviews, white papers, literature reviews, and so on. Table 1.1 provides an overview of my corpus.

I submitted an IRB protocol to my institution and the project was given "not human subjects" status by an administrative review. In a discussion of issues of consent in corpus studies using Internet data, Tao and coauthors (2017) argue that accessibility of online research sites is an important determinant in whether informed consent is required (11). The data in my corpus meets the United States Department of Health and Human Services definition of public behavior archived on public web sites where authors do not have expectations of privacy (Office for Human Research Protections 2018). All of the artifacts I collected were existing data, publicly archived on the Internet without password protection. The students who published these portfolios knew their work was going to be publicly available on the Internet, and most of the portfolios include a welcome page in which the students introduce themselves to a potential broader readership beyond the course and welcome readers to their website. An additional ethical issue in online research that Tao and coauthors (2017) discuss is the sensitivity of the topic being researched. I do not criticize the students or their writing in my research but rather provide examples primarily of the benefits of giving students a greater role in the response construct.

Though the data in my corpus is public and not focused on a sensitive topic, as Tao and coauthors (2017) point out, even Internet research focused on public data that is not classified by an institution's Institutional Review Board (IRB) as human subjects status is on a continuum between private and public (13). Although they are not private or password protected, the ePortfolios in my corpus were published to meet a course requirement. Students using Digication might have had the option of choosing password protection or publishing for solely an institutional audience, whereas students using Google Sites or Weebly or WordPress did not have a privacy option. In the interest of protecting the privacy of the students and teachers, I anonymized all of the data, and I do not identify students, teachers, or writing center tutors by name or institution. In some portfolios students display graded work, which is technically a violation of the Family Educational Rights and Privacy Act (FERPA), and I did not include in my examples shared in this book rough or final drafts that are graded.

Data Analysis

As I was collecting responses from ePortfolios, I also began reviewing the literature on response. Given the scope of my data, my constructivist theoretical framework, and my desire to design a heuristic that fully engages the response construct, I made the decision to conduct a comprehensive review of the literature on teacher and peer response to college writing and college students' self-assessment of their writing that had been published since the early 1980s—the first wave of empirical scholarship on response in Writing Studies that was ushered in by the work of Nancy Sommers and the research team of Lil Brannon and C. H. Knoblauch. Another motivating factor in undertaking a comprehensive review of the literature was that I knew of no other review of response literature that attempted to (a) synthesize the findings of not just the literature on teacher response but also peer response and student self-assessment of college writing; (b) integrate research and theory from Writing Studies, WAC, and ESL/EFL scholarship; and (c) include a comprehensive overview of both US and international literature on response to college writing published in English. Never far from my thoughts as I researched and wrote this book was the memory of one of my mentors when I was in graduate school, Richard Straub, who always encouraged me to be comprehensive in my thinking and my research-ing, and whose work on response has strongly influenced my perspective and the perspectives of Writing Studies teachers and scholars. Because my research corpus consists of college-level writing, I did limit the scope of my literature review to research on undergraduate college writing. I began by developing a heuristic based on predominant themes and areas of focus of the response literature. When I applied the heuristic to my corpus, I found that my analysis of my data caused me to revise my initial heuristic. Namely, the amount of student self-assessment and self-reflection on transfer of writing in my corpus, and the ways that my own pedagogy was shifting based on the evidence of the quality of self-assessment in my research, caused me to integrate metacognition and transfer more prominently into subsequent drafts of the heuristic.

My process of analyzing the data consisted of three cycles. In the first cycle, I read the portfolio artifacts quickly, noting in a spreadsheet the extent to which they connected to or differed from the components of my heuristic of themes from the literature. In the second cycle, I read the artifacts more closely, noting both representative and dis-crepant example comments and making brief analytic memos in the spreadsheet. In this second cycle, I revised the heuristic so that it had a greater focus on metacognition and transfer, based on the patterns I noted in the corpus. In order to peer check the reliability of my analysis and to check my own reliability over time, six months after complet-ing my analysis of the data I engaged in a third cycle of analysis and shared a random sample of twenty portfolios with two graduate students who were at the time pursuing a PhD in Education at the University of California, Davis, Amy Lombardi and DJ Quinn. I gave Lombardi and Quinn a stipend to participate in a three-hour reliability "sense-checking" (Creswell 2009, 192) activity in which I asked them to check the validity of my findings by reading a proportional stratified sample of ten portfolios each (seven first-year writing portfolios and three WAC course portfolios randomized within each stratum, for a total of 170 pieces of student writing responded to by peers or the teacher). During this activity, I reread all twenty portfolios. We then did a thirty-minute peer debriefing and discussed the extent to which Lombardi and Quinn perceived the themes from the literature and the questions in my heuris-tic matched the data. They felt my heuristic accounted for response con-structs in the corpus and they were in broad agreement with my analysis of the data in relation to the themes from the literature, although they noted additional discrepant examples and also pointed out additional findings of interest.

Although I used my heuristic to categorize qualitative patterns in my corpus, I made a conscious choice not to create a taxonomy of types of response and code discrete comments. The evolution of research on response is a gradual movement away from focusing solely on analyzing teacher comments and toward incorporating ethnographic methods and considering student writing and student reflections after receiving response. Earlier research—and some current studies—are focused on creating taxonomies for coding and assessing teacher response. However, Ferris (2003) warns that "counting schemes . . . may not capture the complexities of revision" (36), and other prominent response scholars have emphasized that coding and interpreting teacher comments in isolation is reductive (Fife and O'Neill 2001; Knoblauch and Brannon 1981; Newkirk 1984; Phelps 2000). In light of my constructivist framework, and because I did not have the benefit of being able to member check coded responses with the teachers and students in my research, I elected to focus on broader qualitative patterns within my heuristic rather than use a taxonomy to code discrete comments or student revisions. In this qualitative and constructivist methodology, "labelling is done to manage data rather than to facilitate enumeration" (Spencer et al. 2014, 278). As Creswell (2013) notes, quantitative coding may not always work in a qualitative and constructivist research project, as "counting conveys a quantitative orientation of magnitude and frequency contrary to qualitative research" (185). However, I do attempt to provide enough qualitative evidence from the ePortfolios to establish the patterns in my corpus and their connection to the themes from the literature and the components of my heuristic. This evidence includes teacher and peer response, excerpts from drafts of student writing, and student self-assessment.

In my focus on student reflections on the responses they receive from teachers and peers, I hope to begin to address, on a large scale, the call for more response research that considers students' perspectives. This call for more student voices is ubiquitous in recent response research. Lee (2014) asserts that "research that explores students' role in evaluating their peers' writing and in self-monitoring of their own learning is much needed to add new knowledge to the current research base on feedback in writing" (1). Chris Anson (2012) calls for research that answers the question, "What do students *do* with teachers' responses to their writing? How do they read and interpret those responses, and with what subsequent effects on their improvement as writers?" (192). Edgington (2004) expresses concern that "the focus on response has continued to be on teachers and the comments they write. Few scholars have focused their studies on how students react to responses" (287), a concern shared by Formo and Stallings (2014), who argue, "We have not studied the writer as solicitor of feedback" (48). Zigmond (2012) echoes these concerns about the lack of student voice in response research: "Most research in writing response theory examines the different types of comments that teachers write but falls short of understanding students' perceptions of those comments" (112). My research builds on the limited number of response studies that focus attention on student perspectives on response. Teacher comments are an important component of my study, but whenever possible I consider these comments in the context of student reflections on teacher comments.

Limitations of the Study

I believe the large scale of my data, the amount of student self-reflection on response that is included in most of the ePortfolios I collected, and the fact that my data is unsolicited are strengths of this study. The limitations of the research are in many respects similar to the limitations of the research I conducted in *Assignments across the Curriculum*. Despite the size of my corpus, I certainly cannot generalize from my data to all of college response to writing in the United States. This is especially true given that my corpus includes more than twice as many ePortfolios from first-year writing courses than courses in the disciplines. In *Assignments across the Curriculum* I noted strong patterns in the over two thousand writing assignments, and I argued that these patterns provided broader insight into college writing than smaller scale studies. I believe the same is true for *Reconstructing Response to Student Writing.* Although some of the responses in my corpus are from undergraduate career portfolios that students assembled themselves, the majority of the portfolios are from courses in which the teacher required ePortfolios and asked students to include rough drafts, peer response, and artifacts of self-reflection. The fact that most of the responses in my research are from teachers who have adopted portfolio pedagogy and writing as a social process further limits my corpus from being representative of college response as a whole.

A study of over a thousand responses, hundreds of student self-reflections, and tens of thousands of comments cannot include the level of context of smaller-scale, ethnographic research. As was true of *Assignments across the Curriculum,* I do not have data from interviews with students or teachers or observations of classes. In this respect, my research is similar to other large-scale studies of response, including Connors and Lunsford's (1988, 1993) studies of comments in 3,000 essays solicited from writing teachers across the United States, Dixon and Moxley's (2013) analysis of 118,611 writing teachers' comments on 17,433 essays at one institution, Ian Anson and Chris Anson's (2017) lexically based index of 50,000 first-year writing students' peer response comments at one institution, Lang's (2018) analysis of five years of first-year writing TA comments on 17,534 pieces of student writing at one institution, and an analysis by Wärnsby and coauthors (2018) of 50,000 peer reviews at three institutions. As was true for these researchers, I did not have access to teachers to ask them what the intent behind their comments was, or what theory of response informed their feedback practices. It is certain that the teachers in my corpus responded to students in ways that I could not capture using my research methods: for example, in class discussions, office hours, conferences with students, and so on. It is also highly likely that there were teacher responses that students chose not to include in their ePortfolios, or that came after they had completed their ePortfolios. I did not observe any of the courses in my research, and I cannot connect peer and teacher responses to classroom conversations, except to the extent that classroom contexts were discussed in student reflections. Because of this, I try to avoid speculating on teachers' intentions as I analyze their comments, and I focus instead on student uptake of teacher and peer response, since unlike prior large-scale response studies, I do have students' testimonies in the form of portfolio reflection essays, process memos, metacommentary directly on responses, and introductory statements on web pages.

It is not my intention in *Assignments across the Curriculum* and *Reconstructing Response to Student Writing* to provide an in-depth look at the writing assignments and responses of individual teachers, courses, or institutions. Rather, my goal in these two books is to zoom out and provide a panoramic view of college writing and responding in the United States. I consider my work in these two books to be a compliment to ethnographic research into college writing, helping to sketch a large-scale picture of writing and response across the college curriculum at a variety of types of institutions across the country. If my work as a researcher is taken as a two-part investigation of college writing, over the last decade I have analyzed over 2,000 writing assignments and over 1,000 responses to student writing at 170 institutions of higher education. Throughout this book, I consider my findings regarding response in the context of my prior research on college writing in order to present a comprehensive perspective on writing and responding in higher education in the United States. I end this book with a postscript in which I reflect on what I have learned studying college writing and responding on a national scale and offer advice for composition teachers, faculty in the disciplines, writing center tutors, writing program administrators, and upper-level administrators regarding teaching writing, responding to writing, and designing impactful writing programs.

OUTLINE OF THE BOOK

Chapter 2, "A Constructivist Heuristic for Response," explores the theory and research behind each question included in my constructivist heuristic for response. This review includes research from Writing Studies, ESL/EFL, WAC, and international scholarship published in English. The literature review I undertook for *Reconstructing Response to Student Writing* includes over 1,300 books and articles on the topics of teacher and peer response to college writing and student self-assessment of their writing. My constructivist heuristic is both a tool for researchers to take an expansive approach to studying response and a conceptual reframing of response research that encourages scholars to shift their attention from the role of teachers to the role of students in response constructs. This shift will encourage researchers to include peer response and student self-assessment in studies of classroom response, and it will benefit teachers and students by giving students a more central role in the response construct.

In chapter 3, "Teacher Response to Writing," I discuss patterns in the 635 teacher responses to student writing in my research. My constructivist heuristic for response serves as an organizing device for the chapter. Because my data includes student reflections on teacher response, I discuss how students react to the responses provided by their teachers on rough and final drafts. The data reinforces prior research that shows that teachers construct their responses in limited ways and often focus on correctness, but my research also shows that teachers are quick to praise student writing. My research reveals that teachers connect their responses to the genres they are assigning, but there is a lack of teacher comments that can be applied to students' future writing contexts. In chapter 3 I highlight the extent to which the teacher as evaluator dominates students' thinking about writing and revision, with many students expressing their desire to achieve a good grade and please the teacher rather than seeing teacher response as an opportunity for growth and learning.

Chapter 4, "Peer Response to Writing," focuses on patterns in the 419 peer responses to student writing in my research. As with chapters 2 and 3, my constructivist heuristic for response serves as an organizing device. Because my data includes student reflections on peer response, I discuss how students react to their peers' comments on their drafts. The data supports prior research that shows that with scaffolding and guidance, students can respond effectively to their peers' writing. In chapter 4, I push this concept further than most prior researchers who have investigated peer response, and I argue that the peer response in my study is just as effective, and often more effective, than the teacher response.

In chapter 5, "Students' Self-Assessment of Their Writing," I present patterns regarding student self-assessment of their writing in the 128 portfolio reflection essays in my corpus, with the heuristic once again acting as an organizing device. Most of these essays are extensive and detailed, and they are supplemented by other forms of reflective writing in many of the ePortfolios, such as process memos and revision plans included with drafts. Chapter 5 presents evidence that not only are students capable of effectively assessing their own writing but they are often as insightful as teachers. I emphasize that students express a desire for response that they can apply to future writing contexts, and that they are thoughtful about reflecting on issues of growth and transfer when they assess themselves as writers.

In chapter 6, "Reconstructing Response," I review the major findings of the study, consider the implications of my findings, and suggest future areas for research in response. Chapter 6 reminds readers of the ways my research builds on, expands, and sometimes contradicts the prior research on response that I synthesize in chapter 2. In chapter 6, I suggest future directions in response research, with an emphasis on research that examines the full response construct and that considers aspects of response that were prominent in my study but have been less prominent in prior research, including response and transfer; the role of grades in student uptake of response; and the importance of socially constructed elements of response such as genre conventions, discourse community, and student and teacher sociocultural contexts. I make the argument that the future of response should mark a shift from an emphasis on teacher as primary responder and rough and final drafts as the focus of response to student self-assessment as the primary form of response and artifacts of self-assessment, such as portfolio reflection essays, as the primary focus of teacher response. Chapter 6 expands the purpose of my constructivist heuristic for response from a tool for response researchers to a pedagogical tool to aid faculty across disciplines in designing more effective and more expansive response constructs.

In the postscript, "Reflections on Two Decades of Researching College Writing and Responding," I provide final reflections on college writing and responding based on my research in *Assignments across the Curriculum* and *Reconstructing Response to Student Writing*, which taken together represent an analysis of over 2,000 writing assignments and over 1,000 responses to student writing at 170 institutions of higher education. I consider the implications of my research into college writing and responding for teachers, writing center tutors, writing program administrators, and upper-level administrators.

2

A CONSTRUCTIVIST
HEURISTIC FOR RESPONSE

This chapter describes the components of the constructivist heuristic for response to writing that I developed as a tool to analyze the data in my corpus of teacher and peer response and student self-assessment artifacts from ePortfolios across the college curriculum. The heuristic, which I introduced in chapter 1 (see figure 1.1), can be used by researchers as a means to consider the full range of actors, contexts, and components of response constructs when conducting studies of response to writing, and it can be used by teachers in any discipline to design response in their courses. The heuristic is organized around fundamental questions that researchers and teachers can ask themselves as they study response or design response in their classes. With the heuristic I aim to accomplish a variety of purposes in relation to the literature on response: to organize, distill, and synthesize what we know about response from empirical research in Writing Studies, ESL/EFL, WAC, and international scholarship published in English; to address gaps in the literature on response by highlighting related research on writing transfer and student self-assessment; and to encourage future researchers investigating response and teachers designing the response construct in their courses to shift their focus of attention from teacher response to peer response and student self-assessment.

To develop the heuristic, I used a snowballing research technique, reading all of the relevant research cited in each reference section of books and articles I located through library database searching. This resulted in a review of over 1,300 books and articles on teacher and peer response to writing and student self-assessment of their writing that focus on undergraduate postsecondary education. Ferris (2003) as well as Biber and coauthors (2011) note that results from empirical studies of response must be viewed in the context of the quality and robustness of the research design of each study, and to begin to address this concern I make it clear where the research points to definitive findings from

https://doi.org/10.7330/9781646423682.c002

multiple, well-received studies and where the research is mixed and inconclusive. My comprehensive, snowballing approach to reviewing the literature on response helped me gain perspective on which research was the most highly cited, which areas of research have been neglected, and which areas of research are emerging.

The research that shapes my heuristic dates back to the initial empirical scholarship on response in Writing Studies that began with the work of Nancy Sommers, Lil Brannon, and C. H. Knoblauch in the 1980s. Empirical research on response in the 1980s focused on teacher comments, and in the following decades the focus of response research expanded to include considerations of peer response and analysis of richer contextual data than just teacher comments, including information from interviews with teachers and students and analysis of drafts of student writing. Recent response research is influenced by the social turn in the study of writing, with researchers drawing on socio-epistemic theories of writing and responding to frame their research questions and designs (Anderson 1998; Askew and Lodge 2000; Crook 2022, Evans 2013; Price and O'Donovan 2006; Villamil and de Guerrero 2020). I draw on social constructivism in the design of my response heuristic, and I consider the entire social construct of responding: the student, teacher, course, assignment genre, discipline, and sociocultural context. I aim to both capture important areas of research in response and reframe response research using a constructivist lens. A number of areas of my heuristic overlap with themes noted by Stephanie Crook (2022) in an article in which she reviews the literature on response from a social-constructionist lens, "A Social-Constructionist Review of Feedback and Revision Research." *Reconstructing Response* was in the final editing process when Crook's article appeared in *College Composition and Communication.*

A constructivist approach to research in response takes into consideration the roles of the student author, peers, writing center tutors, teacher, and potential responders outside the classroom, such as writing center tutors, friends, and family. Constructivist research in response investigates the role of genre and discourse community in shaping response as well as the personal and social contexts of the student and teacher. Constructivism emphasizes the central role of the learner in the creation of knowledge and the value of self-regulation. My heuristic emphasizes students' role in the response construct by focusing on self-assessment, peer response, and the students' personal and social contexts.

This chapter is organized around the six questions that make up the heuristic:

1. Who should respond? (self, peers, tutors, teachers, wider audiences)
2. What should response focus on? (metacognition, transfer, growth, processes, products)
3. What contexts should responders consider? (student, responder, course, assignment genre, discourse community, institution, sociocultural context)
4. What type of feedback should responders give? (directive to facilitative, praise to critique, local to global, generic to specific, minimal to extensive)
5. When should response occur? (before drafting, during drafting, final draft)
6. What modalities should responders use? (face-to-face, print, electronic, audio, video)

As I synthesize prior research on response to explore each question in my heuristic, I point to definitive findings, highlight gaps in the response research, and reframe the literature to encourage a constructivist shift in our research emphasis: from teachers to students, from grading to self-assessment, and from rough and final drafts of discrete writing genres to far reaching transfer and growth.

WHO SHOULD RESPOND?
Self

Most models of response to writing emphasize the teacher/student dyad as central to response (Beaumont et al. 2011; Evans 2011; Goldstein 2005; Huot 2002; Phelps 2000; Rae and Cochrane 2008). The exception to this is a handful of models of assessment and feedback from international scholars that make student self-assessment central (Hattie and Timperley 2007; Juwah et al. 2004). Nicol and Macfarlane-Dick (2006) argue that "conceptions of assessment have lagged behind conceptions of learning in higher education. While students have been given more responsibility for learning in recent years, there has been far greater reluctance to give them increased responsibility for assessment processes (even low-stakes formative processes)" (215). In considering the question, "Who should respond?" my response heuristic addresses this lag between theory and practice, and in my heuristic I encourage researchers and teachers to begin to address the question of who should respond to student writing with the students themselves. In Andrade and Evans's (2013) conception of response and assessment, "Students occupy a central and active role in all feedback processes, including and especially monitoring and regulating their progress toward desired goals and evaluating the efficacy of the strategies used to reach those goals" (21). In a stronger assertion—and one that aligns with a constructivist framework for researching response—Probst (1989) asserts, "The responsibility for making judgments about the quality of their work must become the students'" (76).

The most prominent voices in the scholarship on student self-assessment and writing, David Boud, Nancy Falchikov, and Kathleen Yancey, define self-assessment in similar ways. In *Enhancing Learning through Self-Assessment*, Boud (1995) outlines features of effective self-assessment tasks: deep learning, consideration of evaluative criteria, taking into account student's goals and experiences, and synthesizing learning and thinking about future applications (35). Boud (1991) emphasizes students playing a role in shaping evaluative criteria, arguing that self-assessment should include "the involvement of students in identifying standards and/or criteria to apply to their work and making judgments about the extent to which they have met these criteria and standards" (159). Falchikov also emphasizes the centrality of student judgements in feedback and assessment. Falchikov's (2005) definition of self-assessment in the Self-assessment in Professional and Higher Education project helps us further consider the different possible dimensions of self-assessment:

- a way for students to become involved in assessing their own development and learning
- a way of introducing students to the concept of individual judgment
- involving the students in dialogue with teachers and peers
- involving individual reflection about what constitutes good work
- requiring learners to think about what they have learned so far, identifying gaps and ways in which these can be filled and take steps toward remediation. (120)

Kathleen Yancey's work is focused on reflection, and as Brew (1999) notes, "All self-assessment involves reflection, but not all reflection leads to self-assessment" (160). However, I discuss Yancey's work alongside Boud's and Falchikov's because Yancey's conceptions of self-reflection typically involve the kind of evaluation and judgment that is associated with self-assessment. Like Boud and Falchikov, Yancey emphasizes students setting goals, revising based on retrospective judgment, and considering future steps. She argues that reflection includes "processes of projection, retrospection (or review), and revision" (1996, 85). Yancey (1998b) describes reflection as:

1. goal-setting, revisiting, and refining
2. text-revising in the light of retrospection
3. the articulation of what learning has taken place, as embodied in various texts as well as in the processes used by the writer (6)

Like Boud, Yancey emphasizes the connections between self-reflection and growth and transfer. Yancey (1998b) writes that the self-reflection encouraged by portfolio assessment can "help writers think about and articulate their response to their own writing and to see it longitudinally, to see it as the story of their development as thinkers and writers, as creators and composers" (104). Yancey (2016) cautions us not to view this development as merely assimilation to academic discourse norms. She argues for a conception of reflection that is both individual and social and engages with cultural contexts in a process of not just replicating the university but reinventing it (10–11). A constructivist framework for self-reflection focuses on the sociopolitical factors that impact student reflection.

Researchers have found that students are fully capable of self-assessment as writers (Thorpe 2000; Tolar Collins 2000), and that self-assessment improves student writing performance (Pope 2005; Ziegler and Moeller 2012) and leads to increased higher-order thinking in their writing (Lo 2010; Thompson et al. 2005). Recent research on the relationships among writing, metacognition, and transfer has shown that self-assessment increases the likelihood students will transfer rhetorical knowledge and skills to future writing contexts (Beaufort 2007; Dively and Nelms 2007; Downs and Wardle 2007; Mikulecky et al. 1994; Yancey et al. 2014). As Hilgers and coauthors (2000) argue, to be effective, self-assessment needs to be systematic, frequent, integrated, and guided (6). Self-assessment is a growing area of interest in response research, and the value of assigning students a central role in response has been validated by empirical studies. In my constructivist heuristic, the answer to the question, "Who should respond to student writing?" begins with the student, through both self-assessment and peer response.

Peers

If students are at the center of researching and designing the response construct in a constructivist conception of response, peer response is second only to student self-assessment as an area of focus for response research. Researchers studying peer response have found that in most cases peer response is not only just as effective as teacher response but *more* effective than teacher response. One of the most important findings of the research on peer response is that in studies where students received substantial training for responding to their peers, where the teacher provided a thoughtfully designed peer response script to students, and where students received responses from more than one peer,

peer response was similar to teacher response, and often more useful than teacher response.

There are multiple examples of empirical studies from WAC researchers who have found that peer and teacher comments are similar in courses across disciplines. Patchan and coauthors (2009) studied peer and teacher response in a large history course and found that students using the Scaffolded Writing and Rewriting in the Discipline (SWoRD) rubric-based system for peer response gave feedback that was "quantitatively and qualitatively similar to teacher feedback" (139). In a study of a large undergraduate engineering course, Hamer and coauthors (2015) also found that students give similar feedback to teachers. Beason (1993) studied peer and teacher comments in four WAC courses and found that 90 percent of the teachers' concerns in their comments were addressed in student comments (413).

In ESL/EFL courses, where there might be an expectation that teacher response would lead to more significant revisions than response from peers who are language learners, researchers have found that, with the exception of courses made up of beginning English language learners, peer response is nearly equivalent to and sometimes even more helpful than teacher response. Yang and coauthors (2006) compared a group of students in an EFL course at a Chinese university who received feedback from the teacher and a group who received feedback from peers and found that the peer feedback group made more comments that led to changes in meaning. Similar to Yang and coauthors' findings, in a study of thirty-nine University of Hawaii ESL students and thirteen teachers, Devenney (1989) found that teachers were much more likely to focus on grammar, and that "there was a greater tendency for teachers to respond to a paper as a 'finished' piece of writing; whereas students responded to papers as 'works in progress'" (86). Devenney found that student comments were similar to teacher comments in tone and substance. In a self-study of an ESL course in Germany, Caulk (1994) noted that 40 percent of teacher comments were reinforced in peer response papers that received responses from at least three students. In a study of seventy-five ESL college students in Korea, Choi (2013) found that peer response was far more positive than teacher response, although students struggled to respond to sentence-level issues, a finding that was also true for N. Diab (2010), Ruegg (2015), and Wang (2014). Peer response implemented with adequate training has also been shown by the research to be a highly effective pedagogy in nonsheltered first-year writing courses (N. Diab 2011; McGroarty and Zhu 1997; Tannacito and Tuzi 2002; Zhu 1994).

Perhaps the most important benefit of peer response is its connection to student self-reflection: giving feedback to peers helps students improve their own writing. Nicol and coauthors (2014) noted that 68 percent of students in an engineering design course reported that participating in peer response "resulted in their reflecting back on their own work and/or in their transferring ideas generated through the reviewing process to inform that work" (111), a result that Purchase (2000) also found in the implementation of peer response in a large engineering course. In a study of nine intensive English writing courses and 91 students, Lundstrom and Baker (2009) found that students who only gave peer feedback made more significant gains in their writing than students who only received peer feedback. Ballantyne and coauthors (2002) collected a questionnaire about peer response from 939 students, and the students reported that "peer assessment was an awareness-raising exercise because it made them consider their own work more closely" and "helped them make a realistic assessment of their own abilities" (434). Students also appreciated "viewing others' work and having the opportunity to see how others had approached the assessment task (mentioned by 50% of respondents)" (434).

Even though studies of both mainstreamed students and sheltered language learners have found that students appreciate and benefit from peer response, the ESL/EFL research does mention some specific considerations for peer response and language learners. English language learners in sheltered courses may be skeptical of the value of peer feedback and may value teacher feedback far more than peer feedback (Amores 1997; Berger 1990; Leki 1990; Nelson and Murphy 1992; Paulus 1999; Saito 1994; Tsui and Ng 2000; Zhang 1995). Studies indicate that writers who have less experience with English are less likely to make substantial revisions based on response from peers (Allen and Mills 2016; Van Steendam et al. 2010) and need more training and direction in order to be able to make useful comments on the content of their peers' writing (Guardado and Shi 2007). Some Non-Native English Speakers (NNES) from collectivist cultures may be focused on group harmony and therefore less comfortable giving constructive criticism (Carson and Nelson 1996; Hu 2005; Nelson 1997; Nelson and Carson 1995; Nelson and Murphy 1992), although in some studies that involved substantial training and scaffolding this collectivist mindset was not a barrier to providing useful suggestions for revisions and had a positive rather than negative effect (Kamimura 2006; Yang et al. 2006).

The issue of training is a key consideration when synthesizing the results of the research on peer response. There are some empirical studies that have shown students do not find peer response helpful and that feedback from peers does not result in substantial revision. However, the one feature that most of the research studies that found less-positive effects of peer response have in common is that they involve a peer response treatment without any, or with very little, training. Covill (2010) found that peer response had a minimal effect on 61 students in a psychology course, but Covill acknowledges that "for peer review to support significant improvements in students' writing, teachers must commit to using a system that is much more intensive and interactive than the one used here" (221). Guardado and Shi (2007) found that NNES students in a sheltered course had little confidence in their peers' ability to provide feedback, but they conclude that face-to-face discussion with the teacher's guidance to clarify comments could have improved the online peer response. Other studies that found peer response was not effective also involved little or no training for peer response (Amores 1997; Connor and Asenavage 1994; Mangelsdorf and Schlumberger 1992) or not frequent enough use of peer response by teachers for it to be taken seriously by students (Brammer and Rees 2007).

Ken and Fiona Hyland (2006), in a review of L2 teacher and peer response, state that "studies generally suggest that careful preparation and training are essential for successful peer response" (85). In separate studies with similar research designs (a control group of students who did not receive peer response training and a treatment group that did receive training), Berg (1999), McGroarty and Zhu (1997), Rahimi (2013), Sluijsmans and coauthors (2002), and Zhu (1994) all found that students who receive extensive peer response training report more positive experiences with peer response, receive more substantial feedback, and make more meaning-changing revisions. Researchers who have examined the quality of peer response through a design in which peer response was conducted without training and then with training within the same course all note that peer response improves dramatically with extensive training (Choi 2014; McMahon 2010; Min 2006, 2007).

Although level of training of students appears to be the most critical factor in the success of peer response, the way the teacher designs peer response is also important. Peer response done in pairs is far less effective than peer response designed so that students get feedback from three or four of their peers (Bouzidi and Jaillet 2009; Caulk 1994; Cho and MacArthur 2010; Van den Berg et al. 2006). The research is less definitive on the question of whether or not peer response is more effective if it is anonymous. Many studies have found anonymous peer review to be more effective (Coté 2014; Garner and Hadingham 2019; Howard et al.

2010; Lu and Bol 2007; Zhao 1998), but Strijbos and coauthors (2009) argue against anonymous peer review on the grounds that "we are inclined to rate familiar persons more positively and we are more prone to accept feedback from a familiar person than someone unfamiliar" (389). Regardless of whether peer response is anonymous or not, as long as students receive adequate training and are given a thoughtful script by the teacher, peer response is likely to be as effective as teacher response.

Despite the consistent and convincing findings from the literature that peer response is effective, my heuristic does not imply that we should replace teacher response with peer response. In extensive reviews of the literature on response, C. Y. Chang (2016), Ferris and Hedgcock (1998), and Ken and Fiona Hyland (2006) found that studies strongly indicate students prefer to have both peer and teacher response. In a study of 250 students in ten courses across six universities, Kauffman and Schunn (2011) found that students had more positive views of peer response when teachers also responded. In a constructivist response framework, student self-assessment and peer response are at the center of the response construct, but teachers as disciplinary experts remain in dialogue with peers. Before discussing teacher response, it is important to note an important actor in the response construct that lies somewhere between teacher and peer: writing center tutors.

Tutors

The potential impact of writing center tutors is not often considered in research focused on studying the response occurring in individual courses, even though students in those courses may be visiting campus writing centers for additional feedback. However, writing center scholars have investigated the impacts of writing center tutoring indirectly through student surveys and directly through analyzing student drafts, and these researchers have found definitively positive effects. Bromley and coauthors (2018) conducted a qualitative study of three institutions using an exit survey to gauge student perceptions of satisfaction and intellectual engagement with writing center tutoring. The researchers received a total of 2,262 responses, and students reported that they were satisfied with the tutoring they received and would recommend the center to a friend. Thompson and coauthors (2009) collected survey responses from 1,490 students, and like Bromley and coauthors the researchers found that students were highly satisfied with the tutoring sessions. Students also reported that they incorporated feedback from tutoring sessions in their revised drafts. Carino and Enders (2001) also collected survey data from students regarding their experiences with the campus writing center, with nearly 400 students responding. The researchers found that students were highly satisfied with the Center and gained confidence as writers from peer tutoring, with confidence increasing the more students visited. Bell (2000) conducted a phone survey of 104 students who had visited the writing center, and found that nearly all of the students agreed or strongly agreed that the tutoring session was useful and they learned things that would help them in future writing assignments (20). Davis (1988) collected measurements of attitude toward writing from 121 first-year writing students and found that students who visited the writing center over the course of a semester had a significantly higher increase in positive attitude toward writing than students who did not visit the center.

In addition to student perception studies, researchers have examined students' writing processes and final drafts to investigate the effects of writing center tutoring. Young and Fritzsche (2002) examined the drafting habits of 206 students, 30 percent of whom received feedback from a writing center tutor. The researchers found that students who visited the writing center procrastinated less and had a higher level of satisfaction with their writing. Tiruchittampalam and coauthors (2018) studied sixty-five English language learners, thirty-five of whom had received feedback from a writing center tutor. The students who visited the writing center made significantly higher gains in their writing in regard to purpose, organization, and coherence. Henson and Stephenson (2009) reported similar results from a mixed methods study of students in two writing courses. Students who visited the writing center showed statistically significant greater improvement in aspects of their writing such as purpose, development, and organization than students who did not visit the center. Less definitive than research on the impacts of writing center tutor response, and less uniformly positive, are the findings of research on teacher response.

Teachers

In reviews of the literature on teacher response that span from the 1980s to the present, most scholars have taken a dim view of the effectiveness of teacher response to student writing. Knoblauch and Brannon (1981) state that some implications of previous research on response are that "(1) students often do not comprehend teacher responses to their writing; (2) even when they do, they do not always use those responses and may not know how to use them; (3) when they use them, they do not necessarily write more effectively as a result" (1). In a meta-analysis of research on response, Biber and coauthors (2011) found that gains from teacher feedback are small. In another literature review, Ferris and Hedgcock (1998) note, "Teacher response is problematic and tends to be prescriptive, vague, inconsistent, and confusing. . . . Response may often appropriate student texts by being too directive or prescriptive" (124). Similarly, Goldstein (2005) says of the research on ESL/EFL teacher response that students "have difficulties understanding teacher feedback, difficulty knowing what to do with teacher feedback, and degrees of willingness to use teacher feedback" (42). In their updated review of the response literature, Knoblauch and Brannon (2006) claim that whether or not response to student writing is a meaningful activity is inconclusive. Knoblauch and Brannon argue "there is scant evidence that students routinely use comments on one draft to make rhetorically important, and in the end qualitatively superior, changes in a subsequent draft, although students will make limited, usually superficial corrections in order to comply with overt or tacit instructions" (1).

This notion that teachers often make superficial comments and students make superficial revisions is supported by research by Rysdam and Johnson-Shull (2016), Stern and Solomon (2006), Jeffery and Selting (1999), Dohrer (1991), and Cohen (1987). Rysdam and Johnson-Shull conducted a content analysis of nearly one thousand student papers from across disciplines and found that comments were largely focused on pointing out problems and making surface-level corrections. Stern and Solomon also conducted a content analysis of faculty comments from across disciplines, analyzing 598 graded papers written from hundreds of courses from thirty different departments. They found that "most comments were technical corrections that addressed spelling, grammar, word choice, and missing words. Macro- and mid-level comments that addressed paper organization and quality of the ideas contained in it were surprisingly absent" (22). Jeffery and Selting studied the responses to student writing of seven faculty from across disciplines and also found that faculty comments focused on correctness. Dohrer analyzed the comments of a faculty member in speech and a faculty member in history and reported that most teacher comments (from 52% to 80%) dealt with surface-level features. Cohen looked at the teacher feedback received by 217 students in writing and language courses and found that 83 percent of comments were focused on grammar (65). Other researchers have found that many students do not pay enough attention to and do not use teacher feedback (Carless 2006; Glover and Brown 2006; Sinclair and Cleland 2007; Wingate 2010) and that students are often confused by teacher comments (Bowden 2018; Hedgcock and Lefkowitz 1996; Zamel 1985).

One of the challenges teachers face in responding is that they are being asked to play many and often conflicting roles. Leki (1990) says, "The role of the writing teacher is schizophrenic, split into three incompatible personas: teacher as real reader (i.e., audience), teacher as coach, and teacher as evaluator" (59). Straub (2002) outlines six roles teachers play as readers of student writing:

1. *Teacher-reader* as evaluator (focused on assessment)

2. *Teacher-reader* as educator (focused on instruction)

3. *Teacher-reader* as universal audience (representing readers in general)

4. *Teacher-reader* as target audience (representing a specific group of readers).

5. *Teacher-reader* as a common reader (presenting herself as an individual reader)

6. *Teacher-reader* as an implied reader (assuming the role suggested by the text) (40)

Research indicates that the most problematic conflict is between our roles as educator and evaluator. Researchers have found that teachers' comments often focus on justifying grades rather than on student growth (Brannon and Knoblauch 1982; Orrell 2006), that many students care about feedback only as it relates to improving their grade (Brown 2007; Burkland and Grimm 1986; Cunningham 2019), that grading often dictates how much time a student decides to spend on a paper (Caroll 2002; Dohrer 1991), that because of grading many students become obsessed with correctness (Bitchener and Ferris 2012; McMartin-Miller 2014; Richardson 2000), that grading has the effect of reducing self-efficacy and decreasing motivation to learn (Bowden 2018; Lipnevich and Smith 2009), and that grading is racist when it relies on a single, dominant white standard (Inoue 2019; S. Wood 2020).

Although there is ample evidence of a lack of effectiveness of teacher response and negative outcomes when response is connected to a final grade, there is enough evidence from the literature of the usefulness of teacher response that at best we can conclude that the value of teacher response is mixed. In a chapter focused on teacher feedback in *Developing Writers in Higher Education*, a longitudinal study of 169 student writers at the University of Michigan, Wilson and Post (2019) report that the students in their study valued teacher feedback and it played an important role in their development as writers. Bevan and coauthors (2008) found that students in the first year of a biological sciences degree at the University of Leicester linked feedback and learning in a positive way, stating that feedback led to improvement. Ferris (1995) also found that students believed teacher feedback led to improvement, with 93.5 percent of 155 students surveyed in an ESL program feeling that teacher response helped them improve as writers (46). A number of additional studies also found that students value teacher feedback (Bowden 2018; Calhoon-Dillahunt and Forrest 2013; Enginarlar 1993; Leki 1991; Mahfoodh and Pandian 2011; Saito 1994; Small and Attree 2015; Spencer 1998; Zhang 1995), that students make substantial changes based on teacher feedback on drafts (Cunningham 2019; Donovan 2014; F. Hyland 1998; Paulus 1999; Walvoord and McCarthy 1991), and that teachers make global, substantive comments (Dixon and Moxley 2013; Radecki and Swales 1988). Teacher feedback is not always helpful, especially when it is tied to a grade, but the research shows that it certainly has the potential to be helpful and lead to meaning-changing revisions.

Wider Audiences

In many college courses the response construct does not extend beyond the teacher, but it is common for students to seek out audiences beyond the classroom, including family members and peers. In a longitudinal study of twenty undergraduate students at Pepperdine University, Carroll (2002) found that much informal peer response happens in residence halls and student apartments, as students share their writing with friends and ask for feedback before turning it in to a professor. Fiona Hyland (2003) also found that students use spouses or friends "as informants to help them revise their assignments" (223). In a study of the drafting habits of 206 undergraduate students, Young and Fritzsche (2002) found that 42 percent sought out feedback from a friend (49). Séror (2011) found that Japanese students studying at a Canadian university frequently reached out to friends for additional feedback on their writing, and that a distinct advantage of getting feedback from friends was the face-to-face nature of the dialogue. The influence of family and friends as responders to college students' writing has been relatively unexplored by researchers, as has the question of what kind of feedback students receive when they write for wider disciplinary and professional audiences beyond the classroom.

In *Assignments across the Curriculum* (2014), I found that most of the over two thousand writing assignments in my corpus were written for the teacher as audience, but there were some assignments written for a broader audience beyond the classroom. What kind of feedback do students receive if they are asked to write a newsletter for a nonprofit as part of a service-learning project, or if they are asked to submit an editorial to their campus newspaper in a journalism course? How does feedback from broader audiences compare to teacher feedback? To what extent does feedback from wider audiences motivate students to revise? These questions have not been a focus of the research into response to college writing.

WHAT SHOULD RESPONSE FOCUS ON?

Metacognition

Andrade and Evans (2013) reviewed the literature on self-regulation and came to the conclusion, "Learners who possess self-regulated behaviors (i.e., set goals, use and modify learning strategies, and monitor their progress) are higher achievers than those who do not" (16). Ellis (2001) also reviewed the self-assessment literature and argued that practicing metacognition is helpful to students both within and beyond school: "the research literature suggests that opportunities for self-assessment and peer assessment will help students to develop abilities for self-monitoring that they will need in their professional lives" (298). Even though research on metacognition is beginning to be integrated into recent conceptions of assessment and response, this knowledge has not necessarily translated to response practice. Yancey (1998a) bemoans the situation that despite what we know about the research on metacognition, when we do ask students to self-reflect on their writing, "it tends to function as a supplemental or optional task, not as an integral and critical one" (par. 11).

Based on my review of the literature on self-assessment summarized in the previous section of this chapter, my heuristic begins to answer the question, "What should our response focus on?" by prioritizing students' metacognition. Frankenberg-Garcia (1999) notes that "feedback teachers give to students is usually based on first, second, or final drafts. This means that it is based on the outcome of the students' writing decisions, and does not address the decisions themselves" (101). My constructivist response heuristic encourages researchers to focus not just on rough and final drafts of any particular genres, but on the writer's metacognition. Rough and final drafts provide evidence of the rhetorical choices students make and of the labor they put in to writing processes, but a constructivist framework for response research turns our attention to the students' own critical self-reflections on these choices and processes.

Transfer

Shifting the focus of response research and teacher feedback from final products of the particular genres teachers assign to artifacts of student self-reflection will involve shifting our research and teaching focus to transfer of learning. Yancey's scholarship on metacognition has important implications for writing transfer, but transfer has been a neglected subject in US research on response, with the exception of a recent increased interest in transfer and writing center tutoring, including a transfer-themed issue of *The Writing Lab Newsletter* (Devet and Driscoll 2020). Transfer has been a more prominent area of focus in international literature on response, and especially the concept of *feedforward*, which has been primarily concerned with students applying teacher comments from one assignment to another within the same class. This research has found that students desire comments they can apply to their next assignment, but rarely receive such comments.

In a study of undergraduates from across the curriculum at the University of Wolverhampton in the UK, Duncan (2007) found that sixteen students who participated in an activity that involved reflecting on teacher comments and additional teacher support focused on helping students feed comments forward made gains compared to a control group. Vardi (2012) collected a survey from 2,163 students in a first-year business unit in an Australian university and noted that comments on one task that were specific to the next task and also shared performance standards with the next task were effectively applied forward by students, a result also found by Martini and DiBattista (2014).

Carless (2006) surveyed and interviewed students and faculty from eight Hong Kong universities and found that a little over 38 percent of teachers thought "students were often given detailed feedback which helped them improve their next assignment," but only a little over 10 percent of students responded in the same way. Nearly 38 percent of students "felt that feedback was rarely followed by actions to improve student learning," as opposed to 16.1 percent of teachers (224). Orsmond and Merry (2011) interviewed nineteen biological sciences students and six teachers at a UK university about feedback and also noted a disconnect between teacher feedback and students' desires to transfer learning. Students wanted feedback they could apply to the next assignment, but teachers did not focus on this application and did not provide the type of comments that could lead to transfer. Similar to Vardi (2012) and Orsmond and Merry (2011), in focus group discussions with eighteen business students in a London university, Pokorny and

Pickford (2010) found that students desired feedback they could apply to the next assignment but rarely received such feedback.

Researchers who study response are just beginning to consider the value of more far-reaching transfer that students can apply not just to the next assignment but to future writing contexts beyond the classroom. Cunningham (2019) surveyed students in fifteen sections of first-year writing at a large, Midwestern university, yielding 272 survey responses. Nearly half of the students were what Cunningham labels *Writing-Driven*, meaning they wanted response that helped them improve writing abilities overall. Twenty-seven percent of the students also met the subcategory "Improved Writing Skills for Future," which meant students indicated they desired feedback they could apply to future classes (15–16). Lizzio and Wilson (2008), in a study of 334 students from across disciplines, found that "students endorsed the importance of feedback that supported transferable learning" (266). Feedback focused on development as a writer was most strongly correlated with students' perceptions of effectiveness. Freestone (2009) found that when pharmacy and chemistry students at Kingston University were given feedback in one course that could apply to a future course, they were able to act upon that feedback and improve their performance in the future task (101). Freestone's research involved an intentional vertical curriculum design with built-in feedforward, an approach that Irons (2008) argues is critical to ensure that students transfer what they've learned from teachers' comments from one course to the next. The literature on response and transfer has begun to establish that students want response that will aid in transfer, but teachers rarely focus on transfer in their comments.

Growth and Processes versus Products

Focusing on metacognition and transfer in constructing response means focusing on growth and processes rather than products. However, from the early empirical response research to the present, there is evidence that outside of first-year writing courses, teachers across disciplines do not often focus on growth and writing processes. Yancey (1992) argues, "Teachers read to see how the students did (how the assignment functioned) and how the students responded to the assignment (how they did on it). Only secondarily are students' essays read relative to the authors' growth in writing, if at all" (106). Robinson and coauthors (2013) surveyed 166 first-year undergraduate students and found that the largest group of student comments from the survey were related to a lack of information about how to improve their work, coupled with teachers focusing on summative assessment (267). Orrell (2006) observed and interviewed sixteen experienced teachers who all believed that they were focused on students' growth, but in actuality most of their comments were in justification of a grade.

A genre of college writing that is often focused on growth is the portfolio reflection essay/letter/memo. Artifacts of self-reflection, and especially more extensive reflective writing assignments such as port-folio reflection essays, provide teachers the affordance of responding to students' own assessment of their growth. However, the research on portfolio reflection letters indicates that students are not always able to articulate their growth as writers or provide evidence of that growth, and that students sometimes exaggerate their growth in an attempt to impress the teacher as evaluator (Bower 2003; Emmons 2003; Latta and Lauer 2000; Neal 2016). Latta and Lauer (2000) emphasize that due to a lack of experience with self-reflective writing, most students need guid-ance in how to examine their own growth as writers (31). The research indicates that students' growth as writers is at best a secondary consider-ation in response, and that student self-assessment of growth needs to be given greater attention in the design of response constructs.

WHAT CONTEXTS SHOULD RESPONDERS CONSIDER?

A constructivist approach to the response construct emphasizes aware-ness and integration of a variety of personal and social contexts in our response to student writing. Ken Hyland and Fiona Hyland (2006) argue, "The kind of institution, the ethos of the classroom, students' purposes in learning to write, their proficiencies, and the genres they are studying are often important though neglected variables in feedback studies" (14). Paul Prior (1998) notes that contexts we should consider in our responding include the teacher's personal history, the class, the institution, the discipline, and wider social contexts (173). Straub and Lunsford (1995) outline five overlapping contexts for student writing: formal text, rhetorical situation, student's writing processes, student's personal contexts, and the larger social setting, including the classroom setting, genre conventions, and the institutional setting (167). I draw on the work of Hyland and Hyland, Prior, and Straub and Lunsford to settle in my own research on the context categories of student, responder (teacher, peer, tutor, etc.), course, assignment genre, discourse commu-nity, institution, and sociocultural context. I begin with students because in a constructivist model of response the students' personal contexts are a primary consideration in response.

Student

Ferris (2003, 2011) argues that it is critical for teachers to tailor their responses to individual students and to get to know students' writing backgrounds and their strengths and challenges as writers. Ken Hyland and Fiona Hyland (2006) note that tailoring our response is important because the research shows that "students vary considerably in what they want from their teachers in the form of feedback" (222). Goldstein (2005, 18) provides a list of the major student factors we might consider in responding:

- personality
- age
- goals and expectations
- motivations
- proficiency level
- past learning experiences
- preferred learning styles and strategies
- content knowledge and interest
- time constraints
- attitudes toward the teacher, the class, the content, the writing assignment, and the commentary itself

Some of the primary themes in the literature on response regarding students' contexts that teachers should be aware of include students' tendency to think dualistically (correct or incorrect, right or wrong) when interpreting teacher response (Anson 2000), the importance of a trusting relationships with the teacher (Dowden et al. 2013; Lee and Schallert 2008; Sutton and Gill 2010), and the influence of students' prior experiences with response (Elbow 1997; O'Neill and Mathison-Fife 1999). Although response researchers sometimes fail to consider students' literacy histories in studies of response, and teachers do not always take the initiative to get to know students' prior experiences with writing before responding to them, the literature makes the argument that prior literacy experiences will have a significant impact on students' reception of our response.

Responder

Responders to student writing may include peers, teachers, writing center tutors, and a variety of wider audiences. Since the response litera-ture focuses on teacher contexts, and since I discuss peer response and writing center tutor response in other sections of my heuristic, in this section I focus on some of the primary teacher contexts that researchers have investigated: the role of personal emotions in teacher response and teacher biases regarding race and gender. An additional potential bias that is not well researched in the response literature is ableism. These contexts are also relevant for peer and tutor response.

No scholar has explored the primacy of the personal context of the teacher as deeply as Lad Tobin. In *Reading Student Writing*, Tobin (2004) analyzes the central role his personal emotions play when he responds to student writing. Tobin's political beliefs, his prior experiences as a student, and his emotional connections (or disconnections) with students all play a crucial role in how he responds. Caswell's (2018) case study of one community college teacher provides another example of the extent to which teachers' personal feelings can color their responses. Caswell describes a series of emotional episodes during the response process that "reveal the underlying affective tensions between individual emotions, cultural constructions, and institutional contexts that [the teacher] is negotiating while responding to student writing" (71). In research that involved a protocol analysis of eight writing teachers as they read and responded to student texts, Edgington (2005) also found that teachers' emotions, and especially their feelings about individual students, played a central role in how they responded to student writing.

The response literature has found that teacher biases also play a role in shaping response. A prominent type of bias explored in the literature is racial bias. Implicit biases of white privilege shape teacher response, and scholars focused on antiracist teaching and responding have investigated the many ways that white college teachers exhibit implicit bias when responding to BIPOC students (Condon and Young 2017; Grimm 1999; Reddy and TuSmith 2002; S. Wood 2020). Coleman and coauthors (1991) studied ninety Black undergraduates and compared their response to positive feedback, negative feedback, and no feedback from Black and white teachers. They found that the race of the teacher influenced students' perceptions of feedback, with Black female students especially having less positive perceptions about the assessments of white teachers than about the assessments of Black teachers. Kynard (2006) discusses the benefits of taking an Afrodialogic approach and the importance of her own ideologies and background in responding to student writing as a Black teacher at a predominantly Black college. Kynard cites Robert Schwegler (1991), who asserts that the response process is "grounded in personal, social, and cultural ideology and experience" (212) and stresses "the interaction of values and ideologies" in response to student writing (221). Shane Wood (2020) argues that traditionally response has favored white, middle-class, monolingual English users. Wood encourages teachers and students to interrogate the racialized structures that privilege whiteness in response and assessment.

Another context that is prominent in the response literature is gender. Barnes (1990) analyzed the response of forty-four first-year writing teachers to essays written by males and females and found that the gender of the teacher played a significant role in the comments. Barnes notes that male teachers were generally "intolerant of emotional writing, especially when the author was female" (151). Vann and coauthors (1991) conducted a study similar to Barnes's in which teachers from sixty departments responded to essays provided by the researchers. Vann and coauthors found that women in the humanities, education, and social sciences were more tolerant of error than were men. Research on the influence of teacher gender on response is mixed, however, and at least one study has found no difference between the response of male and female teachers (Read et al. 2005). One further complication of the findings of the research on response and gender is the binary thinking that has limited studies to reductive gender categories of male and female.

Another student population that can be negatively impacted by teacher bias is students with disabilities. In the response literature, there is an unfortunate absence of research focused on students with disabilities and neurodiverse students, but Writing Studies scholars who focus on disability provide insights that have significant implications for the design of the response construct. Tara Wood (2017) argues for "cripping time," which involves "approaching the construction of time in writing classrooms in such a way that doesn't rely on compulsory able-bodiedness" (269–70). Teachers' normative conceptions of deadlines for receiving response and for revising based on feedback can put students with disabilities and neurodiversities at a significant disadvantage. Teachers' normative biases regarding production can also be problematic for students with disabilities and neurodiverse students. Later in this book I argue the merits of contract grading as a way to lessen the negative impact grading has on response, but Tara Wood (2017) and Kryger and Zimmerman (2020) expose potential biases teachers may have regarding the ways they conceive of and evaluate production/labor. As these scholars argue, neurodiverse students' ability to complete labor may differ from normative labor standards used by a contract grading system—and for that matter a traditional grading system. Like biases of race and gender, ableism is often unaccounted for in response research, and certainly understudied.

Contexts beyond the Student and Responder: Course, Assignment Genre, Discourse Community, Institution, and Sociocultural Context

Chris Anson (1989) argues that "we must begin to think of response as part of the social and interpersonal dynamics of the classroom community. Our focus must therefore widen to include all that surrounds the texts we read, write, and discuss" (333). Response research would benefit from more studies of the dynamics of the classroom and the effects of those dynamics on student uptake of response, but researchers who have studied classroom contexts have found that students' experiences with and attitudes about the class influence their uptake of peer and teacher response. McAlexander (2000) compared three writing courses and found that the personality of the class as a whole was a greater predictor of what kinds of peer response students preferred than personality traits of individual students. Ken and Fiona Hyland (2019) and Jeff Sommers (2012) argue for the importance of connecting our response to the work of the classroom.

Another context for response that researchers could focus more attention on is the role of assignment genre and discourse community contexts in shaping feedback. Ferris (2003) notes this lack of consideration of genre in her extensive review of the L1 and L2 literature on response, and she comes to the conclusion that "researchers and reviewers should consider the specifications of particular writing tasks and text types in the analysis of teacher feedback and its effects" (34). Straub and Lunsford's (1995) contexts for response model includes genre, and genre is one component of Goldstein's (2005) response model, but despite the many ways that genre and discourse communities shape the response construct, genre and discourse community as factors are not often prominent in theories and models of response or in empirical studies focused on response.

An additional aspect of response that deserves more attention from researchers is the ways that institutions shape response. Goldstein (2005) argues, "Programmatic and institutional attitudes toward writing, toward writing teachers, and toward different multilingual populations can greatly affect how teachers provide written commentary" (11). Teachers in studies of response by Bailey and Garner (2010), Orrell (2006), and Tuck (2012) cite institutional concerns such as campus policies regarding feedback, awareness that comments might be read by a colleague, and the need to provide grade justification in case of a student appeal. Séror (2009) found that institutional factors such as departmental budgets, class sizes, the nature of merit structures for teachers, and prescribed grade distributions were a powerful constraint on learning to write for international university students. Like Séror, Lee (2009) found that faculty workload has a significant effect on response, with briefer and less rhetorically focused comments from teachers with the largest course loads. Hester (2007) explores the negative impacts on students and teachers of a labor-intensive, anonymous response and grading system that was implemented in a FYC program due in part to institutional budget constraints.

A response context that shapes students, teachers, genres, discourse communities, and institutions is the broader sociocultural context that is not left behind when we close the doors of our classrooms or sit alone in our office reading students' writing. Chris Anson (2012) notes, "Text itself is part of a complex interaction involving students' and teachers' construction of each other's identities in the context of a particular activity system layered with multiple intentions and influenced by the 'ideologies of pedagogy' entailed in particular classes located in particular kinds of institutions, themselves influenced by educational values of the broader society" (194). In this chapter I have already discussed a number of factors in response that are heavily influenced by sociocultural contexts, including teacher biases and race and gender. Another sociocultural context that is prominent in response research, and especially the research on peer response, is the influence of culture. Many researchers have noted that some students from collectivist cultures may be less likely to give constructive criticism in peer response and to value harmony over critique (Carson and Nelson 1994, 1996; Nelson and Carson 1995; Nelson and Murphy 1992). Students from more teacher-centered cultures may be less receptive to and confident in their peers' feedback (Mangelsdorf 1992; Paulus 1999; Ruegg 2015). Ruecker (2014) argues that native speakerist discourse can shape NNES students' attitudes, making them less confident in giving feedback to their peers.

Despite the social turn in Writing Studies and the recent application of socio-epistemic frameworks in response research, personal and social contexts for response are not always fully considered in studies of response. Response researchers could focus more attention on the ways that the individual personalities, beliefs, and ideologies of students and teachers shape response, as well as factors such as race and gender and disability. The influences of genre and discourse community could be given more consideration in response research and in models of response and assessment. Studies of response could also make more of the influence of the institution on how teachers respond. The ESL/EFL response literature has devoted a great deal of attention to cultural influences on response, but Writing Studies literature on response would benefit from more attention to the cultural backgrounds of both students and teachers.

WHAT TYPE OF FEEDBACK SHOULD RESPONDERS GIVE?

Shifting our focus from teacher response to student self-assessment puts less emphasis and pressure on the amount and type of comments teachers make in response to student writing and less weight for researchers on the study of teacher comments in isolation. However, the quality of the comments that students receive from peers, writing center tutors, and teachers is still a critical component of the response construct. Investigations of the type of feedback that is most effective have been the dominant focus of response research, and for the sake of ease of use for researchers and for teachers across disciplines, I have narrowed this aspect of my heuristic down to what I interpret as the primary continuums of focus in the literature on response regarding type of comments: directive to facilitative, praise to critique, local to global, generic to specific, and minimal to extensive. I organize these areas of focus in continuums to avoid binary thinking about what type of feedback responders should give.

Directive to Facilitative Comments

Straub (1996) advises us not to think about teacher control in comments as dualistic, and he argues, "Given the power relations that adhere in the classroom, all teacher comments are in some way evaluative and directive" (247). With this caveat in mind, the research does tend to show that comments that fall on the facilitative end of the continuum are more effective than extremely directive comments that wrestle control of the student's text. Scrocco (2012) used think-aloud protocols to analyze students' uptake of teacher response and found that "open-ended, cooperative suggestions on students' drafts can encourage writers to brainstorm, critically consider their ideas, and plan revisions, whereas imperative, critically directive, and closed remarks that instruct students to implement particular changes may stifle their active engagement in their writing process" (288). Surveys have shown that students prefer feedback that is not overly directive (Arndt 1993; Straub 1997).

Despite the value of facilitative comments, researchers have found that teacher comments are often highly directive, even when teachers claim that they value facilitative response. Ferris (2014) used a mixed methods approach to study the response of 129 community college and university writing teachers. Many of the teachers claimed that they used primarily questioning techniques, but Ferris found that statements and imperatives dominated their actual comments. Since Nancy Sommers's (1982) seminal article "Responding to Student Writing," Writing Studies and ESL/EFL researchers have found that teacher comments are often highly directive (Ferris et al. 2011; Ferris and Hedgcock 1998; Rysdam and Johnson-Shull 2016; Stern and Solomon 2006).

A number of scholars have questioned the advice from the response literature that we should always avoid being directive in our comments. These scholars focus on the ways that certain types of courses and certain student populations might benefit from more directive response from the teacher. For example, some researchers have argued that courses that introduce students to a specific discipline may require more directive feedback. Wingard and Geosits (2014) analyzed teacher comments from seven Writing in the Disciplines (WID) courses and came to the conclusion that "directive commentary is appropriate when students who are novices in a discipline are trying to learn the conventions of a disciplinary genre" (11). Patton and Taylor (2013) argue that directive commentary may be more appropriate in engineering courses. Another student population that appears to benefit from more directive response is language learners. Researchers have found that NNES benefit from response that is more directive and contains less hedging (Baker and Bricker 2006; Cohen and Cavalcanti 1990; Fathman and Whalley 1990; Leki 1990; Sugita 2006). Students from cultures that value more direct speech patterns may also benefit from more directive feedback (Leijen and Leontjeva 2012). Reid (1994) argues that ESL teachers should accept their role as "cultural informants" and thus be less concerned about appropriating student texts (275). ESL research especially points to the need for teachers and researchers to consider a variety of contextual factors, including students' cultural backgrounds, when considering how effective more directive comments might be.

Praise to Critique

Researchers have found that comments that offer praise and explain why a student has been successful can increase confidence and motivation. Daiker (1989) notes that one benefit of praise is that it helps students who suffer from writing apprehension. Research on student perceptions of teacher comments has shown that most students value praise, and not just apprehensive writers. Hayes and Daiker (1984) conducted protocol analyses of seventeen first-year writing students' responses to teacher comments and said that they "cannot overstate how highly students value positive comments and how clearly they remember them from draft to draft" (4). Jones and coauthors (2012) also found praise was highly valued by students. The researchers studied perceptions of teacher feedback of 518 undergraduate bioscience students at three UK universities and found "the most motivating feedback was, unsurprisingly, praise words such as 'very good' or 'excellent' (accounting for 41% of the motivational factors)" (10). The students did accept and value negative comments "if they were constructive and indicated where they could improve" (15), but researchers have found that response that is only criticism or too much criticism can demoralize students (Jones et al. 2012; Mahfoodh 2017; Poulos and Mahony 2008; Weaver 2006).

The research shows that most teachers do not offer much praise in their comments to student writing. Rysdam and Johnson-Shull (2016) go as far as to say that the literature indicates that "response is not only frequently negative, it is frequently cruel" (70). Whether teacher response is too often only critical or sometimes even cruel, it appears that praise is rare in response to college writing. Dragga (1988) found that four writing teachers at Texas A&M in a control group that did not receive instruction on strategies for praising student writing averaged a little over one praise comment per student essay. Beason (1993) studied the feedback of eighteen teachers from across disciplines and found that just 11 percent of teacher comments were praise (411). Ruegg (2018) noted that praise made up just over 4 percent of comments by ESL teachers at a Japanese university on thirty-seven students' essays (96).

Nancy Sommers (2006) argues that praise and constructive criticism should be in balance, and both types of commentary should be in service to helping students improve as writers and develop strategies for future writing contexts. In a constructivist conception of response, the extent to which teachers offer praise or constructive criticism will depend on the student, the stage of the draft, the genre of the assignment, and the many other factors of the response construct. But the research does indicate that in most cases a balance of praise and constructive criticism, and concrete explanations for why something a student has written is effective or would benefit from further revision, is a best practice in response.

Local to Global

Perhaps no other topic in the response literature has received more attention than the extent to which teachers should comment on local (sentence-level) versus global concerns. In *Reconstructing Response to*

Student Writing, I wish to turn both researchers and teachers' attention away from this debate, given the constructivist shift of emphasis from comments on final drafts of discrete genres to students' self-reflection about the processes of composing in those genres, and the shift from particular revisions and edits that students have made in a rough or final draft to what students have learned about revising and editing that they can transfer to future writing contexts. However, there are courses in which evidence of facility in composing certain genres and in editing those genres appropriately for the target audience is a priority (for example, an upper-division business writing course or an engineering communications course), or courses where sentence-level style is of special emphasis (for example, a poetry or fiction course). In these kinds of courses, more attention might be given to sentence-level effectiveness. But certainly, regardless of the discipline or the course, empirical studies of teacher comments shows that college teachers across disciplines have tended to err on the side of focusing on local over global concerns when responding to student drafts.

Nancy Sommers (1982) studied the comments of thirty-five teachers at New York University and the University of Oklahoma and found that even when commenting on rough drafts teachers focused on usage, diction, and style. Chris Anson (1989) and Ferris and coauthors (2011) found a similar focus on surface features in the responses of writing teachers. Stern and Solomon (2006) conducted a content analysis of faculty comments from 598 graded papers written for hundreds of courses from thirty departments at one university and found that most comments were "technical corrections that addressed spelling, grammar, word choice, and missing words" (22). Rysdam and Johnson-Shull (2016) conducted a similar study of nearly one thousand student papers from across disciplines, and like Stern and Solomon, they found that comments were largely focused on pointing out problems and making surface-level corrections. A similar focus on error was found in research by Dohrer (1991), Glover and Brown (2006), and Snymanski (2014).

The ESL/EFL literature shows definitively that instructors teaching language learners focus on correctness more often than content (Ferris et al. 2011; Ferris and Hedgcock 1998; Lee et al. 2018). Researchers who have surveyed and interviewed NNES about teacher feedback have consistently found that students most often receive local and not global comments from teachers (Cohen 1987; Cohen and Cavalcanti 1990; Hedgcock and Lefkowitz 1996). A pattern in the research on response is that teachers often claim to value content over correctness and believe that their comments are focused on global concerns, but in their actual responses they wind up focusing on grammar, diction, and syntax (F. Hyland 2003; Junqueira and Payant 2015; Lee et al. 2018; Montgomery and Baker 2007; Séror 2011; Taylor and Patton 2006).

ESL/EFL research on error and Writing Studies scholars' concerns regarding teachers' obsession with local issues of grammar and syntax intersect in complex ways. Nancy Sommers (1982) argues that "the student's misunderstanding of the revision process as a rewording activity is reinforced by their teachers' comments" (151), and the Writing Studies research has shown that students have come to associate good writing with correct writing due to teachers' focus on correctness in their response and grading. But many ESL/EFL scholars argue that language learners, and especially students from teacher-centered cultures, strongly desire feedback on grammar and syntax and will feel resentful of teachers who do not provide adequate feedback on error (Ferris 2004; K. Hyland and F. Hyland 2006), a claim that is supported by studies of students' feedback preferences (R. Diab 2005; Ferris 1995; Leki 1991; McMartin-Miller 2014; Radecki and Swales 1988; Seker and Dincer 2014). Truscott (1999) complicates this notion of student preference for error correction, noting, "To some extent, the argument from students' beliefs is circular: By using correction, teachers encourage students to believe in it; because students believe in it, teachers must continue using it" (116). Research on student preferences has certainly shown that grades are a strong factor in why students want teachers to mark errors, and it appears that teachers across disciplines are often sending students the message that correctness is more important than content and will factor heavily into the final assessment of their writing. This idea that sentence-level errors will stigmatize language learners in courses in the disciplines is commonly presented by ESL/EFL scholars as evidence for the argument for responding to error (Ferris 2006; K. Hyland and F. Hyland 2006).

Guénette (2007) states that success or failure of feedback on error "will depend on the classroom context, the type of errors students make, their proficiency level, the type of writing they are asked to do, and a collection of other variables that are as of yet unknown" (51–52). In a constructivist response framework, the extent to which the teacher focuses on local or global comments will be influenced by all of the other factors in the response construct. It is important to note, however, that in a constructivist conception of response, knowledge students learn about their own editing processes that they can transfer to future writing contexts is more important than any specific strategies that teachers use to comment on local concerns.

Generic to Specific

Nancy Sommers (1982) found in her early research on response that "most teachers' comments are not text-specific and could be interchanged, rubber-stamped, from text to text" (152). Researchers who have interviewed and surveyed students about what types of response are most effective have consistently found that students prefer specific comments to generic or vague comments (Jones et al. 2012; Lipnevich and Smith 2009; Murphy and Cornell 2010; Poulos and Mahony 2008; Still and Koerber 2010; Straub 1997; Walker 2013; Weaver 2006; Ziv 1984).

The research indicates that students make more substantial revisions when they receive text-specific comments. Ferris (1997) analyzed 1,600 comments on rough drafts of 47 ESL students' essays and then compared the rough drafts to the final drafts and found that comments that were text specific "were associated with major changes more than were shorter, general comments" (330). Ziv (1984) studied the effect of teacher comments on successive drafts of four first-year students and discovered that students responded favorably and revised more thoroughly when they received specific cues and specific suggestions from the teacher. Vardi (2009) found that the one hundred students in an Australian business course were far more likely to make substantial changes to their writing when teacher comments were text specific. Other researchers have noted similar results regarding the value of text-specific feedback (Beason 1993; Carless 2006; Fathman and Whalley 1990; Hedgcock and Lefkowitz 1996; Lipnevich and Smith 2009; Price et al. 2010; Sitko 1993).

Students may prefer specific rather than generic comments, but that does not mean that it is effective to cover their writing in comments. Research shows that students are often overwhelmed by the number of comments teachers make (Dohrer 1991; Ferris 2003; Glover and Brown 2006; Mahfoodh 2017; Vardi 2009) and that students who receive an overwhelming amount of comments perceive that the teacher has a negative impression of them (Ackerman and Gross 2010). Extensive commenting that overwhelms students often amounts to marks noting every grammatical and syntax issue (Glover and Brown 2006). Some studies indicate that students may prefer for teachers to mark every grammatical error (Bitchener and Ferris 2012; McMartin-Miller 2014), but the reasoning behind this desire is often merely the wish to get a better grade. Throughout their published work, prominent scholars of ESL/EFL theory and practice, such as Dana Ferris, Ilona Leki, and Fiona and Ken Hyland, recommend responding to patterns of sentence-level concerns in NNES students' writing rather than noting every possible grammatical or syntactic confusion for the reader, thus putting more of the onus on students to practice editing processes.

WHEN SHOULD RESPONSE OCCUR?

Before and during Drafting

In a sense, teachers begin responding to student writing before students even begin the process of drafting. Teachers' assignments point to their expectations and assessment criteria, scaffolding activities may include asking students to engage in invention tasks such as freewriting or journaling or research proposals, and teachers might meet with students to brainstorm in one-on-one conferences or students might visit with a writing center tutor to discuss their plans for writing before they have a draft. However, once students have begun to generate drafts, the research shows that the most effective pedagogical tool teachers have for providing students response during drafting is peer response.

Empirical research indicates that the majority of students make substantial revisions after receiving peer feedback. Price and coauthors (2007) reported that 55.9 percent of students made some or many changes based on peer response feedback (147). Leijen (2017) studied forty-three Estonian students in an English language academic writing course and found that 458 of 885 peer feedback instances led to revision (43). Allen and Mills (2016), Mendonca and Johnson (1994), and Villamil and de Guerrero (1996, 2020) all found that more than half of peer response comments were incorporated into revised drafts. Paulus (1999) found that 32 percent of the changes made to a second draft of an essay were a result of peer feedback, and 63 percent of these second draft peer-influenced revisions were meaning changes (281).

Research has also shown that students make substantial revisions based on teacher response on ungraded drafts. In looking closely at the revisions made as a result of comments from a business teacher, Walvoord and McCarthy (1991) found that 96 percent of meaning-changing suggestions resulted in student revision (93). Donovan (2014), in a self-study of her physics courses, found similar results: 95 percent of students in one course and 100 percent of students in another course used her feedback to revise (1021). Cunningham (2019) studied writing courses and found that 94 percent of the students read teacher feedback, and that students who earned A's and B's consistently applied feedback in revising (14). Paulus (1999) found that NNES in a single course made meaning-level changes as a result of teacher feedback, a result that Fiona Hyland (1998) also reported in a study of two ESL courses. Ferris (1995) found that across an ESL program, students valued teacher feedback and used it to improve their writing. Ferris notes that 93.5 percent of the 155 students surveyed felt that teacher response helped them improve as writers (46). A number of other ESL/EFL studies confirm that students make use of teacher comments to revise (Connor and Asenavage 1994; Ferris 1997).

Final Draft

The research indicates that comments on final drafts are the least efficient use of teacher feedback because they have the least effect on student learning. Students tend to focus on the grade rather than comments when teacher response includes grades (Burkland and Grimm 1986). Students are far more likely to pay attention to feedback provided on preliminary drafts than final drafts and far less likely to apply comments made on final drafts to future writing contexts (Ferris 1995; Polio 2012; Price et al. 2010). When teachers comment on final drafts, they often wind up simply justifying a grade. Connors and Lunsford (1993) found that, in their analysis of teacher feedback on 3,000 papers, "the majority of the comments at the beginning or end of the papers served one purpose: to justify and explain final grades. Over 59% of the initial and terminal comments were grade justifications" (213). Orrell (2006) found a similar focus on justifying grades in a study of sixteen teacher education and nursing teachers. The research is definitive regarding when to respond. Responding to drafts in progress is far more beneficial to students than response on a final draft, especially when that response is attached to a final grade.

WHAT MODALITIES SHOULD RESPONDERS USE?

The modalities teachers use to provide feedback on student writing range from the traditional practice of writing on students' printed work in pen or pencil to the commenting function of electronic word processing or online file sharing programs to face-to-face conferences to audio files to screencasting. There is a temptation to ask which of these modes are most effective, and much of the research on response modalities is focused on the effectiveness of a particular modality or a comparison of the effectiveness of two or more different modalities. The data from this research is useful, and it can help teachers decide which modes to use in responding, but Breuch (2004) encourages us to ask not which response mode is best but rather what are the differences between the modes. This requires thinking carefully about the affordances and constraints of each mode of response. Universal Design for Learning also highlights the value of offering students multiple modes for receiving response, and a constructivist framework encourages teachers to provide students with agency in choosing which mode of response they would prefer. In a constructivist conception of response, choosing a response mode is influenced not just by its affordances and constraints but by all of the other factors of the response construct as well, from the students to the teacher to the genre of the assignment to the type of response being given.

Face to Face

It appears that one of the affordances of the mode of face-to-face feedback is that it is more likely to lead to a focus on global comments. Ho (2015) studied peer review in an EFL course and found that there were significantly more content-focused comments in face-to-face peer response than computer-mediated peer response. Ho and Savignon (2007) found that students preferred face-to-face peer response because they were more easily able to seek clarification and negotiate meaning. Pitts (2005) surveyed students in the department of music at the University of Sheffield and found that a central request from students was increased face-to-face feedback from teachers. The research indicates that offering students the opportunity for face-to-face feedback should be a central factor in constructing response, and the negotiation and dialogue that is frequently a central feature of the face-to-face mode of response aligns with a constructivist conception of the response construct.

Print versus Electronic

With electronic modes of response replacing traditional pen or pencil comments on student papers, few current studies are concerned with print as a mode of response, although older research does note students' frustrations with teachers' poor handwriting and fear of the red pen. A more pressing question for current response research has been not whether print or electronic modes of response are more effective but rather what types of electronic modes do students prefer? In studies where students received adequate training, both synchronous and asynchronous uses of computer-mediated peer response have been shown to be effective modes (C.-F. Chang 2009; Li et al. 2008; Liang and Tsai 2010; Lin et al. 2001; Tannacito and Tuzi 2002; Tuzi 2004; Ware and

Warschauer 2006). Honeycutt (2001) found that students preferred asynchrounous response and that it led to more revision, a point emphasized by Breuch (2004), who argues that asynchronous interactions may "allow reviewers to think more carefully about their responses" (40). This extra time is especially beneficial for NNES students (Ruecker 2014). Asynchronous computer-mediated peer review may also be welcomed by introverted or apprehensive students (Mabrito 1991).

Audio

Audio feedback has been a subject of interest since the 1980s and the introduction of cassettes in response, with MP3 and podcasting the focus of current research on audio response. Researchers have found that audio feedback typically provides greater depth, is more personalized, and is easier for students to understand than written feedback (Ahern-Dodson and Reisinger 2017; Bauer 2011; Bourgault et al. 2013; Cooper 2008; Hennessy and Forester 2014; King et al. 2008; Kirschner et al. 1991; Knauf 2016; Macgregor et al. 2011; Olesova et al. 2011; Pearce and Ackley 1995; Rhind et al. 2013; Rodway-Dyer et al. 2011; Sipple 2007; J. Sommers 1989). The research has consistently found that students especially appreciate how personal audio feedback is and the depth of audio comments as compared to written comments.

Video

Video has also proven to be an effective mode for response to student writing, with screencast technologies being the primary medium used and studied. One of the significant affordances of using screencasting for response is the ability to make a personal connection to students, in part because of the tendency for teachers to use a more conversational tone when they use screencasting (Anson 2016, 2017; Grigoryan 2017; Hase and Saenger 1997; Silva 2012). Screencasting feedback has also been found to be lengthier than written feedback (Elola and Oskoz 2016; Hase and Saenger 1997). Surveys of students indicate that they have a positive response to screencasting as a mode of response (Anson 2017; Grigoryan 2017; Thompson and Lee 2012; Vincelette and Bostic 2013).

Regardless of the mode of response studied, researchers have consistently found that students' comfort with and attitude about the technology used for peer response, and teachers' beliefs about and confidence in using the technology used to deliver teacher feedback, play a role in the response construct (Grouling 2018; Jin and Zhu 2010; Lin et al. 2001;

Matsumura and Hann 2004). The research indicates that students benefit when teachers take advantage of the affordances of multiple modes of
response, especially when students are given some choice about which
mode to give and receive feedback in.

APPLYING A CONSTRUCTIVIST HEURISTIC
TO RESPONSE RESEARCH

The response heuristic I described in this chapter can help researchers
investigate the response construct in its full cognitive and sociocultural
contexts. The heuristic emphasizes that decisions about who should
respond, what response should focus on, when response should occur, and
what modes should be used in responding are interrelated and socially
constructed. The heuristic, and the forty years of empirical research in
response that it is based on, turns the focus of response research and the
design of the response construct away from teachers and toward student
self-assessment and peer response—a reflection of the broader evolution
of response research from decontextualized studies of teacher comments
to more ethnographic methods that include social factors and a broader
variety of actors in the response scene, including student uptake of
teacher response, peer response, and student self-assessment.

Despite the size of my corpus, as I apply the heuristic to the artifacts of the ePortfolios in the following chapters I am able to discuss
some factors in more depth than others, namely because my data does
not include observations or interviews. However, because my corpus
includes teacher response, peer response, and student self-reflections on
response they received both within the course and from friends, family,
and writing center tutors, I am able to discuss my constructivist heuristic
with a degree of context that has not been possible in prior large-scale
studies. In the chapters that follow, I apply the heuristic to my corpus of
teacher and student responses, focusing on teacher response in chapter
3, peer response in chapter 4, and student self-assessment in chapter 5.
The order of the chapters corresponds to the shift in attention that a
constructivist framework for response encourages, moving us away from
the centrality of the teacher as responder and shifting the focus of the
response construct to peer response and student self-assessment.

3

TEACHER RESPONSE TO WRITING

In this chapter, I focus on the 635 pieces of student writing in my corpus that received teacher response. I use my constructivist response heuristic (see figure 1.1) as a tool to analyze my data, and similar to chapter 2, this chapter is organized around the six questions of my heuristic. In applying my heuristic to the data, I aim to capture as fully as possible the multiple contexts of the teacher response in my research. However, because I only have the teacher comments that students chose to include in their ePortfolios, and because I do not have evidence from classroom observations or interviews with the teachers in my study, my analysis, although large in scale, is limited in context. In order to provide an additional layer of context, I include in this chapter student reflections on their teachers' responses. I also examine revisions students made to their drafts after receiving teacher comments to gain a better understanding of what impact teacher comments had on students' drafts.

Before I discuss the teacher comments from my research, a few notes about the presentation of student, teacher, and writing center tutor comments in this chapter and throughout the rest of the book. Because I do not know which pronouns each student and teacher in my research uses to refer to themselves, I use "they" and "their" to refer to a single student or teacher as well as plural students and teachers. In order to keep the names of teachers and writing center tutors confidential, whenever a student refers to a teacher or a tutor in a comment I cite, I use "X" in place of the teacher's or tutor's name. When a teacher refers to a student, I also use "X" in place of the student's name. Sometimes student reflections or teacher comments had minor grammar or punctuation errors or were written in a dialect or accent that differs from standardized edited academic English, and I chose not to edit typos or accent variations.

WHO SHOULD RESPOND?

In my constructivist response heuristic, teachers are not the default primary responder to student writing. Teachers are only one actor in

https://doi.org/10.7330/9781646423682.c003

the response construct, and as I discussed in chapter 2, when teachers put themselves at the center of response, the results are decidedly mixed. But because the organization of this book moves from teacher response to peer response to student self-assessment, in considering the question, "Who should respond?" in this chapter, I focus on teacher response. In *Assignments across the Curriculum* (2014), I noted that two-thirds of the over two thousand college writing assignments in my study were written for the teacher playing the role of examiner, looking for correct answers to textbook or lecture material. My research on response adds further evidence of the narrow, examiner role that teachers often set for themselves. The most striking pattern in my analysis of teacher response, and students' reflections on teacher response, is the teacher playing a judging role and the impact this appears to have on the students in my research.

Although I do not include in my research graded drafts due to the FERPA-related concerns I mentioned in chapter 1, even on drafts in progress teachers in my study frequently play the role of evaluator and use their comments to simply rewrite students' work. A first-year writing teacher admits to a student, "I've made some drastic revisions to some paragraphs, to try to make them clearer, but I'm not sure that I haven't distorted your ideas in doing so." A photography teacher tells a student, "I went ahead and played with your photo. I moved the horizon line closer to the rule of thirds. I brought up the shadows to show more detail, and sharpened the image some." Often teachers simply scratch out student sentences and write in the teacher's own ideas, such as a teacher who tells a student that the first sentence of an essay "could be something like, 'While most people think becoming healthy is only about eating healthier foods and working out at the gym, they often overlook the importance of mental health.'" Figure 3.1 is the first page of a teacher response that illustrates this kind of response as rewriting.

Frequently in my corpus, teachers judge student writing in a harsh tone and express frustration that students are not writing in "correct" or "proper" ways, as these comments illustrate:

You MUST correct your format.

You should not make the same technical mistakes—citation, formatting, grammar, punctuation, and syntax errors—that you made in Major Essays 1 and 2.

You MUST put your Works Cited list in proper MLA format to receive a grade on the essay!!!

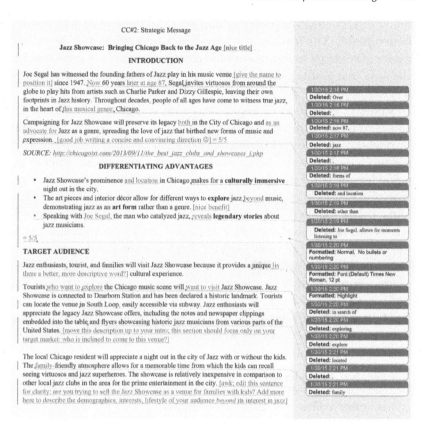

Figure 3.1. Teacher response as rewriting.

Students in my corpus frequently reflect on trying to please teachers in their role of judge. A student from my research spells out this narrow view of the teacher as judge in their portfolio reflection, stating, "As far as the essays that are included in my E-portfolio, again they are developed and fixed to please my target audience, Professor X." In a final reflection on their teacher's comments, a student with a similar philosophy writes, "Knowing what the teacher wants from an assignment is really helpful. You can alter your work to fit the teacher's expectations." In a final portfolio reflection, another student shares a similar approach: "After the midterm and as the quarter has moved on I feel like I have a better understanding for my target audience for this class, which is my teacher Professor X. I have been focusing more on making my paper geared toward her ideals of a solid paper. I have been following her rubric more closely and have been making sure I have everything in the paper that she is expecting to be in there. By doing this it makes my professor happy and ultimately sets me up for a better grade." The teacher as sole audience for writing, and the related desire of students to figure out what the teacher wants, is connected to the ways that grading impacts how the students in my research uptake teacher response.

Students' conflation of teacher response and grading, even when it comes to teacher comments on ungraded drafts, is a consistent theme throughout my study. At times students seem to plead with teachers to simply focus their response on what students need to do in order to get a good grade. In a process report that asks the student to share what type of feedback the student wants, one student writes, "I just want to know if I've followed the rubric. I don't want another average grade, tell me if I've followed the rubric correctly." A different student says in the last line of their process memo, "This is the improved version of my essay and I hope it will help me to attain a decent grade." Students are at times surprisingly honest about the connection between grades and their motivation to write, as is evident in the following passages from portfolio reflection essays—the first from a student reflecting on prior experiences in school and the second from a student reflecting on their current first-year writing course:

> I had thought grades were far more important than what I was actually writing or how I really viewed something. I didn't really care about what I was writing as long as my grade was satisfactory.

> My first goal, sadly, was to receive an A grade in the class. I say sadly because that is not what writing is all about. Writing is about expressing one's idea on a specific idea without any thought of evaluation, but I must be honest when I say that my effort was important for me to receive an exceptional grade.

Students in my research were motivated to put more effort into their writing in order to get a better grade, but this effort was typically described not in terms of a genuine desire to improve or to communicate with an audience but simply as a robotic exercise in pleasing the teacher as judge.

Assigning students recognizable disciplinary, professional, or public genres written to specific wider audiences is one way that a handful of teachers in my corpus discourage students from seeing them as merely graders. A first-year writing teacher illustrates this point with their response to an assignment that asks students to write a proposal to a campus organization. The teacher writes in an end comment of a proposal aimed at the university's student government: "The only suggestion I have for you is to consider your audience as you revise, especially the beginning of the essay. I think your introduction would appeal to a general audience, but where and when does SGA step in? Try to make the first couple of paragraphs more relevant to the specific situation you are writing for."

The more precise the target audience of the rhetorical situation of teachers' assignments, the more precise the feedback teachers provided. Consider, for example, the teacher who asks students to create a public service announcement and writes in their comments to a student, "My only suggestion would be to leave a contact name/number/email address/website, etc. so that your audience can actually go and do something about this." The marginal comments of a first-year writing teacher who is responding to a student's sales pitch for a commercial include, "Remember, you're pitching this commercial to your boss, so you can be more concise with this information and therefore more convincing," and "Here you're moving away from pitching the commercial to your boss."

In *Assignments across the Curriculum,* I noted that a handful of the assignments I collected were written not to a hypothetical wider audience but to an actual audience beyond the classroom. A professional writing student in my current research, reflecting on feedback they received from the teacher on a resume, speaks to students' perceptions of the usefulness of feedback that is given on an assignment that will eventually be circulated to an audience beyond the classroom: "I feel that after having this assignment I will be better equipped to make sure my resume isn't one of those that gets thrown in the trash because of a simple formatting mistake. I used Dr. X's advice to update my own resume and feel that it is more useful after having done so." This student's appreciation for the teacher's advice is a stark contrast to the attitude of the students I cited earlier in this section who are focused on pleasing the teacher in order to get a good grade.

Other responders to student writing in my research who occupy a space between teacher and peers are tutors in campus writing centers. I did not have enough data in my corpus focused on response from writing center tutors to merit a separate chapter on the topic, but there were nineteen ePortfolios in my research that included response from writing center tutors, and discussion of tutor response was common in portfolio reflection essays. Students in my study consistently mention in their portfolio reflections that tutor response helped them rethink their focus and organization and improve their writing. Consider the significant effect of a tutor's response described in this first-year writing student's portfolio introduction:

> In paper one, I had a difficult time thinking of a solid thesis. My initial thesis was just to talk about how Tilliamook Cheddar could be considered an expressionist artist according to Rosenberg's definition. . . . So, I took my essay to a tutor who helped me to create a thesis that had more meaning. My new thesis, questioned Rosenberg's definition and stated how there should be new guidelines to what Rosenberg considered an abstract artist, otherwise anyone, even dogs, could be considered abstract expressionists. Finally understanding how to create a paper with meaning was an important step for me; it was an 'AHA! Moment.'

In the revised draft the student composed after following the tutor's guidance, the thesis is changed from summarizing Rosenberg's definition of abstract art to critiquing and redefining it. In the revised thesis the student states, "By comparing the art of Pollock and Tilliamook Cheddar, Rosenberg's definition of abstract art will be criticized and redefined to include the intelligence factor that goes into creating abstract expression which separates Pollock from Tilliamook Cheddar."

A similar rethinking of content is reported in a reflection on a writing center visit by another first-year writing student: "In order for me to better understand the difference between 'showing' and 'telling' my audience my claim, X from the X Writing Center gave me some advice. He told me that the claim should 'never be given away' and that it should be open to 'interpretation.' He taught me how to incorporate more creative and descriptive ways to show my audience my claim. He advised me to 'think about my claim' and then to think about how I can 'deliver the claim in different ways.'" In the draft the student shared with the tutor, the final paragraph contains a mechanical thesis statement in the last sentence: "Reading a book, article, poem, or comment of a YouTube video, can cause an emotional reaction such as happiness, heartbreak, or sadness in order to cause a person to conduct an action that can change their life." In the revised draft, the student opens with a new, extended narrative that is followed by a three-sentence statement of the controlling idea of the essay that is more nuanced and developed than the pat thesis statement from the first draft.

Another student explains that a visit to the writing center not only helped them refocus an essay but gave them a powerful rhetorical approach that they transferred to other academic writing assignments:

> While at the Writing Center, I was really taught how to decide whether or not my paragraphs were focused. My tutor would ask what persuasive strategy each of my paragraphs was discussing in order to enhance my thesis statement. I was also taught that making the claim that contradicts my thesis can be powerful to my thesis if I can offer why that claim is

inherently wrong. In this paper I decided to bring up the claim of shock factor and how the use of bold or even disturbing images may deter some but will attract many in the long run. I had never used a counter-argument as a persuasive strategy in writing before, but now it is something I try to include in all my papers for more positive overall conclusions.

Throughout my study, in the reflections students include in their portfolios, they highlight feedback from tutors as being especially helpful in gaining confidence as writers, rethinking content and organization of ideas, imagining the needs of a reader as dramatized by the tutor, and transferring rhetorical strategies and knowledge to other academic writing contexts.

Although most of the students in my research who reflect on writing center visits describe the writing center as a place to get help with the content of their writing, many of the teachers give students the impression that the writing center is a fix-it shop for writers struggling with sentence-level issues. The following end comments are representative:

> Next time, work with a tutor in the writing center for proofreading purposes before submitting your final paper.

> Your revision should also address the many grammatical and mechanical errors in the draft. . . . I would definitely encourage you to work with a Writing Center tutor, review some of these problem areas, and make sure you know how to correct them and avoid them in the future.

> Nice improvement, but the number of awkward and incorrectly structured sentences really impede the communication of your thesis. I strongly suggest going to the writing center for tutoring.

> Similarly, you have some grammatical issues with comma splice run-ons and your choice of preposition (using 'of' when you mean 'about' for example). In your future papers make sure to edit with an eye for these errors, and consider using the writing center.

The writing center tutors in my research do not act as judges, and they resist focusing on rewriting students' words or merely correcting their sentences. But the teachers in my study often describe the purpose of working with a tutor in these more narrow editing terms.

Another source of feedback beyond the teacher for the students in my study is friends and family. Even if teachers create a response construct that limits students to the student/teacher dyad, students will reject this limitation and seek out feedback on their own, not just at campus writing centers but in dorm rooms and communications with family members. I include a discussion of response from friends and family in this chapter because, in a sense, students are using friends and family as additional teachers, hoping for an extra layer of feedback on organization, development, and editing.

It is common for students in my study to mention family members as sources of additional feedback or second opinions regarding a teacher's advice, as these passages from student ePortfolio reflections illustrate:

> Along with having my workshop group edit this paper; I also had my mother and older sister edit it.

> My last step is I give my paper to either a family member or my roommate to get their opinion on the content and see if they catch any grammatical mistakes.

> When I would sit down to write the first step would always be to first call my mother.

> After I completed the draft and did some self edits I usually went to the writing center or asked my twin sister for feedback.

Students also turned to friends and roommates for additional feedback, as these portfolio reflections articulate:

> After visiting the writing center I made a few changes and had one of my friends review my paper before submitting it.

> My roommate helps me a lot about editing, because my grammar has lots of mistakes need to fix it.

> Every time when I finish my paper, I will give to my roommate or other friend, they gave me many useful advices. Like the research paper, at the beginning, I could not decide which kind of topic I will choose for my paper, I want to find something unique and special. My roommate gave me the idea and I found that is definitely what I want do for my project.

In many of the courses in my research, the teacher is at the very center of response, and the primary emphasis is on the student/teacher dyad, but even in these teacher-centered courses students seek out feedback from writing center tutors and from friends and family.

WHAT SHOULD RESPONSE FOCUS ON?

Scholarship that explores the question of what response should focus on tends to turn our attention to the sentences and paragraphs of drafts of student writing rather than focusing on student self-reflection and students' own assessment of their drafts. Response scholars such as David Boud, Nancy Falchikov, and Kathleen Yancey have encouraged researchers and teachers to refocus their attention and consider the central role metacognition plays in students' growth as writers and their ability to transfer what they have learned to new contexts. Yancey (1998a) argues that most researchers and most teachers have not caught up to this shift from a focus on products to a focus on student self-assessment, and in line with Yancey's assertion, most of the teachers in my corpus focus far more often on sentences and paragraphs of discrete drafts than on student self-reflection.

Despite the fact that there are 128 student midterm and final self-reflection essays in my corpus, and many student process memos included with rough drafts, I have evidence of only seven teacher responses to students' self-assessments. These responses to student metacognition are primarily teachers engaging in dialogue with students during drafts through the use of process memos. For example, in one first-year writing course, a student notes in their process memo that they are struggling to verbalize the connection between theories from the readings and the student's discussion of jargon. The teacher responds, "I agree that the paper read at times like an argument about jargon in general rather than an argument about what Klas says about jargon, which is a bit more complex than you've made it out to be." A student in a different course expresses concerns about organization in a self-reflection, and the teacher writes in an end comment, "You were concerned about organization. My advice is to consider how each and every paragraph can support the overarching argument that will be the backbone of your essay." In answering a postscript question posed by the teacher, "How did you challenge yourself to leave your comfort zone during the revision process?" a student writes, "I think I challenged myself more in the writing itself by trying to add quotes or dialogue because I usually am not good with that stuff." The teacher responds directly to this reflection, writing, "good—this is what your memoir needed." In each of these cases of response to students' metacognitive writing, there is evidence of the student exhibiting self-efficacy as an author and the teacher entering into a dialogue with the student in such a way that teacher response builds on student self-assessment.

Closely related to metacognition is transfer of learning. Of the 635 pieces of writing in my corpus that teachers responded to, and the thousands of teacher comments I analyzed, there are only a dozen comments that focus on transfer to future writing contexts. Most of these are end comments that focus on the transfer of writing strategies to the next assignment within the course. What follows are examples of these type of feedforward comments:

In future papers, I encourage you to use your opening paragraphs to set the stakes and extent of your argument, using your concluding paragraphs to build on those ideas in the context of the evidence and reasoning you've laid out.

Next time, please allow time toward the end of your revision process to find your clearest presentation of your claim, and add it to the introduction.

In Paper 2, build on your strong eye for literary detail by applying it to a clearly-articulated debate.

In Paper 3, be sure to ground any argument or theory sources with a clear explanation before you apply them to the other sources.

It is certainly likely that the teachers in my study commented on transfer to future writing contexts in response I was not able to capture due to the limitations of my study, such as one-on-one conferences or class discussions. But it is rare in teacher comments on the drafts in my corpus for transfer from one assignment to the next to be a focus, and rarer still for teachers to discuss more far-reaching transfer to contexts beyond the course.

In the 635 student drafts with teacher comments in my corpus, there were only two content-focused teacher comments that focus on the student as a writer beyond the current course. These more far-reaching transfer comments emphasize strengths students can build on in their future academic careers:

This is a poetic move, you have some bold language moments in this paper, you might try to grow this impulse as your write at university more and more, balancing it with acute thinking. The tension this would create will take you far.

You write with a sense of purpose and you make really excellent connections to other texts we've read in class. These are your strengths as a writer and something you should be proud of and keep in mind when you compose your next papers in your academic career.

Perhaps more teachers in my study focused on transfer to future writing contexts in responses given after final portfolios were submitted and thus were not available to me, but these examples are the only evidence of far-reaching transfer comments in my corpus.

In their portfolio reflection essays, students express an appreciation for comments they can transfer to the next assignment in the course or to future courses. A student who received a comment from the teacher regarding a source that lacked credibility commented, "I now know for future papers that sources like this are not reliable for a research paper." Another student mentions in a reflection on teacher comments on a draft, "On the second page of my paper, I was given this comment: 'Do you think this is a reasonable definition? Is there another, more sociological definition you can use to augment this popular understanding?' If I were to rewrite this paper, I would certainly address these questions. Nevertheless, in my third paper, I tried to find the best, most widely accepted definition of a 'social movement' to avoid receiving this comment again." In a similar comment, a student reflects, "The professor's comments on my final draft indicated that I had much room for improvement. Although the professor did like my quote integration, my overall argument had no strong guiding claim or problem statement." The student says that "to do better on paper 2, I knew I had to alter my approach to writing."

One strategy for improving transfer is to give students feedback focused on their growth as learners. Just as teachers in my research rarely make comments focused on writing and transfer, only a handful of comments focus on growth. Despite requiring an emphasis on process in students' presentation of their ePortfolios, which often include rough drafts, process memos, and reflection essays, teacher comments in my study rarely acknowledge the ways students improve (or continue to struggle) from draft to draft and assignment to assignment.

The teachers who do comment on students' growth as writers typically do so to emphasize positive growth, as these end comments from business writing, education, and first-year writing teachers illustrate:

> Overall, X, your commitment to your learning is quite impressive, and we truly appreciate your efforts to improve your writing and your work. It is quite evident that you are, no doubt, growing as a student, a writer, and a thinker. Keep up the good work!

> This is a solid essay. It contains your best writing and thinking of the semester.

> I am very pleased with your progress from draft to draft in this essay as well as overall progress throughout the course of the semester. Your analysis and structure grew increasingly sophisticated with each project.

Students in my study appreciate these types of comments on their growth as writers. In an introduction to their ePortfolio one student says, "I am extremely proud of how the essay was received. To see the growth of my writing skills and argumentation from the first essay to the last is a great tool to continue the growing process." The teacher reinforces this student's pride in their growth in an end comment on one of the student's essays, writing, "You made good use of your sources, and employed a much stronger conceptual layout for the presentation of your ideas than you have in earlier assignments." Another student writes in a reflective note in their ePortfolio, "I was very glad to see that my Professor noticed my improvement in writing and the hard work I put into the Second paper." On a marginal comment on this second paper the teacher writes, "Thanks for making the changes; this is a much better intro paragraph—good job!" and in the end comment, "You make some good improvements from your previous draft."

Commenting on students' growth will often mean commenting on students' drafts and being aware of their revision processes. I discuss teacher comments on drafts, and the revisions students made based on teacher comments on drafts, later in this chapter when I explore the heuristic question, "When should response occur?" In this section, I consider the ways that teachers integrate (or fail to integrate) peer response feedback in their comments. Many of the ePortfolios in my research include peer response, and I collected 419 peer responses. Despite the ubiquity of peer response, teachers rarely focus on this aspect of students' writing processes in their responses. Only five teachers comment on the relationship between a student's revised draft and their feedback from peers:

> Your use of the peer edit to glean advice from your fellow students . . . served your paper exceedingly well.

> I agree with [the peer responder], though, that the idea about the Other at the end needs further development.

> Your midterm portfolio, on a literal level, addresses many of your essay drafts and peer commentary on major assignments.

> It may be in your best interest to reread your peers' comments and to seriously reflect on enhancing the amount of description in your story.

> I agree with whoever edited this for you, that your topic of characters' assumptions is a rich one that you could do a lot with.

Many of the teachers in my study use rubrics to respond to their students' writing, but only one rubric, which is from an advanced composition course, mentions revision based on peer response: "The evidence clearly indicates where you have made progress and how you have transformed your writing throughout the peer review process and evaluation cycles." It is certainly likely that some teachers in my corpus engage in dialogue with peer response in feedback to students that I did not capture in my research, such as class discussions or one-on-one conferences. But it is notable that as central as peer response is in many of the courses in my research, teachers rarely engage in dialogue with peer feedback in their responses on student drafts in my corpus and rarely assess students' use of peer feedback in their rubrics.

WHAT CONTEXTS SHOULD RESPONDERS CONSIDER?

Taking a constructivist approach to response means being aware of the many contexts that shape response to student writing, from students' personal literacy histories to our own biases as teachers to the genre and discourse communities of our writing projects to wider sociocultural contexts. In a constructivist approach, just as student self-assessment and growth is central in response, students' personal contexts are a primary consideration for researchers and teachers when taking into account the contexts of the response construct.

Self-reflection artifacts found throughout students' portfolios in my corpus provide valuable information about students' literacy histories. For example, consider how the following excerpts from student self-reflective artifacts regarding their language backgrounds might inform teachers' response to their writing:

> As a bilingual student who speaks Korean at home and English in the social scene, communicating my thoughts through an alternative language is a major success for me, especially in Advanced Writing for the Health Professions.

> As a student speaking English as a second language, I have always had issues with writing papers and communicating with people effectively. This has been a continuing interest for me while taking this course. Consider how difficult it would be to communicate words that have not direct translation into another language.

> Growing up in an Indian immigrant household, I did not have many opportunities to converse in the English language. Since English is my third language, I face many challenges both speaking and writing the language on a daily basis. When I began Writing 39C, I was nervous that I would not be able to survive through the ten weeks of rigorous research and writing.

> I love painting, writing and reading. However, writing in English is a challenge for me because that is my second language. At the beginning, I was totally lost and didn't know how to help myself out of my problems. . . . I cannot remember how many times I feel bad about myself when I failed on writing assignments in my first year.

In response to the final passage in these examples of student reflections, the teacher wrote, "Don't worry about your English and writing. Just put forth the effort and do the assignments and we'll make sure that your meaning is coming across and that you're putting thought into your work. You'll do fine. I'm very glad you're in my class." This teacher's awareness of the students' context of someone who has been taught to see their multilingualism as a deficit rather than an asset created an opportunity to provide reassurance and encouragement to the student prior to responding to drafts of formal writing assignments.

It is apparent in the reflective writing in my research that one critical aspect of understanding students' contexts as writers is understanding their fears about writing. One student reveals in a self-assessment essay that they "had the biggest fear of writing, especially when it came to grammar." In a similar statement another student writes in their self-analysis essay, "I constantly worry about the grammar rather than focusing on the voice and flow of my words." A number of students in my research express a general fear of writing, including a student who says in the introduction to their portfolio that they were "terrified of writing at a collegiate level. Possessing severely limited experience in writing, having written only 4 essays in my high school career, I feared I would struggle to write even an acceptable paper let alone a spectacular one." Another student writes about their initial feelings regarding their first-year writing course, admitting, "Quite frankly, I was frightened. I was not a strong writer; in fact, writing was my weakest subject."

In addition to expressing fear about writing, a number of students in my corpus comment on rigid writing formulas learned in high school that would not necessarily transfer (or would negatively transfer) to college writing contexts, as these passages from three different students' reflective writing illustrate:

> To me, English was always boring and redundant. There were always dumb rules that we had to follow as students. Like Jane Schaffer. I loathed having to chunk my sentences, always being restricted to the same monotony of CD, CM, CM. Where was the expression and freedom in that?

> Also, in high school I've always been told that in my conclusion I just rephrase my introduction. So I don't understand what Dr. X means by 'your conclusion should rest your case, not repeat your argument.' To me, resting my case simply means repeating my argument and then saying I win.

> My regimented five-paragraph essays had always earned crappy grades because I would not stick to the regimented requirements set forth by my teachers. I would write free-flowing six-, seven-, or eight-paragraph essays as early as seventh grade, merely because I was emulating writers who I'd read before.

Perhaps one reason students in my research note that writing formulas learned in high school do not transfer to college-level writing is the variety of genres they are asked to write in for their college courses.

In *Assignments across the Curriculum*, I found that teachers across disciplines assign a wide variety of genres, and in my corpus of ePortfolios there is also an array of assignment genres. The teachers in my research frequently consider the context of genre in their responses, and their feedback focused on genre concerns is nuanced. For example, a student who wrote a formulaic five-paragraph theme introduction in response to a literacy autobiography assignment received an end comment from the teacher that states, "A literacy autobiography is not a typical academic essay and you would need to think of a different introduction that sets the stage for your personal literacy narrative but so in a way that works well in a genre where the writers tell the story of their literacy development." Another teacher also differentiates between formulaic writing and composing in an authentic genre, writing in an end comment, "So, you would not normally introduce your gap in the introduction. Literature reviews work differently than a traditional 5 paragraph essay where you forecast the whole paper at the end of the first paragraph. For this project, you should only deal with one gap, because the research gap is what leads to the project proposal; in most cases, academic research doesn't try to tackle all the gaps at once, but instead does research in one particular area at a time."

Teachers in my study often ask students to revise in order to meet genre expectations. Consider the way genre influences a first-year writing teacher's suggestions when the teacher writes in an end comment, "When revising, just reorient your discussion of the data your research uncovered so that it justifies your claim. Then you will have transformed this from a summary of research into an argument essay." This student was able to revise to meet genre conventions and receive a high grade on the final draft. The student added a thesis sentence that made a claim about the necessity of a consistent measure of the Internet's energy consumption, an argument regarding needed mandates for creating energy efficiency, and a footnote elaborating on technical information regarding energy standards.

Revising for genre conventions is the focus of another teacher's end comments on a student's rough draft: "X, your enthusiasm for Princess Diana is clear, however, you must understand that this is a biographical research essay, an overview of her life. You are writing this as if it is an opinion piece on what a generous person Diana Spencer was. What you need to do is write about the facts and events of Spencer's entire life. It is not appropriate for you to express how wonderful she was." The teacher suggests that the student tone down their language and quote and paraphrase the perspectives of secondary sources rather than make so many of their own evaluative judgments. The student's final draft reflects the struggles students may encounter writing in a new genre, even when teachers make clear and helpful comments regarding genre conventions. The student does add paraphrasing and citation, but the paper becomes a string of paraphrases, intermixed with strong personal opinions that the student decided to keep in the final draft, despite the teacher's advice that personal opinion was not appropriate for this genre.

The genre conventions of a white paper play the primary role in constructing an end comment with advice for revision from a first-year writing teacher: "My main suggestion for a revision of this draft is the following: this has a wonderful argument and tone, but it's not really a white paper in its current form. It's reading more now as an argumentative paper, where your stance on the issue appears in the introduction and throughout the draft. It's wonderful that you have this stance identified, and you do argue from this viewpoint quite effectively, but I do want to see more identification of key players and their opinions on either side of the research question." This student did not include the final, revised draft in their portfolio, so I do not have evidence of whether or not they revised based on the teacher's genre convention comments. But there is evidence in the students' final portfolio reflection essay of an awareness of how the genre conventions of a white paper can help the writer keep information organized. The student writes, "In my White Paper I had a section called Environmental Benefits of a Plant Based Diet, and another called Health Benefits of a Plant Based Diet these sections were helpful because it allowed me to place the ideas into categories. This idea of organizing my thoughts into different sections of the paper allowed me to channel my thoughts into one area at a time."

As I discuss in chapter 5, many students in my research reflect on genre conventions in their final portfolio reflection essays, especially in first-year writing courses where the prompts for reflection essays often explicitly asked students to do so.

Genre contexts are a common focus of response in my corpus, but teachers rarely consider the classroom context when they give students feedback. Occasionally teachers refer students back to course readings as models of the genre students are attempting to write, but other than these occasional references to class readings, there are only three instances in tens of thousands of comments from teachers in which connections are made to the work of the class:

> You participate well in class, and do the assigned reading, so I have confidence that in the future your essay will improve.

> You have a fondness for passive voice verb constructions that would be much clearer in an active voice construction. We'll go over this together in class.

In your first body paragraph and beyond it isn't clear that the symbolism associated with the handkerchief has nothing to do with its physical reality. As we discussed in class, handkerchiefs are prosthetic devices that serve as a kind of membrane in that they help to absorb bodily fluids and thus serve to regulate the boundaries between the body's outside and inside. For Othello, Desdemona's inability to produce the handkerchief on demand signifies the dangerous openness of her body.

Although I did not observe any of the courses in my research, and I cannot know the extent to which teachers responded to students' questions about their writing in class, I can say that the work of the class is not often referred to in teachers' comments on drafts.

Teachers also rarely make the connection between the work of the class and the work of academic discourse communities. The potential for connecting the classroom and the larger discourse community is articulated nicely in language from a first-year writing teacher's writing assignment: "Keep in mind that discussion of the materials we contemplate in this course extends far beyond the walls of the classroom. Scholars and critics refine their understanding of artistic works and develop their own arguments by responding to one another, just as we do during class discussions and peer-review sessions." In *Assignments across the Curriculum*, I found that teachers rarely connect their writing assignments to the work of a broader discourse community, and teachers in the present study rarely connect their response to the work of the classroom as a discourse community. But a handful of teachers in my corpus do provide feedback that references the audience expectations of broader discourse communities beyond the course. One rubric criterion from an assignment in a technical writing course states, "Sophisticated, consistent design enriches the text's message. iFixit conventions are followed." In a philosophy course, the teacher writes in a marginal comment, "Please do not use questions when you are writing philosophical argument. An argument is a set of statements." And in a clinical practicum course, the teacher says in an end comment, "Change management is the life of an Informatics Specialist. X was able to see this in action and identify some of the change management methodologies that were in use."

One strategy for emphasizing discourse community in response is to couch individual teacher response in the context of a sequence of courses at an institution or within a major. Only a single response in my corpus references another course the student has taken previously, when a teacher mentions to a student in a marginal comment that they "should be pulling from your research class" to identify strategies for measuring correlation between nurses' participation in professional development and their incomes. Although students sometimes mention in their portfolio reflection essays the ways that the writing they completed in one course in a sequence is connected to the next course, a pattern of my corpus I discuss in chapter 5, teachers rarely make this connection in their response. Teachers in my study also fail to consider the sociocultural contexts of writing in their response, perhaps partly due to the fact that few of the assignments are connected to a wider public audience beyond the classroom.

WHAT TYPE OF FEEDBACK SHOULD RESPONDERS GIVE?

From Nancy Sommers's seminal "Responding to Student Writing" (1982) to current studies on teacher feedback (Ferris 2014; Ferris et al. 2011; Ferris and Hedgcock 1998; Rysdam and Johnson-Shull 2016; Stern and Solomon 2006), researchers have found that teachers generally give directive response, often wrestling control of the writing from students. It is common for the teachers in my study to take control of the student's work, deleting and rewriting as a form of response. Screenshots of responses to paragraphs from two different teachers exemplify this directive approach to responding (see figures 3.2 and 3.3).

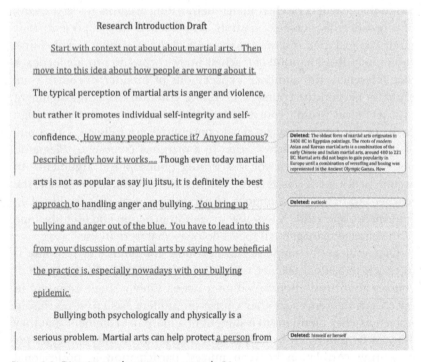

Figure 3.2. Directive teacher response example #1.

The Romans were known to build public or civic works, both for the cities they conquered outside of Rome as well as within the city of Rome itself. These public works were meant to take care of the physical and emotional needs of the people, and were often done by the wealthy or even the Imperial family. Senators and Emperors who wanted to cultivate or influence the public would build civic projects, such as theaters, to improve the quality of life for the Roman people as well as to win their favor. Daily life for the Roman people was far from comfortable, and the theaters were a way to temporarily forget about the squalor they came from and enjoy life. Two prime examples of theaters built as civic projects are the Theatre Marcellus and the Flavian Amphitheater. To understand the similarities and differences in these pieces, it's important to take a look at where, when, and why they were built, as well as who built them. Though built by different emperors at different times, they share a number of similar characteristics, including architectural elements, location, and purpose.

The Theater Marcellus was built by the emperor Augustus in Rome between 23 B.C. and 17 A.D., during the Imperial Augustan period. When Augustus came to power, he had a vision for Rome. He stated that he came to Rome, a city of brick, and would leave it a city of marble. He brought about a time of peace and prosperity for the Roman Empire following the turbulent time of the Late Republic. The Roman Empire had expanded, and needed a new form of governance to accommodate the increasing number of territories. Augustus was chosen by Julius Caesar as heir and successor, and as such Augustus comes to power and created a successive form of government and leadership. Augustus is highly ambitious, wanting to make his mark on the Roman

Figure 3.3. Directive teacher response example #2.

These kinds of directive responses would have fit side-by-side with the directive comments Sommers shared in her research from forty years ago, and I will not belabor with further examples the point that has been well-established in the response research: teachers across disciplines often wrestle control of students' writing and cross out and rewrite as a typical response technique.

Overly directive response can reinforce students' misconception that a teacher's purpose in responding is to correct students' writing. One student in a reflection memo says, "I made the corrections the professor suggested," and another student says in a reflection on teacher comments, "Dr. X does a very good job of pointing out what is wrong in a draft so that we know exactly what needs to be fixed." Another student states in their portfolio reflection essay that they prefer the teacher's comments to peers' comments because the teacher "always gave me the feedback I needed to understand the mistakes I made in order to make them right." These comments add further evidence for an observation I made at the beginning of this chapter: students focus on grades and perceive teachers as judges to be obeyed.

There is a stark contrast between the highly directive comments I shared in the previous two excerpts and the examples of teachers in my research asking open-ended questions that put the onus on the student to make content revision decisions. What follows are examples from my research of these open-ended questions:

> Why should savers compromise? Doesn't an investment of $1mm or $2mm deprive them of an opportunity to create more wealth??

> What is the prevailing scholarly interpretation of the film? How does your own analysis fit alongside these others?

> As I note in the one of the bubbles above, the dog's paintings could present a real challenge to Rosenberg and other fans of abstract painting. Do you think that the dog's art delegitimizes the value of abstract art? What do you think about Rosenberg's criteria for "good" abstract art, if a dog can fulfill it?

It is notable that the directive comments in my corpus tend to focus on sentence-level issues, while the open-ended questions are almost always focused on global content.

Although I found that the teachers in my study generally give directive response, I also conversely found that teachers in my corpus frequently praise students. Teachers' words of praise for students are often effusive, as these comments from teachers across disciplines illustrate:

> I think you have done an excellent job researching, as I've read it so far. Such apt source selection!

> You have the beginning of a great post here!

> You will need to develop these thoughts a little, however your basic idea is FANTASTIC!!

Thank you for your revision. Your storyboard is quite thorough, and your use of screen shots is both clever and effective. Additionally, your revised phrasing strengthens and clarifies your points. Well done!

This paper was a joy to read. You are a fantastic, thoughtful scholar. This kind of writing from one of our students fills me with hope and pride.

I LOVED your paper.

Students in my study appreciate praise comments of any kind. One student notes in a portfolio reflection, "My self-esteem increased when I received the comments from my peers and professor. Most of the comments were positive."

Perhaps the most effective way to offer praise is to use it as a motivating factor for further revision, as these teachers in my research do:

I think you do a good job leading your reader through his argument here. You might use this as a model for some of my earlier comments.

If you agree with Caruth's descriptions of trauma, then how does applying that description to these texts help us understand the texts in a new way, or how does the use of the texts expand or change Caruth's claims? Your focus on imagery and textual (or filmic) detail is a great place to start, so build on that instinct.

Good story! it shows instead of tells. can you do this more?

Praise can be used as a starting point for further revision and also as a means to emphasize to students the types of knowledge and skills that will transfer to future writing contexts. The two more far-reaching transfer comments from my research that I cited earlier are examples of praise comments:

This is a poetic move, you have some bold language moments in this paper, you might try to grow this impulse as your write at university more and more, balancing it with acute thinking. The tension this would create will take you far.

You write with a sense of purpose and you make really excellent connections to other texts we've read in class. These are your strengths as a writer and something you should be proud of and keep in mind when you compose your next papers in your academic career.

In *Assignments across the Curriculum,* I found that teachers give students mixed signals regarding their assessment criteria in their writing assignments and rubrics, and there are many instances in the teacher responses in my corpus of confusion regarding praise and critique.

One teacher covers a student's essay in marginal comments focused on critique, but begins the end comment, "This has the makings of a really great paper." I noted a similar disconnect in an engineering communication teacher's response that focuses on marking errors throughout the student's essay but ends with the comment "Nice job!"

During the sense-checking activity for this research, one of the two graduate students who read a sampling of my data, DJ Quinn, noticed that when teachers offer praise in their comments to students, it is often followed by "but" or "however" and a critical comment. After DJ pointed this out, I reread the teacher praise comments and found that his observation was true of the entire corpus. The following teacher end comments illustrate this pattern:

> I like how you have developed the responses to Greene and Khan. However, try not to over do the contrast.

> You have a nice beginning, however you need to make some significant adjustments.

> X, your enthusiasm is clear; however, your essay as not as clear as it needs to be.

> Nice info overall although your spacing is awkward.

The last two examples of teacher end comments point to a pattern in my research that when teachers do immediately follow a praise comment with critique, that critique is often focused on sentence-level concerns.

The assignment prompts and rubrics I collected in *Assignments across the Curriculum* revealed teachers' obsession with grammatical and formatting correctness. Response research has found that teachers tend to focus on local, sentence-level concerns in their response, but just as I found a balance of directive and facilitative teacher comments in my research, I found a balance of attention to local and global concerns. However, there are many teachers in my study who focus their response almost exclusively on local concerns, and sometimes these comments have a tone of frustration or even anger:

> You did no editing?

> Poor use of punctuation; review online handbook for use of commas.

> Fused, choppy sentence. You should have reviewed your paper for grammatical correctness and syntax errors.

> Your paper suffered from a lack of clarity throughout due to poor syntax.

> You have got to stop putting sentences together this awkwardly.

Although I do not have extensive demographic information about the students in my research, in portfolio introductions, reflection essays, and literacy narratives, many students discuss their backgrounds as multilingual writers. One problematic response from my corpus was a case of a teacher's comment that a multilingual student's use of punctuation is "strange."

Although the response literature I cite in chapter 2 recommends that teachers avoid focusing only on sentence-level concerns, the students in my study often express an appreciation for editing feedback. These passages from three students' portfolio introductions exemplify students' desire for local, sentence-level feedback:

> In Writing 098, I learned that my writing skills are not sufficient even at the end of the class. I believe that my professor from Writing 098 had not corrected me or marked my mistakes enough. Thankfully, Professor X marked almost all the mistakes that I had in my papers. It was easier for me to see what my errors are clearly and try to find the ways to fix them.

> The criticisms that I received during WR100 allowed me to focus on my errors with writing. By resolving the issues that were pointed out in my writing I was able change my writing process to one that created less errors, more clarity, and more focus.

> I would like you to know that I appreciate the time you take to give feedback as I feel like it really helps because with things like run on paragraphs and spelling errors I wouldn't notice stuff like that and you really help me to stay on top of it.

It is worth noting that the students represented in these excerpts are highly focused on grades and had experienced being harshly penalized for editing errors. When students in my research reflect on the local editing comments they receive from teachers, they tend to talk about meeting the teacher's demands and trying not to lose points on their next piece of writing for the course.

Unlike students' uptake of teacher comments focused on local concerns, when students reflect on global revision suggestions they receive from teachers, they tend to talk about re-envisioning their work and growing as writers:

> My professor pushed me throughout the semester asking questions such as, what in the piece made me feel that specific emotion. She taught me important aspects to look for in paintings besides the subject of imitation. . . . When considering all of these aspects of art, my analyses became more deep and well thought out.

The comments made on my essay two draft by Dr. X, made me realize that I had lost sight of a great deal of my essay. I realized that while I did spend a long time, and alot of effort, looking up new sources and expanding my Eaton argument, I lost sight of the Ethicism and Separatism part of my essay. For the final draft I aim to revamp that part of my essay, and incorporate those ideas in a more organized and apparent fashion.

X felt the same way as she writes in the comments, "I'm not sure exactly what your thesis/problem statement/ significance are going to be, so make sure you clarify." I took this comments into deep consideration and focused on significance and clarity to make sure my point came across more clearly in peer edits and the final draft.

Global comments from teachers led to global revisions from students. The student who claims their analyses of art "became more deep and well thought out" due to the teachers' comments added entire paragraphs of analysis to final drafts, considering the paintings with a more critical eye and addressing each of the teachers' open-ended questions regarding the analysis of the artworks. The student who acknowledges that their professor was right in commenting that they had "lost sight of the Ethicism and Separatism part" in their essay added two full paragraphs on Ethicism and Separatism to the final draft, both of which contain support from additional secondary sources. The student who reflects that they took their teachers' suggestions regarding a lack of thesis/problem statement/significance "into deep consideration and focused on significance and clarity" was not overstating their revisions: this student transformed a simple approach to summarizing how symbols in two novels express trauma as defined by a psychologist into a sophisticated and nuanced argument. The student argues that the psychologist's discussion of trauma is lacking reflections on how trauma is resolved, and the student shows how trauma is resolved in the two novels through acts of repetition.

Whether teachers are providing local or global feedback, students in my research appreciate specific feedback and articulate ways they made global revisions based on specific feedback. One example of specific feedback comes from end comments from a first-year writing teacher: "The best way to bring this to the next level is to summarize each paragraph's point in a single sentence. Think about how well those sentences flow together. Try rearranging them until they flow as well as possible. If you still find gaps or rough spots in the logical sequence of the sentences, compose a new sentence to fill that gap." In a reflection on this teacher's comments, the student writes, "Another example of rearranging and reworking my paragraphs. Thanks for the specific examples of where I can improve my essay!" Another first-year writing teacher writes in an end comment, "For yours, it would be cool if you could convince a few people to let you study their actual online interactions, like an IM chat and/or FB statuses, etc. You could also talk with them (interview) to see what they think about what they do. Long story short, I think a deep study of a few individuals would be MUCH more interesting than a survey." The student reflects, "I took her advice, and conducted interviews with four different people about their online activities and how they feel about what they do online." Other students mention in portfolio reflection essays how they revised based on specific feedback:

> Also, when Dr. X comments on my view that Vertov's use of montage doesn't affect emotions as does Eisenstein's use of montage, I rethought my analysis. I decided that I can't really say much about emotions because the situation in Battleship Potemkin is different than Man with a Movie Camera.

> On page 2 X tells me where I should do more research and where to include that information. In this case, X told me, "Research and discuss how this book has been hailed by preservationists and environmentalists and used as an educational tool." Before, I would have never thought to include that in my paper, but now I know how to look at things from a different angle and offer a new concept to help the quality of my paper. Therefore, I've learned that the key component in the writing process is the revision.

The student who says they rethought their analysis after reading their teacher's comments concerning emotions in the films of Vertov and Eisenstein is not overstating their revision process. The first draft that the teacher commented on was focused in the thesis and in every paragraph on showing the ways that films from these two directors used montage to affect emotions in similar ways, but the revised draft takes a different and more nuanced approach, arguing that the film *Man with a Movie Camera* approaches emotions in a much different way. The entire organization of the second draft reflects this major change, and in the revised draft the essay is set up as a series of contrasts between the two directors rather than as a series of connections. A comparison of the introduction from the first draft of this student's essay and the revised introduction illustrates this major revision:

Original Introduction

In his essay "The Montage of Film Attractions," Sergei M. Eisenstein states that cinema is used "for exercising emotional influence over the masses." He believes that the order in which certain sequences are put together is able to influence the audience's emotions; this happens when "montage fragments" that, by themselves, provoke several preconceived associations or emotions in the audience, are juxtaposed to create a stronger emotional effect parallel to the effect of just the fragments alone. By examining the use of montage fragments in Eisenstein's film *Battleship Potemkin*, it can be concluded that Eisenstein's theory is correct. It is also possible, by observing the lack of montage fragments in Dziga Vertov's film *Man with a Movie Camera*, to see how without the correct arrangement of shots it is impossible to arouse any emotion in the audience.

Revised Introduction

In his essay "The Montage of Film Attractions," Sergei M. Eisenstein asserts that cinema is used "for exercising emotional influence over the masses." He believes that the order in which sequences are put together influences the audience's emotions. More specifically, juxtaposed "montage fragments" that provoke several preconceived associations or emotions in the audience create a similar, yet stronger emotional effect than the effect of just the fragments alone. Eisenstein uses this type of montage to propagandize the Soviet Union in his film *Battleship Potemkin*. Another very propagandistic film, Dziga Vertov's *Man with a Movie Camera*, also makes use of montage to portray the Soviet Union as a progressive utopia. However, while Eisenstein manipulates the audience's emotions with montage until they dislike and fear the previous monarchy, Vertov's method of montage has less to do with the emotional effect on the audience and more with the amplification of movement to imply the magnificence of the Soviet Union.

Although the students in my study appreciate specific feedback and are able to revise based on specific suggestions, it was common in my corpus to find pieces of writing that are blanketed in comments, or Word documents with numbered comments that reach into the thirties and forties. The excerpts from teacher responses to student essays shown in figures 3.4 and 3.5 are emblematic of many teachers' tendency to overwhelm students with comments.

Students report feeling stress and a loss of confidence when teachers provide this many comments. In a portfolio reflection essay a student says, "After Professor X corrected my draft, I was mortified! There was red ink all over the paper! Not only did this make my confidence level drop, but it made my stress level increase as well." Another student reflecting on teacher comments writes, "I couldn't believe it: 53 comments. I must have done something horribly wrong."

[MS1]Next Time, keep Tile page together with the rest of the paper; this heading is not necessary when using a title page properly.

[MS2]According to whom or to which set of statistics? By whom are you being influence? It is important to acknowledge sources. Your opinions, assessments, evaluations, or claims have little value if not provided within the context of credible sources.

[MS3]The politically correct nomenclature is "black Americans" or "African Americans." Black people are also referred to as "persons of color," but such is used in a specific context and not limited to only blacks.

[MS4]Which decision? Be specific!

[MS5]Poor use of punctuation; review online handbook for use of commas and hyphens (dashes).

[MS6]Review use of conjuction"and" at the beginning of a sentence???

[MS7]Conjunction "and" used again in this sentence (see previous comment) creates repetitive construction.

[MS8]Review use of "but" versus "however" to begin a sentence. Try using a more appropriate transitional word or phrase which presents contrast to the preceding statement..

[MS9]AN appropriate TRANSITIONAL WORD OR PHRASE WOULD MAKE THIS CONSTRUCTION MORE LOGICAL AND LESS CHOPPY.

[MS10]Although a choppy introductory paragraph with poor sentence construction, your thesis is clear enough

[MS11]Good topic sentence.

[MS12]You do not have to use his full name every time. The first usage of the name in the essay should be the full name; afterwards, King or Dr. King is sufficient.

[MS13]Document source!

[MS14]This is somewhat repetitive. You have already established this point in your Intro; you now need to clearly define what is King's ethic of love and how he used it (examples or illustrations) to bring about societal change.

[MS15]With an appropriate transitional word, this is a good place to begin a new paragraph.

[MS16]Cite source.

[MS17]Cite source.

[MS18]Cite source.

[MS19]???

[MS20]See MLA for correct citing of sources in your text notes. Also, see my comment on the works cited page.

[MS21]According to whom? Cite source.

[MS22]Be more specific!.

[MS23]According to whom? Cite your source.

[MS24]Remember you are writing a persuasive paper. If you are arguing a case or claim for Dr. King, you need to affirm his claim by asserting King's words and beliefs through the use of direct quotes expressing the same. Otherwise, your paper is based simply on your feelings and beliefs and not sound evidence.

[MS25]You began the paragraph with the past tense. Now you use the present tense; maintain tense continuity as appropriate, within each paragraph.

[MS26]Review MLA for correct citation of text notes; you cite them incorrectly throughout your essay.

[MS27]Validate this claim with a direct quote from King.

[MS28]Review correct use of punctuation for introducing and concluding a direct quote

Figure 3.4. Overwhelming amount of teacher comments example #1.

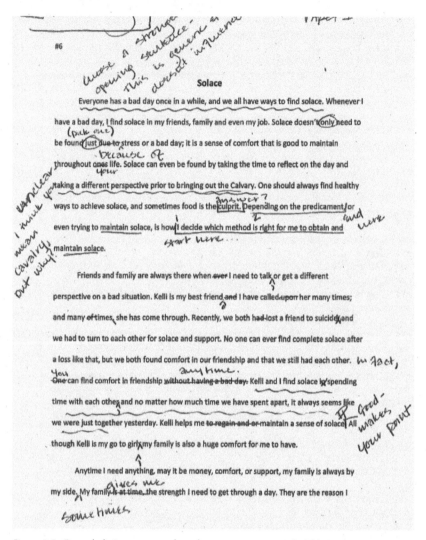

Figure 3.5. Overwhelming amount of teacher comments example #2.

WHEN SHOULD RESPONSE OCCUR?

The student who is worried they have done something "horribly wrong" speaks to the impact teacher comments have on students' motivation and self-confidence, especially when comments are tied to a grade, as I discussed earlier in this chapter. One of the primary advantages to responding to student drafts in progress is that it de-emphasizes summative assessment. In a portfolio introduction, one student writes, "I appreciate Professor X for giving me a chance to rewrite some of the essays. Because by doing it, it is not just about getting a grade but really improving." In one instance a student includes a cover note with a draft and writes to the teacher, "I still have a lot of work to do. I didn't realize how disorganized my thoughts were until I started writing . . . but I think I have a better idea now." The teacher replies in a marginal comment, "That's OK, X. This is part and parcel of the drafting process! The key is that, as you mention, you know have a much better idea of where you want to go, having put these ideas down in writing." Another student points out the benefits of visiting the teacher during office hours and getting feedback that led to global revisions: "I love going to office hours in between each draft. I had Professor X for Writing 39A, her advice and comments during office hours had given me ideas for revisions. I would always record her suggestions with my phone, and listen to them again while I edit my paper." Very few of the teachers in my study grade rough drafts, and teacher comments on drafts tend to focus on what the student could do to improve the writing and not on justifying a grade, as these comments on drafts illustrate:

> If you choose to revisit this project I would suggest that you focus on your grandad's room and personal effects again in addition to his physical portrait.

> For the revision, you might consider evaluating a number of hate speech cases that have already been decided to see if you think Posner's formula can be applied to determine the correctness or incorrectness of these decisions. I've made a few comments about conceptual revisions, but once you move more clearly toward developing your central case study, the reorganizing you'll need to do will become clear.

> Should you decide to revise this piece for the final portfolio, try and rephrase why Motely created his painting in a strong conclusive way (rather than reiterating what you have said throughout your paper).

In reflective ePortfolio artifacts such as metacommentary on teacher comments, reflections on drafts, and portfolio reflection essays, students report that they appreciate comments on drafts and use teachers' comments to make substantial revisions, as in these reflections from first-year writing students:

> Professor X was able to tell me what I had done right, or at least pointed out the things that I had mentioned that were indeed important to the development of my thesis and paper as a whole. I found what I had to explore in a more in-depth manner, and applied much of the advice provided by this comment and other comments in the final edition, found on the next page.

> When I had to revise my literacy analysis for my midterm, I used a lot of the teacher's suggestions to revise it such as not being detailed enough as to why my third grade teacher was unbearable. I then added more examples as to why I did not like the teacher so it made more sense to the audience.

> For my second paper, I was able to draw heavily from the feedback I received from Professor X in order to improve my paper. As you can see in the first two pages of the draft I have included, I worked off each of his comments either checking them off (to indicate that I had made the correction) or crossing them out (to indicate that the comment was no longer relevant). I actively revised this draft and really worked with the comments to make significant improvements to further drafts. This draft helped me to understand the importance of actively responding to drafts rather than merely glancing over comments passively.

Students' claims regarding global revisions in these reflections were supported by evidence from the drafts in their portfolios. Take, for example, the first comment from the student who says, "I found out what I had to explore in a more in-depth manner" and "applied this advice." The teacher had commented on the need to rethink the validity of some arguments, explain other arguments in more detail, and consider more nuances. In the final draft, the student added substantial support from secondary sources, added sentences and paragraphs of explanation for arguments, and revised wording and qualified arguments to create more nuance. The student who was asked to develop their literacy analysis and "used a lot of the teacher's suggestions" added more concrete narrative details for evidence and revised a two-sentence paragraph superficially reflecting on the significance of the narrative to a thirteen-sentence paragraph with an in-depth reflection.

Unlike teacher comments on rough drafts, teacher comments on graded final drafts often focus not on future global revision but on what the student could have and should have done. The following passages from end comments on graded writing represent this sense of lost opportunities:

> More summary and synthesis of your key findings and observations at the end would have been helpful.

> I could not find a clearly stated research question, though you state the motivation for the study was to explore the lived experience of off-campus students related to participation in fitness activities with on-campus recreational facilities. I would have liked to see this purpose turned into an overarching guiding research question.

Overall organization of your argument is sound, although there is some information (noted in text) that would have been helpful to know earlier in the paper.

Where this paper could have been improved is by focusing a little more on specific peoples rather than the early historical progression in which many people groups are lumped under one title for a period of time.

The research I reviewed in chapter 2 suggests that because these comments are written on a final, graded draft, students will be unlikely to address in their future assignments the global revision concerns expressed by these teachers (Ferris 1995; Polio 2012; Price et al. 2010).

WHAT MODALITIES SHOULD RESPONDERS USE?

In chapter 2 I note that the research shows that one of the main complaints students have about teacher response is a lack of clarity, and this is true of both the clarity of teachers' advice and the clarity of their handwriting. In a study conducted in the second decade of the 2000s, I expected to find few handwritten comments. I was surprised that a third of the comments in my corpus are in handwritten form, but not surprised to find that many of these handwritten comments are illegible. Many of the teacher comments that are included in my corpus required me to expand the display on my computer screen 200 percent in order to comprehend them. The brief excerpts from teacher responses shown in figures 3.6 and 3.7 are examples of the kind of scrawl that students have to try to understand.

In addition to a reliance on written comments, teachers in my research rarely take full advantage of the affordances of the digital response modes they do engage in. For example, the commenting function of Word is a common response tool for the teachers in my study, but it is almost always a one-way communication rather than a dialogue. Only a few teachers take advantage of the affordances of Word or PDFs to engage students in a dialogue or ask them to reflect on teacher comments. Figure 3.8 is an excerpt from a response in my corpus illustrating this reflective/dialogic use of the digital mode of response.

Email is another digital tool that lends itself to dialogue. A few of the students in my study include in their ePortfolios email communications between themselves and their teachers. The following excerpted example of one of these email communications illustrates the dialogic potential of email response:

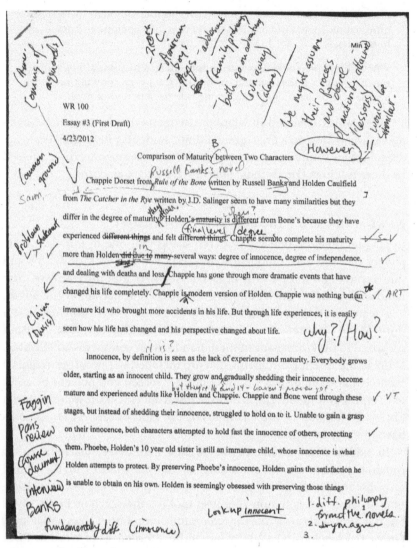

WR 100

Essay #3 (First Draft)

4/23/2012

Comparison of Maturity between Two Characters

Chappie Dorset from *Rule of the Bone* written by Russell Banks and Holden Caulfield from *The Catcher in the Rye* written by J.D. Salinger seem to have many similarities but they differ in the degree of maturity. Holden's maturity is different from Bone's because they have experienced different things and felt different things. Chappie seem to complete his maturity more than Holden did due to many several ways: degree of innocence, degree of independence, and dealing with deaths and loss. Chappie has gone through more dramatic events that have changed his life completely. Chappie is modern version of Holden. Chappie was nothing but an immature kid who brought more accidents in his life. But through life experiences, it is easily seen how his life has changed and his perspective changed about life.

Innocence, by definition is seen as the lack of experience and maturity. Everybody grows older, starting as an innocent child. They grow and gradually shedding their innocence, become mature and experienced adults like Holden and Chappie. Chappie and Bone went through these stages, but instead of shedding their innocence, struggled to hold on to it. Unable to gain a grasp on their innocence, both characters attempted to hold fast the innocence of others, protecting them. Phoebe, Holden's 10 year old sister is still an immature child, whose innocence is what Holden attempts to protect. By preserving Phoebe's innocence, Holden gains the satisfaction he is unable to obtain on his own. Holden is seemingly obsessed with preserving those things

Figure 3.6. Illegible teacher response example #1.

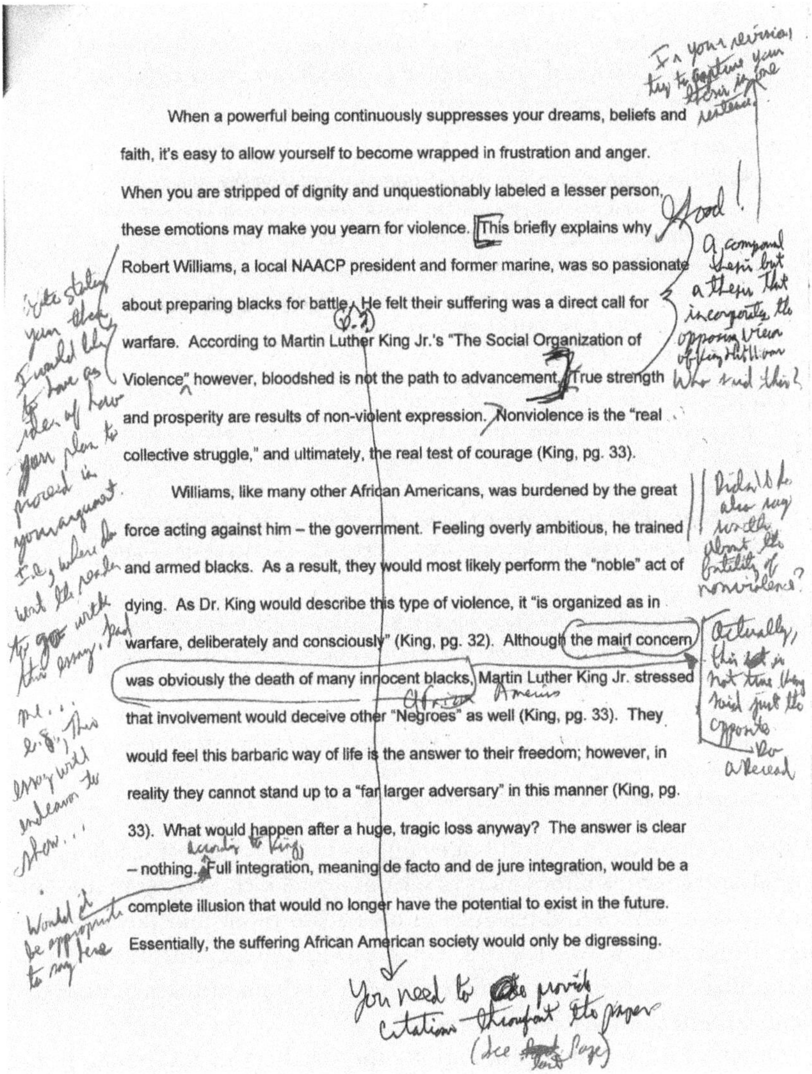

When a powerful being continuously suppresses your dreams, beliefs and

faith, it's easy to allow yourself to become wrapped in frustration and anger.

When you are stripped of dignity and unquestionably labeled a lesser person,

these emotions may make you yearn for violence. This briefly explains why

Robert Williams, a local NAACP president and former marine, was so passionate

about preparing blacks for battle. He felt their suffering was a direct call for

warfare. According to Martin Luther King Jr.'s "The Social Organization of

Violence," however, bloodshed is not the path to advancement. True strength

and prosperity are results of non-violent expression. Nonviolence is the "real

collective struggle," and ultimately, the real test of courage (King, pg. 33).

Williams, like many other African Americans, was burdened by the great

force acting against him – the government. Feeling overly ambitious, he trained

and armed blacks. As a result, they would most likely perform the "noble" act of

dying. As Dr. King would describe this type of violence, it "is organized as in

warfare, deliberately and consciously" (King, pg. 32). Although the main concern

was obviously the death of many innocent blacks, Martin Luther King Jr. stressed

that involvement would deceive other "Negroes" as well (King, pg. 33). They

would feel this barbaric way of life is the answer to their freedom; however, in

reality they cannot stand up to a "far larger adversary" in this manner (King, pg.

33). What would happen after a huge, tragic loss anyway? The answer is clear

– nothing. Full integration, meaning de facto and de jure integration, would be a

complete illusion that would no longer have the potential to exist in the future.

Essentially, the suffering African American society would only be digressing.

Figure 3.7. Illegible teacher response example #2.

On Nov 20, 2010, at 1:43 PM, X wrote:

If I were to look at how Slater uses authority throughout her memoir would I connect this to ethics? I am just slightly confused as to what I would say about her use of authority. Thanks!

Professor X:

Well, Couser says Slater has special authority and therefore ethical responsibility as a psychologist to write about illness in a way that does not stigmatize patients (I'm paraphrasing—look for the lines). He doesn't say much about how she actually evokes (and undermines) scientific authority in Lying. He mentions that she cites an outdated textbook in her preface, but there is a lot more textual evidence to consider.
Does this help?

On Nov 20, 2010, at 5:41 PM, X wrote:

So could my thesis be something along the lines of Couser believes that Slater had an ethical duty as a psychologist to not mislead her readers who would respect her authority. However throughout the novel she undermines scientific authority and through that shows that she cannot be trusted either. It's not quite worded perfectly but hopefully it makes sense. Thanks!

Professor X:

Yes, exactly—she undermines not only her own scientific authority but scientific authority in general. You might consider further how she characterizes her role as a psychologist as an adult (there is only one passage, I think) and what if anything her description of being a psychologist has to do with scientific authority. Then: How does Couser view/rely on scientific authority to make his own argument against her? Continue to explore variations on this theme. It's all interesting.

Although there are a handful of examples in my corpus of teachers taking advantage of the affordances of various digital technologies to respond in a dialogic way, overall teachers in my corpus rarely take advantage of the affordances of Word, PDFs, Google Docs, email, and other digital technologies to engage in a dialogue with students and encourage students to reflect on teacher comments.

Other rare uses of technology by the teachers in my research are audio and screencast responding. The ePortfolios in my corpus include two audio responses (recordings of a teacher's verbal comments to drafts of two different students' writing uploaded to YouTube) and two screencast responses. Because I have so few of these modes of response in my research, I will not comment on them other than to make a pedagogical observation. Research has found that teacher audio and screencast comments generally go into more depth and are more extended than written comments (Elola and Oskoz 2016; Hase and Saenger 1997; Kirschner et al. 1991; Lunt and Curran 2010; Munroe and Hollingworth 2014; Rhind et al. 2013; Rodway-Dyer et al. 2011), and this can certainly

In able to learn other subjects, students need to be literate. Let us take Biology for example. We need to have the ability to read so we can gain knowledge and information. We also need to know how to write so we can practice what we've learned in Biology. I remembered one of my classmates who couldn't read very well in the forth grade. Before exams he would study double the time we spend on studying, because he was a slow reader. So, it is significant, that we learn how to read and write so we can be taught other subjects in schools.

My family was the second reason where I've been influenced to be literate. The reason behind that, was because they valued education. My father is a manager in the "Seaport Customs" in Kuwait. So he really knew how important is it to be literate. He always kept reminding me that literacy is the best weapon to fight unemployment. So enrolling me in a strong private school was his idea in the first place. My dad always kept telling me "Being literate will bring you success". As an example, when I was a kid my father kept teaching me how to read street signs whenever we pass by one. At the house when I ask my father about a new word he will teach me how it is spelled and then ask me to write its definition. In the other hand, my mother taught me how to read some words from my bedtime-story books as a kid.I still remember my favorite story, it was called "Rescuing The Dragon". Because of the fact that my mother always chose a story that really interests me, it made me passionate to read and completethe story on my own.She always tried encouraging me to be literate and well educated in school. Without a second thought my family tried their best to give me the opportunity to be literate and they succeeded.

Commented [J17]: Great recognition of who reading and writing are truly interdisciplinary.

Commented [J18]: Read this aloud.

Commented [OJ19]: Yeah it seems complicated. Although, I do not know what is the mistake but I will rewrite this sentence.

Commented [J20]: We'd (past tense to keep with the rest of this sentence)

Commented [J21]: Watch your tense shift here

Commented [OJ22]: I recognized my mistake.

Commented [J23]: This make sense, but it's more common to say "On the other hand"

Commented [J24]: Italicize book titles.

Commented [OJ25]: What is it that I missed?

Commented [J26]: Great examples of all the ways your family was a great motivator and sponsor of your literacy.

Figure 3.8. Digital response as a dialogue between teacher and student.

be a benefit. But in the few examples of audio and video modes in my research, the comments are so extensive that they may be overwhelming to students. One of the screencasts in my corpus provides a running explanation of ten to twenty written comments per page, as a screen shot of the video illustrates in figure 3.9.

Research has shown that students tend to prefer audio and video response to written response, and although I cannot add anything of substance to this area of response research based on the few examples of these modes of response in my study, I will simply point out that my research further emphasizes the need stressed by Breuch (2004) for teachers to carefully consider the affordances and constraints of whatever mode of response they choose. Teachers in my research might have also kept in mind that engaging in a variety of modes of response is beneficial for students with learning differences and students with disabilities. Giving students some choice in the mode of response they receive is one way to make response more accessible and to follow principles of Universal Design for Learning in constructing response.

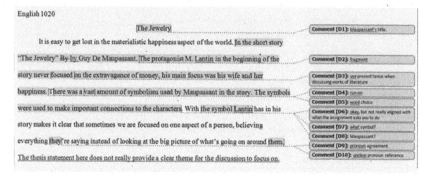

Figure 3.9. Extensive screencast comments.

In this chapter, I have applied my constructivist response heuristic in an attempt to consider the full context and the many factors involved in teacher response. My consideration of this context is limited by the constraints of my data, which does not include classroom observation and does not capture all of the responding that the teachers in my corpus engaged in. However, patterns emerged from my analysis that should be of interest to response researchers and to teachers across disciplines designing response constructs for their courses. The teachers in my corpus often play a narrow and intimidating role of judge and jury, and this results in students perceiving of teachers not as interested readers or representatives of their disciplines or coaches who can provide feedback in order to help students grow as writers, but rather as authority figures to be pleased in order to achieve a good grade. This tendency for students to focus on grades when interpreting teacher response is a focal point of a handful of studies on response (Bowden 2018; Brown 2007; Burkland and Grimm 1986; Cunningham 2019; Dohrer 1991; Richardson 2000), but I believe that not enough has been made in the response literature of the disconnect between teachers' goals of coaching students through their writing processes in their response and students' perceptions of teachers as judge and grader.

Teachers in my research do sometimes play the role of discourse community expert, helping demystify genre conventions for students, but this role is not often explicitly connected to broader disciplinary values. In *Assignments across the Curriculum*, I argue for situating writing assignments in richer rhetorical contexts, whether that means connecting to students' personal lives and professional interests, considering the context of disciplinary and professional genres and discourse communities, or asking students to write for wider public audiences. In the same spirit, I encourage teachers to consider richer contexts when designing the response construct. When teachers respond, they should keep in mind both students' literacy histories and the genre and discourse community contexts that teachers can draw on to show students that they are not merely moving through a series of siloed courses taught by teachers with their own particular sets of seemingly idiosyncratic preferences, but rather that they are being asked to compose in the sophisticated contexts of genre and discourse community expectations.

The teacher response in my corpus is also not often connected to the work of the classroom, to peer response, or to the response students are seeking out from writing center tutors, friends, and family. A handful of the teachers in my corpus make connections between their comments and future context for writing, but responding for transfer was rare in my study. Based on the best practices in response I discussed in chapter 2, there were some positive patterns regarding the teacher response in my study: teachers were quick to offer praise, most teachers balanced local and global comments, and teachers did the bulk of their responding on drafts in progress, with students showing evidence of applying teachers' comments in their revised drafts. However, the teacher response I discuss in this chapter further adds to the literature that indicates the impact and quality of teacher response in college is decidedly mixed, and when teachers play the central role in the response construct, they reinforce students' beliefs that teachers are merely judges, with idiosyncratic demands that must be met, with the ultimate goal of writing as not communication or meaning making but achieving a high grade. My constructivist heuristic encourages researchers and teachers to move beyond the transmission model and beyond response as a teacher/student dyad and place greater emphasis on the role of students in response constructs. In the next chapter, I present evidence from my corpus that supports prior finding from the research regarding the usefulness of peer response as the first step in shifting response from teachers to students.

4

PEER RESPONSE TO WRITING

Study after study shows that when students are given substantial training and a well-designed script, they are capable of providing response that is similar to teacher response, and often more encouraging than teacher response and more focused on global concerns (Beason 1993; Caulk 1994; Choi 2013; Devenney 1989; Hamer et al. 2015; Patchan et al. 2009; Patton 2012; Yang et al. 2006). In this chapter, I consider the extent to which the peer response in my corpus reflects these findings from prior empirical research. I present evidence from the 419 peer responses in my corpus, as well as reflection on peer response from students' portfolio reflection essays. As with chapters 2 and 3, this chapter is organized around the six questions that make up my constructivist heuristic for response. Because constructivist education theory argues that students should play a central role in shaping knowledge, a constructivist heuristic for response encourages teachers and researchers to focus more attention on peer response and conceive of peer response as more than just a supplement to teacher response.

WHO SHOULD RESPOND?

When considering the question, "Who should respond to student writing?" most teachers' and students' thoughts will probably turn to the teacher, not peers. However, I did discover in my research for *Assignments across the Curriculum* that peer response has become more popular across disciplines, and it was not difficult for me to locate examples of peer response for my current study. Despite peer response becoming a more common practice, in much of the response research and in many college courses—including first-year writing courses—peer response is viewed as merely supplementary to teacher response.

Despite its relegation to a supplementary form of feedback in the courses I studied, the peer response in my research tends to reflect the best practices in responding I explored in chapter 2 more often than

https://doi.org/10.7330/9781646423682.c004

the teacher response in my corpus does. Peers focus on global concerns, make specific suggestions, are generous in offering praise, and ask open-ended questions that lead to further content revision. A student from a first-year writing course summarizes the feelings most of the students in my study have about peer response, as revealed in the reflective artifacts included in their ePortfolios:

> Although I did not know him, X was very helpful in providing feedback for my essay. . . . X's greatest contribution was with my connection to Rogers' theory of consequences. In my earliest drafts, I was going to use Samir Amin to argue my point, but switched to Rogers because I felt it would be a stronger argument. I had a lot of trouble simply "adding" Rogers into my paper, as I was not all that familiar with the original reading (at the same level of development as I was with Amin), but through discussions with X I was able to improve my Rogers paragraphs.

The kind of specific, content-focused feedback that this student praises their peer for can be found in my corpus again and again, especially when teachers have designed peer response scripts that encourage specific response focused on content. What follows is an excerpt from a peer response script and student response that is typical of the quality of much of the peer response in my research:

> What is the problem (write it here)? Do you believe it is truly a problem? How could the author be more convincing?
>
> *The problem is overcrowding on the Singapore transportation systems, and the inconvenience this causes its riders. I fully believe this is a problem because the author includes personal touches that make me feel as if I can experience the cramped buses too. I think the author could potentially expand upon the inconvenience that a cramped transportation system creates, other than just talking about the awkwardness of being 'packed like sardines.'*

> Does the essay propose workable, realistic, well-thought out solutions? What are some solutions the author hasn't thought of?
>
> *The solutions proposed are workable and realistic. However, I do think they could be more well-thought out. By this I mean to say that the solutions need a little more backing them. They have a great general framework, but there needs to be more details. A potential solution the author has not thought of might be to run more buses. Although this is not the best option since it would not be environmentally friendly. The author suggested that there be an incentive to riding the buses at dead hours, and I think this idea is great but could use a little more backing it.*

> Does the essay demonstrate sound reasoning and logic with well-supported documentation?
>
> *I would say that it does! I think that the author could potentially draw from other cities and their successes (or even failures) in the realm of transportation. This may help him to gather more information, and also increase the credibility of his paper.*

Does the author discuss one solution more than others, indicating it is the most feasible/reasonable? How could the discussion of the most feasible solution be expanded upon?

I do not feel that the author emphasized one solution more than the others. I felt that there was a disconnect with the solution that was the most logical, and I would like to see that strengthened a bit. I personally would say that the incentive solution was the most reasonable and would be the main solution. If so, then I would expand upon this by drawing from examples of transportation systems from other cities and discusses their successes with it. OR I would just expand upon the success of the current program, what kinds of businesses might profit most from expansion, etc.

In one ePortfolio in my corpus, a student includes teacher and peer response on the same draft side by side. This example speaks to my observation that peer response can be more focused on global issues—and can be even more helpful for revising—than teacher response:

Peer Response #1

I think you have a solid rough draft for your literacy narrative. I liked all the specific details you included about your dad reading your Dr. Seuss at bedtime. I also really like how you included the quote from Dr. Seuss and how you set up your citations. You still gave references but it didn't distract from your paper, and the quote was a great inclusion to your paper.

Throughout your essay, I noticed you kind of repeated certain details and words (like I did in my paper). Instead of repeating them, maybe you could elaborate on it more. For example, you could possibly elaborate more on how the content of the Dr. Seuss books influenced your love for reading. Also, you could possibly make a connection between the books you read when you were younger and the books you read now. Otherwise, it was great and I enjoyed reading it!

Peer Response #2

I think your paper related the concepts we learned in Brant to your own personal experiences very well. However, I do think you should focus more on your experiences first, and then go on to relate them to literacy concepts. In other words, I think you had too much of "because of this, I do that." Try just discussing a single anecdote from your past in full before you start relating it to the present. By doing this, I think you could end up shortening your content and making it more clear and to the point instead of slightly repetitive. Also, I noticed you have a lot of run on sentences that need to be revised and/or eliminated from your essay so that it has more clarity. Overall, your essay did a good job of showing how your past relates to your attitudes of literacy today. It definitely has the potential to be great!

Teacher Response

You have a couple of specific anecdotes, with discussions of two sponsors and some material goods. Great.

I am curious as to why you have chosen to use footnotes. Is this your understanding of how engineers do citations? If so, just let me know. If there's no particular reason, it would be good for you to learn how to do internal citations.

In my study there were a number of examples like the one above of peers providing more thoughtful and useful feedback then the teacher.

Although most of the students in my study spoke glowingly of peer response, there were a handful who were skeptical that peers could help them—at least at first. The most skeptical student in my corpus wrote in a final reflection on the course, "The peer review was the worst part of this course. How could I better my writing from someone who scored lower on his or her essay than I did?" The student intimates that everything peers said would need to be verified with the teacher, writing, "When we had to do peer review I knew that it just meant I had to do more work when writing and bring it to the teacher later."

Although this student has no kind words for peer response, the other students in my research who express skepticism about peer response do begrudgingly acknowledge that they revised their writing based on peers' suggestions. One student writes in a reflection on peer response that they think "it is useless to get comments from someone who is on the same writing level as myself. I would prefer to just receive comments from Professor X because he knows exactly what makes a strong paper." But this same student admits that they completely reorganized a draft and added a link to a video due to two separate peer response comments. Another student says in a process memo, "I should be wary in taking [peers'] opinions into consideration" because "these are my peers and . . . they are students," but this student also admits that "I wouldn't have noticed half the errors if it wasn't for my peer review."

Another student acknowledges that even though they did not trust their peers' responses, they did learn quite a bit from the act of reading and responding to their peers' drafts. In a midterm reflection this student writes, "I personally do not care for peer review because none of my peers are accomplished writers. They are just like me, still discovering the writing world. However what I do like from peer review is reading others papers, especially when having the same prompt. Reading the paper gives me ideas for my own paper or inspires me to write about another topic that is similar. Reading these papers also can show me what does not work too well, which then I reevaluate my own paper to see if I made some of the same mistakes." A similar sentiment is expressed by another student who was initially skeptical of peer response but quickly saw the value in learning by reading a peer's draft:

> The skill that I learned this quarter that I found most beneficial was definitely peer edit. At first I thought the peer review paper was pointless and was just to give us more work. . . . The second I started reading X's paper I realized how much I could learn from this assignment. Reading her paper was the best thing I could have done because it instantly showed me all the things I needed to change about my paper. She was a very strong writer and the paper made so much sense organizationally, it allowed me to see the mistakes I made in my own paper and I am very grateful we did this [peer response].

Certainly some students will remain skeptical of peer response, regardless of the quality of the feedback they get, but my research indicates that even skeptics are often converted to believers in the value of peer response.

Even if some of the peer responders in my research failed to provide helpful feedback to their peers, one of the strongest patterns in my research is students reflecting on how much they learned from reading their peers' drafts and how they were able to apply what they learned to improve their own drafts, regardless of the quality of the feedback they received from peers. I share a substantial number of these reflections to emphasize this point:

> Peer review definitely changed the way I write. When I read over a classmates essay and edit it, I start to think about my essay and if I have that same problem.

> Likewise, reading the work of my peers has helped me see the good and bad in my own writing as well. Through reading others essays and finding similarities to my own writing style, I can see things I should include in my writing as well as things I should avoid.

> Having someone who is doing the same assignment read and critique my paper helps give me new insight into what I need to improve, and reading someone else's draft often helps me think of improvements I need to make in my own paper.

> During most classes we had to sit and read other student's work and I saw that I was becoming a better critic of myself by doing this. I was able to read my work as if I were reading one of my peers' and then make corrections based on the discrepancies I saw.

> I can see techniques a classmate use, and look for ways to apply them to my papers.

In the reflective writing in their ePortfolios, students in my study consistently mentioned the benefit of peer response feedback and the usefulness of reading their peers' drafts and applying techniques that classmates were using in their own writing. It is notable that students' reflections on teacher response are most often associated with pleasing the teacher in order to get a good grade, but reflections on peer response are focused on developing their drafts and growing as a writer.

WHAT SHOULD RESPONSE FOCUS ON?

In chapter 3 I suggested that response researchers and teachers turn their focus of attention to metacognition, and metacognition can also be central to peer response. Students in my research are rarely asked to respond to their peers' metacognitive writing, but there are a handful of teachers who ask students to write process memos with each peer response workshop. These process memos are opportunities for writers to inform their peer responders what they believe to be the strengths and weaknesses of their drafts and to ask their readers questions they would like addressed. In the rare instances in my research that students are asked to engage in this type of metacognition, writers are successful at thoughtfully assessing their strengths and challenges and readers are able to address their peers' concerns. In one example of this dialogue, the writer asks their peer responders if the summary is too long and if there are any points that should be cut out. One peer responder writes, "This is a good summary, however, it doesn't need to be so detailed. . . . I think a lot of the good points you make in your summary can be moved into the later parts of the paper when you discuss why you agree or disagree." Another peer responder advises this student to focus the summary more on the subject of the essay, the PGA's denial of carts for golfers with disabilities.

In another example of a peer response process memo, the writer shows just how capable students are of assessing their drafts, and also how valuable this assessment can be to help guide the peer responder. The student author writes, "I was very torn apart when trying to organize the paper. I wasn't sure if I should just analyze the article in the way it was written, starting with the title and ending with the last paragraph, or if I should use a rhetorical tool to separate my sections. For example, bring up all the ethos, then pathos, then logos." As this example shows, peer response focused on concerns and questions the writer is asked to discuss in a process memo can help direct peer responders to give more focused and useful feedback. Process memos for peer response are rare in my corpus, but since I did not observe peer response, I cannot know how many teachers encouraged students to share questions and concerns they have about their writing just before they engaged in in-class peer response.

Although there is not a single peer response script in my research that contains a question that would lead students to write a comment focused on transfer, I did find some evidence that students were transferring comments they received from peers to future drafts and to future writing tasks. Sometimes transfer meant using a comment made on one section of a piece of writing and applying it to other sections. In a reflection on peer feedback, one student writes, "My first draft for Paper 3 was incomplete. Very incomplete. Therefore the feedback I got on it was only related to the first sub-claim I was arguing. However, the feedback for the first sub-claim guided me through my second sub-claim; I made sure not to make the same mistakes." In this student's second draft after receiving peer response, they organized what were a few rambling paragraphs for the first sub-claim into three focused and developed paragraphs, and they went from including a single reference to a secondary source to support their first sub-claim to drawing on the secondary source multiple times in each paragraph. This same approach was applied to the second sub-claim in the revised draft.

Another student comments that because their peer reviewer "only had time to review four of the six pages, I tried (and succeeded, I think) to apply the main idea behind his criticisms—that I should elaborate more on my ideas and my concluding sentences in the paragraphs—to the last two pages." Although this student did not make major global revisions based on peer feedback, their revised draft does contain additional concluding sentences in each paragraph that elaborate on the main idea of the paragraph—a clear application of the peer response comments. In reflecting on a specific peer comment ("This sentence does not feel like then end of the paragraph"), another student writes, "Although this comment is about a specific paragraph, I tried to apply it to everything so that transitions from idea to idea and paragraph to paragraph were smoother."

One student in my research was able to articulate their ability to transfer peer feedback to future writing assignments. In a reflective portfolio introduction, the student writes, "In the peer review above, my classmate had made great suggestions on how I should improve my paper for the second draft of Comp I. He commented on how I should add transitions sentences to help with the flow of my paper. When I talked about the three different Supreme Court cases, I just listed them out without making connections from one to another. This is something I must be careful of on future papers because I tend to go off on a tangent by not mentioning my evidence's connection with my purpose and claim." Although a limitation of my study is that I do not have evidence to support students' claims that they transferred peer response comments to assignments in future courses, the comments from students I have cited in this section represent the continuation of a pattern I noted in chapter 3: students' appreciation of response they can transfer to future writing tasks.

The teachers in my corpus rarely comment on students' growth, but students are able to see how peer response contributed to their growth as writers, and they are proud of this growth. Students connect their increasing skill at reading and assessing their peers' writing with their own growth as writers. One student writes in a reflective introduction to their portfolio, "Being able to see the growth in others played a substantial role in me being able to see the growth in myself." A similar sentiment is expressed by a student who writes in their final course reflection, "I already discussed my initial shyness about peer review, but my opinion has changed. After recognizing others mistakes, I was quickly able to recognize my own mistakes much faster and in turn, I grew as a writer."

This connection between peer response and growth as a writer is thoughtfully articulated in the final course reflection of a first-year writing student, and I will end this section with the students' reflection on peer response:

> I now understand that peer reviewing is the most important component to my writing process, as I critique my own work along with my classmates work in peer reviews, my writing process has strengthened and evolved. Peer reviewing throughout this quarter has helped me become a more attentive reader, expand my outlooks, and strengthen my writing. The only way to grow is to leave your comfort zone and expand your thinking. I have come to understand that writing is an open process that permits writers to use later invention and re-thinking to revise their work, and all of this began with the sharing that took place in each peer review this quarter. Peer reviews took me out of my comfort zone, and not only would my writing process be incomplete without them, but I would lack many of the skills that I now have.

WHAT CONTEXTS SHOULD RESPONDERS CONSIDER?

Whether it is through process memos or conversations during workshops, peer response can provide useful opportunities for students to get to know their peer writers' contexts. The peer response process memos in my corpus ask students to reflect on the strengths of their drafts, describe their writing processes, and articulate questions for their readers. My research indicates that perhaps the most useful student contexts that should be explored prior to peer response are students' concerns about sharing their writing with their peers. In a final reflection for a first-year writing course, one student expresses their initial anxiety regarding peer response:

> On September 6th, the first day of WRD 103, Professor X had us think about what made us uneasy about English, specifically writing. Without much thought, sharing my writing with others immediately popped into my head. Later, I found out that we would peer review our work weekly. This news made me uneasy to say the least. The anxious feeling increased when I looked around and realized I knew not a single one of the students sitting around me. How was I supposed to share my work with strangers? Would I be judged by my writing before these new faces got to know who I was?

This student goes on to acknowledge that they came to appreciate peer response and overcame their unease, but this reflection is a reminder of the importance of providing students the opportunities to share their fears about peer response before asking them to share their writing.

In a writing process reflection essay, one student expresses how helpful it was that the teacher acknowledged the class's concerns about peer response: "Having to peer edit another classmate's essay, for me, was a challenge. At first I felt as if I wasn't qualified to give feedback to another writer when I, myself, wasn't a good writer. My teacher suspected quite a few students to feel that way, so therefore, she talked to my class about not thinking of it in that way but, instead, think of it as a chance to help each other with the essays in any way we could."

As I noted previously, a limitation of my study is that I was not able to observe students participating in peer response groups, and I do not have information about contexts they shared during peer response activities. However, students' portfolio reflection essays indicate that an important student context for peer response for teachers to consider is students' fears of sharing their writing.

In addition to the personal context of the writer, peer response always involves the contexts of the genres and discourse communities of writing tasks. Just as it was notable that many teachers in my corpus thoughtfully attended to the nuances of genre and discourse community in their responses, it is striking that students in my research frequently reflect on genre and discourse community conventions in their peer responses. Sometimes this means confirming that a peer is succeeding in meeting genre expectations, as in the peer response comment from a first-year writing student who observes, "I thought the language was very fitting for the genre (a magazine) in which it would be published. It was very informal, and I didn't run into any words that I didn't know." At other times students point out the ways that their peers' drafts fail to meet genre expectations, as in the case of the student who comments, "I am not sure it should be called a pamphlet (as the formatting does not reflect a pamphlet). Furthermore, she stated that her piece would be a part of a magazine. Redefining her genre and/or making it more clear would be beneficial to the reader."

A number of students mention that they learned genre conventions through reading peers' drafts. In a reflection on the value of peer response, one student writes:

> When I was peer editing X's rough draft, I found that the mistakes I was recognizing in her paper were also in my own. For example, I thought I was extremely organized when I was putting together my rough draft. I had made an outline! Then I read X's paper, and realized that it was natural to want to incorporate an opinion into the summary section as she had done. In my instance, I wanted right off the bat to prove how credible the authors I had chosen were so that my reader would continue with the rest of the paper. But that is an opinion, therefore it belongs in the evaluation section.

Another student writes in a reflection on the assignment, "When first doing the inquiry proposal I wasn't too sure how to do it or what all I should say. But after reading the ones from my group it gave me a better idea of how to do the proposal."

Although students do not use the term *discourse community* in their peer responses, they are capable of thinking about broader disciplinary audiences even without being prompted to do so by the teacher's peer response script. One student writes in their peer response comments, "In your third paragraph you summarize Frankenstein—think of your audience. Our teacher, and most scholars, know the plot of this book already." In a similar reflection on discourse community contexts, another student writes to a peer, "Interesting way to introduce the paper. It might not translate as being scholarly and professional, and it reminds me more of a newspaper article." My study provides evidence that peer response holds often untapped potential for teaching students about genres and discourse communities.

WHAT TYPE OF FEEDBACK SHOULD RESPONDERS GIVE?

In comparison to the teacher response in my corpus, the types of feedback students give to their peers is less directive and contains more open-ended questions. Peer response is more likely than teacher response to include praise comments, more focused on global rather than local issues, and more specific. Figure 4.1 depicts an excerpt of peer response

School was the first place where I started to learn how to read and write. I was enrolled in a good private school from grade 1 until grade 12. The school is called "Rawd Al-Saleheen Bilingual School". We had an American Curriculum, so we've been taught American English in school. Moreover, the books we had were brought from the United States, such as Math and Science books. Teachers were focused on the way they teach us how to read and write. I found that out by the way they used to assign us a lot of linguistic home works and to practices.

In able to learn about other subjects students had to be literate. Let us take Biology for example. We need to have the ability to read so we can gain knowledge and information. We also need to know how to write so we can practice what we've learned in Biology. So, it is significant that we learn how to read and write so we can be taught other subjects in schools.

My family was the second reason where I've been influenced to be literate. The reason behind that was because they valued education. My father is a manager of the "Seaport Customs" in Kuwait. So he really knew how important is it to be literate. He

Commented [J4]: Maybe talk about how living in a different country but learning an American curriculum affected you. Did you like it? Do you feel it benefitted you or took away from your learning?

Commented [J5]: To make this a little more personal, I would suggest maybe giving some examples of personal experiences you've had with the relationship between being literate and learning other subjects. Did you ever have a hard time with it? Were certain classes easier than others?

Commented [J6]: I found this to be really interesting. I would suggest expanding on what exactly it is your father does and why education is so important in relation to his career.

Figure 4.1. Facilitative peer response comments.

comments on a student draft typical of the kinds of facilitative commentary with use of open-ended questions that is common in my corpus. Open-ended questions focused on developing content were ubiquitous in the peer response feedback in my research. Some examples include:

What is the background on this quote? What point does it prove?

Elaborate here . . . Why is it a secret? What would society think if they found out?

Has you mom's wisdom affected or influenced your ability to write?

Why did you decide to start with the negative aspects here rather than say your positive experiences you've had?

Most students avoid taking control of their peers' drafts, in part through the use of open-ended questions, but that is not to say that all of the peer comments are facilitative. There is one peer responder who demands throughout the draft that a student "rewrite the sentence" with no information about why each sentence might be confusing, and another peer who rewrites sentences throughout a draft. However, I found far more examples of teachers wrestling control of drafts from students than peers wrestling control. Given this pattern, it is not surprising that students are also more generous than teachers with praise comments.

In a reflection on a minimalist praise comment from a peer (the peer responder had simply written "good" next to a sentence), a student explains what kind of praise would have been more helpful: "Even though this comment is a confidence booster, I would have liked my peer reviewer to say specifically what was good about the paragraph." Praise followed by specific reasoning for the praise is common in the peer response in my corpus, as these examples illustrate:

> You begin your paper by bringing up the monotonous world that people live in and introduce the idea of "the academic illusion." I believe this is an effective intro to utilize. This establishes first how you feel about the current condition of the education system. It also allows the reader to see from your point of view and decide whether they agree or not.

> I found the topic very clear, especially in the introduction the way he used the quotes right off the bat grabbed my attention showed the viewpoints right away.

> A lot of your facts are from recent years which is really nice because it allows the class to relate since it is coming from our generation.

> Good beginner! I like how you mentioned and described exactly how you were in elementary school and middle school. It gave the reader more of an idea of how you were and probably gave them someone to relate to in their own high schools.

Students note that these types of detailed praise comments are helpful in giving them the confidence they need to understand and believe in the strengths of their writing. As one student articulates in their portfolio reflection essay:

> One of the peer responses from paper two really helped me learn what my strengths are. During my peer response session, I was told: "The point/counter point is a great set up for this paper because it allows the reader to see both sides almost right next to each other making it easier for them to make comparisons. I don't think you can really improve it, if it ain't broke don't fix it kind of thing. I thought the paper moved great so I don't see any need for additional transition work." Although a big part of peer response is to fix the flaws, it is also just as beneficial to know what I am doing right.

Although praise comments may not always lead to further revision, another common type of praise comment in the peer response in my corpus is praise that encourages further development of strengths. For example, one student notes that their peer's "description of the food and her description of the vile taste of the Pork Rinds is extremely detailed and actually provides humor for the writer. I think that X should dedicate an entire paragraph to the disgusting taste of the food and make it even more descriptive than it already is." Another student writes in a marginal comment, "Maybe you could elaborate on some of the changes? It's quite interesting and it leaves me wanting to know more." In a comment from a peer response script, a student writes, "I like that you mention how the artwork's original audience viewed the painting. It would be interesting if you went into further detail about how this painting affects our contemporary audience."

As generously and deftly as students praised their peers' writing, students testify in their reflection essays that they value constructive criticism from their peers. Excerpts from two different students' portfolio reflection essays speak to this valuing of thoughtful criticism from peers:

> The criticism I got from each peer review was good feedback. The peer review session I found to enhance my critical thinking was during the wake of my person analysis paper of David Grambs "The Like Virus." I got some very good constructive criticism that went beyond the typical "you had a well-written paper" slogan. I was given thorough examples of good phrasing and grammar suggestions; I was given fresh ideas on the different directions I could go in order to find the author's ethos.

> My peer reviewer X notes some confusion he had while reading my paper. These type of constructive comments are what writers need; they help identify to the writer areas in their paper that need to be explained or revised.

A common note that I made in my memos as I analyzed the data from peer response is "balance of praise and constructive criticism." Students often provide a balance of praise and constructive criticism even when there is no peer response script, but in courses where the teacher provides a peer response script that asks for both praise and constructive criticism, students consistently provide this balance. The example peer response in figure 4.2 is representative of the type of balanced feedback students give when the peer response script asks them to note strengths and respond to weaknesses.

As the examples I have provided of facilitative comments, praise comments, and constructive criticism illustrate, students are typically focused on global rather than local revision concerns. The two peer responses that follow contain the kind of global feedback that is found throughout my corpus of peer responses:

> First off this is a great topic. It is something interesting and not well known. The beginning of your paper worked as a hook. I was interested in what the paper was going to talk about, based on the introduction. The idea was brought into perspective with the percentages and factual information. These sources did need some recognition at the end though. These facts would have been much more powerful if some details would have been added to them. The signs of ASD also needed much more detail and expansion. You scratched the surface with all some of their development impairments, but expand on them. How do these

Paper 2 Draft 1 Peer Review

1. Does the introduction have a clear problem statement and respond with a debatable claim?

    Paraphrase the problem that motivates the essay:

    Many people regard Plath as a feminist, but how much of a feminist is she really?

    Paraphrase the writer's proposed solution/thesis:

    Plath is not a "complete" feminist → she is somewhat of a feminist, but not totally pro-woman.

2. If the writer disagrees with an argument source, is this disagreement handled in a balanced way? Does the writer fairly summarize the debated argument source and acknowledge any degree of validity in its claim(s)? Describe:

    She disagrees that Plath is a complete feminist, unlike Perloff and Gill.

3. If the writer *agrees* with an argument source, does the writer agree "creatively"—that is, in a way that clearly distinguishes the writer's ideas from those of the supportive/influential source? Describe:

    She basically agrees with Perloff in that Plath's feminism wasn't militant. She also agrees with Gill about the idea of the fig tree representing the choices women had to face in the 1950s. She makes a unique point that Plath settles down with a family, even though her mirror image, Esther, criticizes men and always shows feelings of disdain for babies.

4. Identify the new source that the writer found independently: ___Gill___ (last name). Does the writer offer enough summary of this source for you to understand its relevance to the problem described in the problem statement? Describe its relevance:

    Yes. In the introduction, she clearly states that Gill discusses the struggles women in the 1950s faced and how The Bell Jar addresses those struggles.

5. How does the writer draw from a source to help move his or her own argument forward? Is there a useful new concept that emerges from the new source? If so, what is this concept?

    She uses Gill to describe Esther's horrible mother to show the juxtaposition of how Esther becomes a mother despite having had such a bad mom.

6. How effective is the close textual analysis of *The Bell Jar* in supporting the writer's main claim? Note any places where evidence is unclear or the writer needs to present more persuasive reasons for his or her interpretation of this evidence.

    Good textual analysis. However, she assumes that Esther marries based on the mention of the baby in the novel's exposition. It is possible, though unlikely, that she had a baby out of wedlock.

7. The most interesting idea I took away from this draft is:

    how sending the bill to Irwin was to "spite all men"

8. The main thing the writer still needs to work on is:

    defining how much of a feminist Plath is. even though she says that Plath isn't a complete feminist, she doesn't specify the exact degree.

Figure 4.2a and 4.2b. Peer response including praise and constructive criticism.

impairments compare to regular development and what does it mean for the child in their everyday activities.

Peer Review: Exploratory Essay
> The paper is concrete, but it could be more solid by narrowing down the topic by just talking about medical use rather than that and crime. The claims are solid. My only concern is that they might overlap each other if you do not branch out on marijuana's medical advantages.
>
> Yes, the writer does have defensible reasons such as brain injuries are more lethal and damaging than marijuana.
>
> There are some statements that come off as bias in the essay. The writer should stay away from certain phrases like "I feel" and make sure to say "they" instead of "he" and "she" unless speaking about a specific person.
>
> The rebuttals were mention, but they should be more specific for the writer to give back a more direct answer.
>
> Overall, the topic is strong and not too broad. You will need a lot of medical evidence and I believe you will have a stronger argument if you provide research from qualified doctors and/or advocates.

In reflections on peer response, students frequently comment on the ways they benefitted from their peers' global comments and how they made substantial revisions based on peer feedback. Students often point out the ways that peer feedback helped them refine or refocus their entire essay, in the form of revisions to their theses:

> The second day X edited my paper. She focused on my thesis, along with the clarity of my paper. The thesis in her mind was too vague and needed to be clarified. She felt that since my thesis was so vague my paper was in turn extremely vague. After this editing session I was able to go back and solidify my thesis. After refining my thesis I was able to narrow in on the key ideas of my paper and make them less vague, making my paper stronger.

> The peer editor for my draft of Man With a Movie Camera reminded me to fix my grammar, to organize my thoughts and not to jump around from technique to technique, to clarify my thesis and make sure it agrees with the rest of my paper and lastly to follow up my claims with examples. Their comment about my thesis is what made me change it from a technical point of view to a social point of view. They made it clear that I stated that I was arguing about one thing but wrote about something totally different.

> The critique that my peer X gave me in Artifact 5 said that my claim was strong, but not strong enough to be supported by enough sub-claims. With this in mind, I was able to approach the final draft of paper 3 and write a thesis that I thought was direct and would be supported by a wide variety of examples, "The radical liberal mentality of the Civil Rights movement transcended onto the second wave of feminism, providing women with the drive to break down the conservative gender barriers that men placed on society."

The student in the first passage who reflects on their peers' suggestions to rework the thesis not only "solidified" the thesis, as they mention, but also added new evidence to support the more focused thesis. The student who received global revision suggestions for their essay about the film *Man with a Movie Camera* shifted focus from film techniques to examining social issues. A comparison between the conclusions of this student's first draft and second draft point to this global change in focus:

> Conclusion of the first draft
>> Dziga Vertov filmed *Man with a Movie Camera* to show how great of a movie maker he was. He turned down other offers to work on other movies so that he could solely work on his new production (Feldman 7). This project was merely a form of entertainment and Vertov's way of trying to show critics what he could really do. Although Carroll argues that this movie is political we actually get a sense of the movie just being a film about people's normal everyday lives not a movie about modernization, unification, utopia, or anything of that sort.

> Conclusion of the second draft after peer response
>> The way that Vertov pieced together his scenes and edited them to work with each other to give an idea of the Soviet Union working as a "machine . . . [and an] implication of causation" further gives it this sense of unification that Carroll explains (Carroll 175,176). Although *Man with a Movie Camera* makes it seem like the Soviet Union is working towards something great, like previously stated, in reality this unification was bringing down the country as serfdom continually rose. As a viewer of the movie and a reader of Carroll's essay one can't help but believe the ideas being thrown at them. After reading Carroll's essay readers gain a better understanding of the movie and what Vertov was trying to do, but we lose a sense of the movie just being a film about people's normal everyday lives and instead turn it into a political film.

Students also testify in their portfolio reflection essays and metacommentary on peer comments that peer response helped them rethink their topics, develop their ideas, and reorganize their entire essays:

> I received some critical feedback from my peers and I decided to change my topic to something I could describe fluently in more detail. Once I had my new topic, my story came to life.

> With my second essay on Designer Babies, my peers suggested that I strengthen my argument by showing more of the dissenting opinion and by strengthening my conclusion. I had not realized that either of these points were weak and on second look realized their insufficiencies and fixed them.

> Peer editing brought to my attention the ambiguity in some of my writing that I felt was clear by reading it on my own. . . . However, when my classmate X was reading mine she noted that my supporting reasons and

evidence were not clear enough but if I better state my claim, than my evidence will become more clear. And so, I rearranged my paper to organize my claims in a more sequential order for better understanding and began to improve my reasonings.

In the case of the first reflection I cited, the student changed their literacy narrative topic from an elementary school talent show in the first draft to the academic struggles of their brother in the next draft, all because peers commented on the lack of detail in the first draft. The student whose peers advised them to "strengthen [their] argument by showing more of the dissenting opinion" integrated other viewpoints throughout the essay for the final draft. The student who was advised by a peer to "better state [their] claim" transformed their focus from a first draft of an essay that mostly summarized the life and work of a photographer to an essay that clearly argues that the artist valued photography as production rather than reproduction, and that this is reflected in the photographer's work.

It is important to note that global revision suggestions from peers do not always lead to substantial revisions, even when students claim in their reflective writing to have made global revisions based on peers' comments. One student claims that a paper helped them "dramatically . . . structure [their essay] to be more effective," but evidence from the peer response draft and the final draft reveal minimal changes to the structure. Another student claims to have included much more analysis of a poem after receiving suggestions from peers, but in the final draft the additional analysis is minimal. My research provides further evidence that to ensure students make global revisions based on peer comments, the teacher still has a role in both reinforcing peer comments and assessing whether students made more than superficial changes to drafts.

Not all of the peer response in my study is focused on global issues. During the reliability sense-checking activity, one of the graduate students, DJ, observed that when students respond by hand directly on a draft, they are more likely to note grammar, syntax, and punctuation issues (93 of the 419 peer responses were images of handwritten responses directly on hard copies of drafts). Additionally, in the cases where the teacher provides no script to guide peer response, students occasionally focus on grammar, spelling, and typos. Students who receive response on only local issues express frustration with their peers, as this reflection on peer review from a first-year writing student illustrates: "I noticed that this peer editor mostly fixed my grammatical errors and awkward word choices. Although I mentioned in the self-assessment essay that

I wanted to reduce the usage of awkward phrases and improper word choices, I felt that I also should have gotten more comments regarding my arguments rather than mechanics." Another student who received only comments on grammar in peer response reflects, "To be perfectly honest I do not find peer reviewing all that helpful. I feel that having a peer look at my paper is almost the same as re-reading it myself."

In addition to being more focused on global issues than their teachers, peers are more specific in their feedback. Just as I have countless examples of useful global peer feedback in my corpus, I have countless examples of specific peer feedback that could lead to concrete revisions. A few examples of specific response from peers will serve as an illustration:

> Organization is one thing to look at. For example, you discuss the significance of the authors' viewpoint before you begin your summary. I can see how that seems like a good place to put it (so that the reader knows what the authors are about when they read the summary) but I think it belongs in the evaluation, where you can evaluate their credibility.

> When you begin to talk about the different subjects within your paper make sure you take some time to go a little more in depth with the arguments that you are making. "Integration is necessary in order to save education systems from falling even further into the impersonal abyss of meaningless knowledge before it is too late." This sentence is very broad which generalizes integration and leaves it up to the reader's imagination to think up of how the integration should take place.

> She should describe the Chinese traditions in full detail and maybe even have a separate paragraph for each benefit the goji berry gives to people. If she does this, the audience will have an extremely clear mindset and will be able to learn many new things about the goji berry.

In their reflections on peer response, students again and again state their appreciation for this type of specific feedback and articulate the substantial revisions they made based on peers' specific advice:

> X in particular, was specific. For example, he told me to describe my observation more, and to explain what different exercises were going on at that time. I was able to look at my paper from the reader's perspective, and realize that if I were reading my paper, the thoughts appeared to be vague.

> For my Community paper X commented in my second paragraph to go deeper about my feelings with my high school and I did. It helped the paper flow better and build a better ethos as well.

> In X's peer review of my analysis, he stated: "Every detail you give about a section should be backed up with analysis. Try not to describe what a

Read through the entire paper *out loud*. Take note of your immediate reactions as you read.

1. Reread the prompt. Does the writer effectively address all of the requirements?

yes, the writer she does

2. Identify the central claim (or thesis) of the paper. Is the argument persuasive, and is it fitting to the scope of the assignment? Does the writer situate his/her hypothesis within the ongoing conversation we've seen in the reading?

That the amount of talking men and women do is very situational.

3. Has the writer done sufficient field work to address his/her claim? Is this evidence presented in a detailed, interesting way? Has the writer effectively analyzed this evidence to show what it means and how it supports/disproves his/her hypothesis?

yes, maybe (not necessary at all) you can add a real life discussion just to further your point, if you want.

4. Is the paper effectively organized? Does the writer provide the necessary cues for you to accurately predict what will come next?

yes, nice use of paragraphs!

5. Will the style, tone, and types of evidence appeal to the intended audience?

yes!

Through your conversation with the writer, prioritize your feedback. Take note of what the writer did well as well as where there is room for revision. Together, map out a plan for revision on the back of this page.

Figure 4.3. Minimal peer response.

certain tab entails just for the sake of making sure you describe every bit of the website." An example X provided was related to the paragraph in which I explained the "issues" tab. When looking back at my paper, I noticed that the whole paragraph only provided a description of the tab.

Despite the overwhelming evidence in my corpus of students providing specific feedback that leads to revision, there are a few examples of students giving generic feedback or feedback that is too minimal to be helpful.

Even a well-designed peer response script does not ensure an adequate amount of feedback, but peer response scripts in my corpus that pose only "yes" or "no" questions almost always led to minimal answers from peer responders, as the peer response script illustrates in figure 4.3.

Although on rare occasions the peer response in my corpus was minimal or focused on sentence-level editing, overall students in my corpus consistently gave global and specific feedback in peer response that was similar to teacher response.

WHEN SHOULD RESPONSE OCCUR?

As I discussed in chapter 2, research indicates that students make substantial revisions when teachers ask them to intervene during the writing process through peer response (Allen and Mills 2016; Leijen 2017; Mendonca and Johnson 1994; Price et al. 2007; Villamil and de Guerrero 1996, 2020). Many students in my corpus mention that peer response changed the way they thought about their writing processes, as these reflections from two different students' portfolios illustrate:

> After peers X and Y peer reviewed my papers—seen in Artifacts 1 and 2—I began to re-evaluate my writing process as a whole. . . . My rough draft of paper 2 served as more of an outline than an actual paper as observed by my peer Y in his peer review. He says, "There is kinda sort a thesis," and "each paragraph kinda relates to the main claim." His inability to understand my paper caused me to re-evaluate my writing process as I began writing Paper 3. I was able to come up with a direction of my paper after writing a detailed outline before I began the writing process for Paper 3.

> I now understand that peer reviewing is the most important component to my writing process, as I critique my own work along with my classmates work in peer reviews, my writing process has strengthened and evolved. Peer reviewing throughout this quarter has helped me become a more attentive reader, expand my outlooks, and strengthen my writing.

Both of these reflections point to students' growing realizations that writing is a social process. It was especially notable to me how often students mention the ways that peer response helped them understand the need to consider readers during drafting and revising processes. A sampling of excerpts from students' reflective writing shows just how critical writing as a social process is to revision for the students in my research:

> I had a hard time developing a claim for my first draft, and this peer editing session enabled me to think out loud to someone about the ideas I had for my paper.

> When someone reads your paper they have a whole different perspective and understanding of it.

> By having peer reviews available from the beginning to end of the process I was forced to consider my audience.

As we had workshop days in this class to revise our paper three times from three completely different people, I slowly came to realize that each reader has a different way of reading and understanding the message you are trying to get across. With that being said, I could no longer write nonsense and "fill in" my paper anymore, which made me start using an outline for my papers.

Through engaging in peer response, the students in my research learned the constructivist lesson that writing is a social process, and this caused many of them to change their entire conception of their writing processes.

WHAT MODALITIES SHOULD RESPONDERS USE?

My corpus includes an even mix of handwritten peer responses, peer responses using the responding functions of Word, and peer responses using course learning management systems. There are no instances of audio or video peer responses included in the ePortfolios in my collection. Given the frequent references in their reflection essays and process memos that students make to productive discussions with their peers, it appears that much of the peer response was conducted face-to-face, or that students were given class time to discuss their feedback even if peer response was conducted online. However, given that due to the scale of this study observations of courses and peer response groups were not a possibility, and given that students in my study do not comment on the affordances and constraints of the modalities of peer response in their reflective artifacts, I will not speculate about the effect of the modality on peer response in the students in my research, or the benefits or challenges of different modalities for peer response. However, I will remind readers of some of the findings from the research literature on response that I summarized in chapter 2: that students appreciate the opportunity for both face-to-face and asynchronous peer response; that digital modes of responding are as effective as more traditional forms of written peer response; and that peer response training and scaffolding is a more critical element of effective peer response than the modality used to respond.

It is clear from the quality of the peer response scripts and the many references students make to scaffolding activities for peer response that my study is made up primarily of teachers who not only believe in the value of peer feedback but are thoughtful in the design of peer response. It is also clear that with training and guidance students are fully capable of giving feedback that is on par with teacher feedback. Even in situations where students do not get helpful feedback from peers, students in my corpus note that just getting a chance to see how other students responded to the assignment prompt helped them make revisions to their own drafts. Courses that do not include peer response as part of the response construct are giving students a narrow view of writing processes and failing to take advantage of one of the best resources teachers have for constructing impactful response. Every course in every discipline should teach writing as a mode of thinking and learning, and every course in every discipline should model the revision processes that professional writers engage in by teaching writing as a social process. It follows, then, that every course in every discipline should not only make use of peer response but should make peer response a central part of the response construct. Perhaps the only pedagogy that is more impactful than peer response in helping students grow as writers and develop the habits of mind and composing processes and strategies they need to succeed in college writing and beyond is student self-assessment. I explore the topic of self-assessment, and the many examples of students' abilities to reflect on their own strengths and challenges as writers, in the next chapter.

5

STUDENTS' SELF-ASSESSMENT OF THEIR WRITING

In chapter 3 I pointed out some of the disadvantages of teachers placing themselves at the center of the response construct, whether that means emphasizing grades or wrestling control of students' drafts. In chapter 4 I suggested that based on my corpus and the findings of prior research on peer response, peer response can replace a great deal of teacher response, to the benefit of both students and teachers. In this chapter, I continue this shift in the focus of response away from teachers and toward students and present evidence of students' ability to assess their own writing and meaningfully reflect on their writing habits, processes, and growth. Just as in chapters 2–4, the six interrelated questions that comprise my heuristic for constructivist response serve as an organizing device for this chapter. Evidence from the 128 portfolio reflection essays in my corpus, as well as additional artifacts of metacognition such as process memos, revision plans, and midterm self-assessments, speak to the value for researchers and teachers in shifting the center of the response construct from teacher comments to student self-assessment.

WHO SHOULD RESPOND?

Most college teachers' cycles of response and assessment begin and end with teacher response, and much of the literature on response is more interested in teacher feedback and assessment than student self-assessment. In a constructivist framework, the attention of researchers and teachers should first be turned to the student's role in knowledge creation and the student's self-efficacy in learning. In a constructivist conception of response, a teacher's primary goal for response is to engage in dialogue with the student's own self-assessment. Examples of this type of dialogue between student self-assessment and teacher response are exceedingly rare in my corpus, but there are a few examples in my research of the type of interaction that a constructivist approach places at the center of the response construct.

https://doi.org/10.7330/9781646423682.c005

A student self-assessment essay in which they reflect on their strengths and challenges as a writer at the beginning of a first-year writing course exemplifies the benefits of designing the response construct to create a dialogue between student self-assessment and teacher response. In their self-assessment essay, the student acknowledges, "My time management has always been poor. I've had trouble writing drafts, because when writing a draft, I don't write as well as I do when I'm cranking out a final. I like to sit down and just crank out a paper." The teacher responds, "Though it's a double-edged sword, of course, the high number of writing assignments in WR 150 (and 100) allow you the opportunity to find the habits and techniques that work for you, through a process of trial and error. I will make a plug for the drafting process, though. Even if you don't use anything from an early draft, each time you grapple with your paper topic you will achieve a greater depth and sophistication, developing your approach in a way you can't in a first draft written under pressure, no matter how elegant or grammatically perfect it should be! I look forward to working with you this semester!" In this example, asking the student to self-assess early in the semester and then responding to this metacognitive writing creates a means to encourage the student to monitor and improve their writing and revising processes.

In my corpus, self-assessment also occurs during drafting processes. An easy to implement tool for self-reflection that is common in my study is a brief process memo submitted with a draft. Despite the fact that process memos were a common task in my research, teachers rarely enter into dialogue with students' self-assessments in their process memos. One example of a teacher interacting with a student's process memo comes from a first-year writing course. In a mid-stage draft process memo a student is asked to assess their strengths and weaknesses and list any questions they have for the teacher. The student mentions that they are concerned about the quality of their argument and that they did not cite two of the authors they are reacting to in their essay. The teacher responds, "I do think you could draw on the theorists more, especially Coles, who can help you develop a more persuasive counterargument." Rather than response as transmission, in this case teacher response affirms the student's self-assessment.

A self-assessment script from a teacher education course is representative of the ability of students in my corpus to self-assess and the benefits of teacher response focusing on students' reflective writing. The following excerpt from a student self-assessment script includes the teacher's response in italics:

1. Effectively provides an introduction that clearly explains the point of the assessment and clarifies the setting (audience, student role, and exactly what students must produce).

    My introduction reminds students of the work they've completed regarding their multi-cultural study on the theme: Identity, and how those works have provided them insight into who the characters are, how they feel, what they think, what's important to them, and why.

    What's particularly striking is the choice afforded students—a real-life or totally fictitious account in any number of formats. The intro, thus, becomes engaging and inviting.

2. Thoughtfully articulates assessment outcomes (standards) in student friendly language (if applicable).

    I restructured the outcomes so that they are written in student-friendly language.

    Yes. Students will clearly understand assessment expectations.

3. Clearly provides a specific set of directions explaining what is required of students from process and in product.

    The directions provide students question(s) they are too consider while developing their short stories, makes it clear to them that, if they're uncomfortable sharing personal stories they may create a fictional piece, and, instead of writing, also gives them the option to create a Podcast or a children's book that is told primarily through illustrations.

    No concerns here; directions also reflect coherence and clarity.

This script provides an example of the ways that students can articulate how they have met assignment criteria, and the benefits of teachers putting themselves in the position of reinforcing students' self-assessments rather than the position of making judgments without considering the context of students' own reflections. As this example illustrates, teacher response can be more minimal and less invasive when teachers engage in dialogue with students' self-assessments.

WHAT SHOULD RESPONSE FOCUS ON?

The research has established that metacognition on writing processes and knowledge increases the likelihood students will transfer rhetorical knowledge and skills to future writing contexts (Beaufort 2007; Dively and Nelms 2007; Downs and Wardle 2007; Mikulecky et al. 1994; Yancey et al. 2014). Even though many teachers in my corpus ask for metacognition in process memos and portfolio reflection essays, they rarely focus on transfer to future writing contexts in their responses, as I discussed in chapter 3. In my research, students are more likely to consider transfer than teachers, even when not prompted to do so. In artifacts of metacognition included in their portfolios, students are very much aware of how they transferred knowledge and skills from one task to the next, as these passages from students' reflective writing illustrate:

> This revision process taught me and helped me a lot in the future with my other essays, also outlined in this portfolio.

> When we moved onto more lengthy papers such as a research paper it was helpful to have the background that the previous papers have provided such as outline techniques, peer edit methods, and writing center advice.

> Also, my goal of being argumentative comes up here as this draft lacked a thesis that was argued through out. This was a point I took to heart and tried improving it not only in the second draft but throughout the rest of the course.

For the most part, teachers in my corpus give feedback in a hermetic seal, rarely pointing out how students' strengths and challenges as writers might be relevant for other courses or for future writing contexts beyond the course. But in their self-assessments and portfolio reflections, students show a desire to connect what they have learned about writing to other contexts beyond the course. A common theme was transfer to other courses:

> What has changed for me this year is the importance of writing an outline, I actually wrote an outline for my final essay in my Mass Communications class which is very unlike me. . . . In my other classes I will also try to work on outlines for my papers as I have discovered that it makes writing a paper much easier.

> The most valuable thing I learned during the process of writing this paper was the thesis progression. . . . This is a process I have already applied to other classes and will continue to use for the rest of my education.

> The knowledge and resources I obtained in this course is helpful in both, my academic and professional career. For example, in my upper-division Sociology course, I was able to successfully apply my skills learned about using credible resources to conduct a literature review regarding the perception of success among children of immigrants.

Students are also able to consider transfer of writing skills and knowledge to their lives after college. In their portfolio reflection essays, students often comment on how what they have learned about writing will be applicable in their future careers:

> As a future educator, I would have to write letters to administrators, parents and my students, so writing is going to be a big part of my teaching career.

I found this assignment to be very practical and helpful. I am planning on using what I have learned from this project to try and get an unsolicited position and The Center for Addiction and Recovery right here on X campus.

Overall, the work involved in performing this research will help me in the future. Identifying reliable sources as well as properly citing the research authors; addressing the appropriate crowd by adjusting the tone, language, construction and form of the review; and lastly, focusing on the main idea of the draft and constantly explaining the relevance of the subject, keeping the interest of the reader alive throughout the writing. These methods of writing skills and outside research will prove beneficial when I enter the health care profession and continue writing academic papers relevant to the suitable audiences.

Whereas teachers are focused primarily on sentences and paragraphs of individual assignments, students tend to focus on transfer and growth.

Students in my study are adept at recognizing the ways they have grown when asked to reflect on their writing for the semester. Students are able to pinpoint specific writing knowledge and specific abilities gained that led to growth. For example, in a process memo, a first-year writing student mentions that a peer presented a counter-argument that forced the writer to refute "with more detail and not dismiss the opposing view," and the writer asserts that this peer feedback "helped me become a better writer as I learned to play devil's advocate with myself." A student in a different first-year writing course observes in their final portfolio reflection that they "came a long way from [their] very first essay" in that they "learned how to organize [their] thoughts, create a convincing point, make the point believable by supporting it with more arguments, and, most of all, to see every side to all arguments." In a midterm reflection, a student from a teacher education course notices that from their first to their seventh weekly writing assignments "there is a difference in length, tone, and vocabulary."

In their midterm and final portfolio reflection essays, students again and again articulated the ways they grew as writers from the start of the course to the finish:

During my few months in WR150, I think it is very fascinating to look at the progress of my work that I have produced: Beginning freshman year if someone told me to write a ten page paper I would have laughed and thought it was a joke but now I have exceeded my expectations as a growing writer and hope to continue to grow at the same rate.

Slowly, I am getting better at being more detailed. With this improvement to my writing, it is more obvious to me when a new idea is being formed and when I should start a different paragraph.

> When comparing my first and my last essay in the class, it appears two separate people had written them. My first casually analyzed a painting and its very obvious artistic elements. My last essay was a thorough assessment of 5 separate works and a detailed, and interesting analysis of their unifying theme.

These student comments on their growth as writers point to the value of asking students to critically self-reflect at various points in the semester. In my corpus, many teachers ask students to assess their progress at midterm, in a final portfolio reflection letter or essay, and throughout the drafting and revising process though process memos that accompany drafts.

One pitfall of asking students to reflect on their growth as writers is what Emmons (2003) refers to as a pat "narrative of progress." In a narrative of progress, a student might write a laundry list of successes, parroting what the student thinks the teacher wants to hear, and may exaggerate the change they experienced as a result of their writing practice in the course. This idea of parroting the teacher in reflective writing is also of concern to Jeff Sommers (2016), who worries that "the reductive classroom dynamic of the student attempting to please the teacher" may trump the metacognitive activity of self-assessment (272). I certainly found narratives of progress that seemed intended to please the teacher in the portfolio reflection essays in my corpus, and I purposefully avoid citing them as evidence of growth. In the previous examples and throughout *Reconstructing Response to Student Writing*, I triangulate students' claims in self-reflections with teacher comments and evidence from revisions of drafts. Through this triangulation of data, I found that in most cases the evidence of growth that students claim in their portfolio reflection essays is present in their drafts.

In addition to being astute in evaluating their growth as writers, students in my research were often perceptive and concrete in their self-assessment of their writing processes. One student points to a specific comment from their teacher, and how that led them to rethink their perspective on revision: "On page 2 she tells me where I should do more research and where to include that information. In this case, she told me, 'Research and discuss how this book has been hailed by preservationists and environmentalists and used as an educational tool.' Before, I would have never thought to include that in my paper, but now I know how to look at things from a different angle and offer a new concept to help the quality of my paper. Therefore, I've learned that the key component in the writing process is the revision." Another student was able to describe in depth the extensive process they learned to apply to research writing:

Through this portfolio, I hope to demonstrate how writing a strong essay is a process. It begins with familiarizing yourself with the text or piece you are arguing for or against. It continues by spending time in the stacks and online trying to find the perfect evidence to support your claim. Then, one must write the paper and revise, revise, revise. . . . This revision process may mean throwing away paragraphs or even scraping your whole thesis. It is evident that the process is a long one (and at times quite tedious), but following the process and completing each step in a thorough, timely manner pays off in the end when you have a solid research paper.

An interesting example of a student providing evidence of a growing awareness of the importance of writing as a process comes from a portfolio transmittal letter in a business writing course. In this example of metacognition on process, the student is able to transfer a situation from a full-class discussion of a peer's draft to the student's own beliefs and understanding regarding revision:

During a peer review session in class, the class suggested that a student cut out a paragraph of unnecessary information in his paper. The class argued that the audience would already know the information. The writer defense to this edit was that he spent a lot of time on this paper and did not want to take anything out. This student was missing the lessons of the revision process as well as considering your audience. As you can see from my draft sections of each paper, I would take out chunks of information if I later decided they were not relevant. When we were editing our proposal papers, I went through many drafts trying to figure out the best ways to be dramatic and show there was a need for my program. I also needed to figure out what was the simplest way to explain my ideas.

In this example, transfer, process, and reflection interact in useful ways, and the evidence of this interaction is in the drafts included in the portfolio.

Perhaps the most powerful examples in my corpus of the benefits of student self-reflection on writing processes come from students who seem to have come to realizations about the importance of writing as a process through their self-reflective writing. The following realization about writing as a process from a student reflecting on two semesters of writing classes involves an analogy that any writing teacher would be happy for a student to make:

I thought about the six academic papers I have written over the year, and I attempted to recall the arguments I made in each paper. I suddenly realized—I couldn't. I panicked. What had I learned after a year of stress, anxiety, hours and hours of revision, tuition? I had no idea. At the time, I was browsing the web, and a delicious-looking dessert caught my eye. I have always loved to cook, and right then I wished that I could make my favorite chocolate cake. Suddenly, I realized that although I didn't remember exactly how many eggs or how much baking soda I use to make the cake, I clearly remembered the process of baking a cake. I then realized that the process of cooking is exactly the same as the process of writing: although I might not remember the sources I used or the key points I developed in each and every academic paper I have written, I will always remember the process of writing.

To extend this analogy, much of the teacher response in my research is focused on how many eggs or how much baking soda is needed to make the cake, but in their reflective writing, students tend to focus their attention on the process of baking.

Even though some students in my research came to realize the inherent value of writing as a process, there were also many students who associate revision with merely trying to get a better grade. Revision is often seen by students in my study as a necessary burden to earn an A grade, as opposed to an important habit of experienced writers. These statements from artifacts of student reflection illustrate this reductive perspective on revision:

> I spent a ridiculous amount of time editing and rewriting and organizing this third essay. But if that's what it takes to earn an A, I think I might be able to do all of it again for future essays.

> I worked the hardest on that essay in particular. I really wanted a good grade more than anything else.

> I worked very hard on this essay to improve my writing and to improve my grade.

> This is my final draft of my third essay, there is great improvement I am sure of that, and I hope it will attain a higher grade.

> For this essay I really strived to improve my writing skills in hopes of raising my grade.

> I put in much more time and effort into this essay, in the hopes of attaining a high grade.

Students in my research often associate satisfaction with their revision processes primarily with the grade they achieved. If significant revision is not required to achieve a good grade, students may not bother to revise. As one student says about their high school writing experiences, "Throughout all my papers I have written in high school and middle school, I did not put that much time into them, so I did not have much time for revision. This has been my mind set in the past: Since I finished a paper, it is done, so what is the sense of spending any more time on it if I know I'm going to get a decent grade in the end?" Only a single student in my corpus articulates a desire to work hard on revision for intrinsic rewards, saying in their portfolio reflection essay, "I hope to cast aside my focus solely on the 'A,' but to create something I will remember." My research points to both the challenges of tapping into students' intrinsic motivation and the many ways that grading distorts motivation and diminishes the effectiveness of self-assessment.

WHAT CONTEXTS SHOULD RESPONDERS CONSIDER?

When the teachers in my research ask students to reflect on their writing and on themselves as writers, teachers gain valuable information about students' literacy histories and their attitudes and approaches to writing that teachers can then consider in responding. For example, in first-year writing courses especially, it was common for teachers to ask students to reflect on the ways their high school and college experiences with writing connect or differ. Consider the first-year writing student who writes in their portfolio reflection essay, "Within the final argumentative paper, I not only had to support my claims but argue them as well. I found this to be a bit hard to do, due to the fact that I was taught in high school for four years that no one cares what I have to say, no one cares how I feel—so how then was I going to construct a convincing and impactful argument on the topic of ACT and SAT testing?" Knowing that this student was not asked to share their perspective in their high school writing assignments could have a significant impact on the kind of feedback a teacher gives to a draft of this student's argumentative paper.

Many teachers in my study ask students to reflect on both their literacy histories and their current contexts. A first-year student in a portfolio reflection reveals, "Coming into this class as a senior who did not do a single English assignment throughout my last year in High School I thought to myself, 'Wow, this class will probably kill me, and I won't be able to focus along with my Calculus 3 class.'" Student reflective writing can help teachers understand students' readiness for meeting our learning outcomes as well as what time constraints students face. I was struck by how many students in my research were willing to reveal their limitations as writers. One student wrote, "Before this writing class my writing process went a little something like this. Day before or morning paper is due; sit down, write paper." Another student admits that in high school they "would stay up the night before and essentially turn in a rough draft the next day. I've never been a huge fan of revising."

Teachers in my corpus rarely make connections to course activities or class discussions in their responses to student writing, but in their self-reflections it is common for students in my research to make connections between their writing and the work of the course. One student articulates a strong connection between class discussions and the argument they make in their paper: "The discussions in class were something I would always think back upon when brainstorming ideas for my paper topics. . . . For one of my first long papers, X had been talking about Richard being an evil character just to be evil. I thought about her idea and thought more about the other characters in the play. Anne popped into my head who really seemed to be a prop for Richard. I quickly wrote this down on the side of one of my assignment sheets and used this as an argument for my paper." Another student is able to point to specific rhetorical strategies discussed in class that they consciously applied in their writing. In their portfolio introduction essay the student mentions, "We talked about incorporating naysayers into our essays extensively in class. In my third essay I implemented a naysayer effectively when I opposed the viewpoint that the exaggeration of the stereotypes of the disabled makes them not offensive." The student further notes, "In class we also learned about the 'who cares?' element of writing. With my development as a writer, in my third essay I incorporated the use of a 'who cares?' to improve my argument by pulling in the importance of the ADA and disabled rights movement today in how it has to deal with an aspect of my essay, how society views people with disabilities." A different student reflects on how class discussions of the Toulmin method encouraged them to examine the warrants in the arguments they made in one of their formal writing assignments. The student writes, "My class notes proved to be very useful in the early phases of my writing and I feel will continue to be throughout the rest of the quarter." Self-assessment provided a context for the students in my research to make connections between their writing and class readings, class discussions, and lecture material.

So few of the assignments in my corpus are written for wider audiences that students do not often reflect on discourse community contexts in their writing—nor are students prompted by teachers to reflect on discourse community contexts in their portfolio reflection essay prompts. I could find only a few cases of students discussing discourse community contexts in assessing their own writing. The following passage from a student reflection essay in a first-year writing course illustrates how capable students are of considering discourse community when prompted to do so by our assignments or by our class readings: "Before I had even started reading and analyzing the Miller-Cochran article, I decided that my second review will most likely be an album review. I didn't have a specific one in mind, but I'm quite familiar with how journalists use rhetoric to review music. It's much different than reviewing literature. After all, they are analyzing with a completely different sense (hearing not reading). I quickly grabbed an Alternative Press magazine from my neatly organized pile of every edition since 2008."

A student in a business writing course is also able to explain in their portfolio transmittal letter how the discourse community context of their research paper affected their rhetorical choices in multiple assignments:

> For my research paper, my audience consisted of people in my business field. This meant that the readers would know the basics of my topic and I did not need to explain background information. . . . I adapted my research paper to appeal to executives in a company. I directed my proposal paper to the co-op program coordinator and took into consideration the information she already knew, how my suggestions would benefit her, and her time. The co-op program coordinator is a busy woman and does not have a lot of time to read a proposal, so I made sure to keep my memo short and clear.

This student also reflects on their prior experiences with writing in the discourse community context of the co-op where they used to work and re-evaluates that writing in light of what they learned in the course. The student reflects on an email they sent to their boss "explaining an accounting situation and the decision [the student] made regarding it." In hindsight the student realizes "the email was long and my solution was not very apparent." The student resolves, "In the future, I will be sure to explain myself more clearly and if needed I will use a table to demonstrate my thought process. I will also cite anything that I used to make my decision, so that my boss can follow how I came to my conclusion." Asking students to reflect on rhetorical choices involving communicating within discourse communities has cultural and political implications, but there is not one instance in my research where students were asked in self-reflections to consider the broader sociocultural contexts of, for example, needing to "adapt" to company executives, or to write more "clearly" to a boss. At the conclusion of this chapter, I consider the implications of this absence of considerations of race, class, and gender in self-assessment activities in my corpus.

WHAT TYPE OF FEEDBACK SHOULD RESPONDERS GIVE?

Earlier in this chapter, I discussed students' ability to recognize their growth as writers and the strengths of their developing writing processes—essentially, students' ability to offer themselves praise. Rodway (2017) argues for the importance of validating self-evaluation with teacher feedback comments to enhance self-assessment competency. One instance of this type of affirmation in my corpus comes from a student's portfolio reflection on an essay. The student writes, "I do, however, think that this paper is an important stepping stone for me, and a prime example of my ability to do very thorough research." The teacher reinforces the students' self-assessment, writing in an end comment on the paper, "Excellent paper . . . *Exceptionally well researched!*" This kind of reinforcement of students' self-assessment of their strengths as writers is rare in my corpus.

In addition to reflecting on their strengths, in portfolio reflection essays and process memos in my corpus students are often skillful at self-critique. Students frequently reflect on the need for both global and local revisions in their drafts. In self-assessing their writing processes in a portfolio introduction, a first-year writing student speaks to both global and local changes they made to their essay:

> In class we critically assessed a sample paper and discussed its strengths and weaknesses. I learned a lot from this exercise because it helped me to be just as critical about my own essay. As I edited this draft, I added more sentences that explained quotations better and more sentences that improved the point I was trying to make in the paragraph. I also made sure that each introductory and conclusion sentence I had in each paragraph was relevant to that paragraph and that it flowed well to the next paragraph.

In comparing this student's first draft to their final draft, the student's self-assessment regarding what they learned from assessing a sample paper and how they applied what they learned is accurate. The final draft has clearer explanations of art works by Mapplethorpe and Serrano and stronger points regarding the significance of the controversies surrounding their work. As the student mentions, paragraphs improved in focus, and much extraneous information was culled from the first draft to the last.

In self-assessment of their global content, students are often more specific and concrete than teachers in their comments. The following excerpts from first-year writing students' portfolio reflection essays illustrate students' adeptness at analyzing the content of their work and their ability to focus in on specific elements of their writing:

> Looking back however, my main problem with the final draft was trying to cover too much material in too few words. For example, I alluded to the potential economic detriments of removing formaldehyde in my claim, but failed to discuss this aspect in depth. I also presented some pieces of evidence with insufficient amounts of explanation. For example, while I chose the relevant facts from Crump et al.'s study, I did not sufficiently describe the context of that study in detail. I also omitted a lot of context regarding Freeman's study as I tried to focus my paragraphs on expressing

my reasons. My argument could have been stronger if I had included more background information on the studies.

> With that, the thesis became a little verbose, but more importantly, result-ed in an absence of significance. I state a claim about death in the poem, but do not answer the question "so what?" Some readers might say that the phrase "characterize the speaker's perspective on dying," communi-cates significance, but I did not analyze the poem from this perspective. One might think that a counterargument will be discussed due to the phrase "rather than a discussion of negative aspects of death." Again, I did not develop this point, which has potential to refute that death is "beauti-ful, eerie, and unstoppable."

Interestingly, although teachers in my study often focus on lower-order concerns in their comments, students focus mostly on global concerns in their artifacts of self-assessment. However, students are also capable of being reflective about their editing processes, as this excerpt from a portfolio reflection reveals:

> I think one of my biggest weaknesses as a writer is editing. I have no prob-lem sitting down and peer reviewing somebody else's work but when it comes to my own work, it just doesn't happen. After sitting down and read-ing and re-reading the same sentences and information over and over, I think that it is difficult to catch my mistakes because my eyes become blinded from them. After receiving a few papers back last quarter, I real-ized that many of the things I turn in have careless mistakes. To prevent this from happening again, this quarter I would wait a few hours or a few days after writing a paper to attempt to review and edit it. I noticed that after not looking at the information for a while and clearing my mind, it became easier to catch silly mistakes.

Many teachers in my study may be more likely to provide generic than specific comments and more likely to focus on sentence-level editing than revision of content, but when provided carefully designed prompts that call for substantial reflection, the students in my study are fully capable of assessing their composing processes from drafting to revising to editing, and of providing concrete examples of the global revisions they made.

WHEN SHOULD RESPONSE OCCUR?

The teachers in my research who require self-assessment most often integrate reflection throughout the course. It is common in my corpus to find first-year writing teachers assign an initial self-assessment of stu-dents' writing skills and habits, or a first assignment that asks students to critically reflect on their literacy experiences in narrative form. In some courses this initial practice in self-assessment is then reinforced

Table 5.1. Self-evaluation sheet

Essay Element:	*Goals for This Element:*	*Greatest Strengths:*	*What to Focus on for the Next Draft:*
Essay Purpose/ Focus (Thesis)	Clear focus; responsive to the prompt; precise; states purpose (answers "why"); forecasts the development of your focus.	I think that my thesis projects a clear opinion and statement.	Maybe focusing more on what the specific aspects of fast food are that is affecting the food supply.
Overall Essay Structure	One idea leads logically to the next; flows.	Some body paragraph thesis statements are well constructed.	Implement more transition statements that make the essay flow better instead of jumping from idea to idea.
Paragraph Unity	Each paragraph develops at least one main idea that connects to your overall focus and purpose; start a new paragraph for each new idea.	Yes	Need to go more in depth in analysis and possible include some personal experiences with the fast food franchises (i.e., Working at inandout)

throughout writing processes as students complete process memos prior to peer and teacher response and revision plans after peer and teacher response. Over half of the ePortfolios in my corpus include a substantial final reflection in the form of a portfolio cover letter or reflection essay.

In this chapter and throughout this book, I have cited passages from student portfolio reflection essays, and these examples have illustrated the value of students engaging in a culminating reflection on their writing processes and what they have learned about writing throughout the course. Rather than cite further examples of the insights students provide when they critically self-reflect at the end of their writing processes, I will focus on the self-assessment that many of the teachers in my corpus ask students to engage in before the final draft. A number of teachers design self-evaluation scripts and rubrics that guide students in their self-assessment, and when students in my study are given this scaffolding, they are often able to accurately assess the strengths of their drafts and find productive areas for revision. See table 5.1 for a representative excerpt from a self-evaluation sheet from a first-year writing course.

This student has located potential areas of revision—being more specific with arguments, improving transitions, going into more depth with analysis, and adding personal experiences—that I myself would have commented on had I responded to this student's draft. If I were this student's teacher, I would feel little need to comment further on this draft. I would be able to simply affirm the student's own assessment.

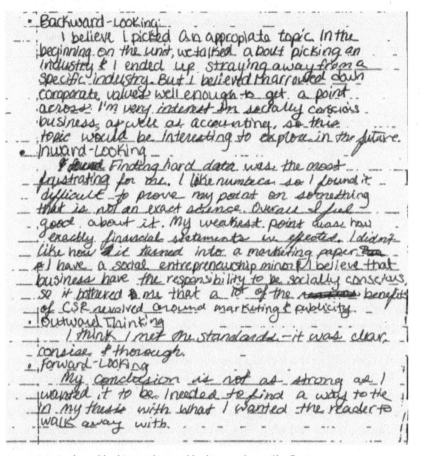

Figure 5.1. Backward-looking and inward-looking student self-reflection.

A business writing teacher in my research asks students to assess their draft through a framework of "backward-looking" and "inward-looking" before the teacher responds. An example student reflection illustrates the usefulness of this framework (see figure 5.1). In responding to this students' draft, the teacher could simply affirm the student's self-assessment of the appropriateness and narrowness of the topic and focus constructive criticism on the weaknesses the student mentions—the discussion of financial statements and the conclusion.

WHAT MODALITIES SHOULD RESPONDERS USE?

Self-assessment can be integrated into any mode teachers choose to deploy in the response construct. A variety of genres of self-assessment

> Moving past the title, when the viewer simply looks at the painting he
> successfully gets a sense of the performance's atmosphere, without having any
> background knowledge of flamenco dancing. The color scheme of *El Jaleo* is the most
> blatant technique Sargent employs to set the mood and tone of the painting. Sargent
> restricts his color palette to black, grey, white, and beige, with accents of red. "His
> powerful use of limited color" (Curry 54) creates a serious, intimate atmosphere
> concurrent with those that Sargent observed firsthand. During his fiv
> Seville, Granada, and Madrid, Spain from 1879-1880, Sargent observ
> performances of the kind depicted in this piece (Heller 10). In a lette
> noted "that the darker, more 'pure' type of flamenco songs appealed
> unusual, since true *cantejondo* (deep, or serious, flamenco singing) a
> (serious flamenco dancing) were seldom appreciated by non-Gypsies" (Heller 13).
> Sargent clearly has an affinity for the traditional, darker flamenco style and this is
> reaffirmed through the mood of *El Jaleo*. The serious atmosphere is certainly achieved
> through the lack of color present in the painting.

Comment bubble: *This citation doesn't tell me anything about Curry's point. I want to know what his point was, not that he used the phrase "powerful use of limited color." And then I want to read your comments on Curry's point, so that I understand how you fit them into your argument.*

Comment bubble: *This is another example of how I struggle with engaging my sources properly. I need to critically analyze their points and incorporate that analysis into my paper. This is something I continue to work on as a writer.*

Figure 5.2. Dialogue between teacher response and student self-reflection.

in my corpus were assigned in print mode: first week self-surveys, literacy narratives, midterm and final reflection, process memos, revision plans. Although teachers in my research rarely take advantage of the affordances of electronic modes for self-reflection, there are a handful of examples in my corpus of students being asked to insert reflective comments on drafts in order to assess their own writing, often with the teacher responding to the reflective comment bubbles students had inserted. Figure 5.2 shows one example from a student's draft where the affordances of the commenting and response function of Word created a dialogue between student self-reflection and teacher response.

Although none of the teachers in my corpus ask students to insert reflective audio comments into their drafts, one teacher asks students to upload self-assessment videos to YouTube that are essentially video process memos. A few of the teachers in my research use screencasting to respond to students, but there are no instances of students being asked to use screencasting to reflect on their drafts in order to provide information for the teacher before responding. It is certainly likely, however, that there were digital modes of response and reflection that the students in the courses in my study engaged in but did not include in their ePortfolios.

In their artifacts of self-assessment in the ePortfolios in my corpus, students are adept at evaluating their strengths and challenges as writers, reflecting on how they have grown over the semester, and considering how what they have learned about writing might transfer to future writing contexts. Teachers in my research deploy a variety of genres in order to encourage self-assessment, from process memos to interactive comments on electronic files to portfolio reflection essays. Regardless of the type of reflective task, the research shows that the most important thing for teachers to keep in mind is integrating self-reflection throughout the course and at every stage of writing processes. As Bower (2003) argues, "Reflection should be integrated into the classroom from beginning to end, progressing from simple to more complex reflective problem-solving questions" (64). Most students have little experience with self-assessment, and it is critical for teachers to guide students' self-assessments and also provide scripts for prompting reflection and models of reflection to emulate.

One important aspect of designing self-assessment that is absent in my corpus is explicitly prompting students to consider sociocultural and sociopolitical contexts in their artifacts of self-assessment. Inoue and Richmond (2016) argue that "most reflective discourses expected in writing classrooms are white discourses" (136), whether that means students of color assessing themselves as deficient when their literacies do not conform to white practices or standards, or students having to fit into white discourse values of individualism, objectivity, and detachment. Similarly, Latta and Lauer (2000) pose the question, "By asking students to assess themselves, are we asking them to internalize the strictures and guidelines of a system that may be discriminatory?" (32). Self-reflection should prompt students to consider not only how they entered a discourse community but the ways their own language and cultural backgrounds both connect to and vary from discourse community norms and expectations. In self-reflection, students should also be given space to question and critique hegemonic discourse norms.

Students' self-assessments of their drafts will not always be accurate and useful, and the teacher has a role to play in not just affirming students' self-assessments but pointing out additional strengths and additional areas for revision. But I believe that the examples of student self-assessment I shared in this chapter, and the example peer responses I shared in the previous chapter, speak to the value of shifting the focus of the response construct from teachers to students. In chapter 6, I summarize my findings and expand on my argument for reconstructing response.

6

RECONSTRUCTING RESPONSE

Throughout *Reconstructing Response to Student Writing* I have applied a constructivist response heuristic that I developed from both a comprehensive review of the literature on response and my national study of teacher response, peer response, and student self-assessment across the college curriculum. The heuristic consists of six interrelated questions that teachers across disciplines can ask themselves as they design the response construct in their courses (see figure 6.1). I have used the heuristic to capture themes from the literature on response, as a framework for analyzing my corpus of teacher and peer responses to over a thousand pieces of college student writing, and as a method of organizing the chapters of this book. But another motivation in creating a constructivist heuristic for response is to provide an accessible tool for faculty across disciplines to help them be more thoughtful, deliberate, and impactful in the design of the response construct in their courses.

A constructivist approach to response encourages us to go well beyond the teacher/student dyad in designing the response construct and consider a variety of contexts that shape response: the students' literacy history, the genres we assign and their discourse community contexts, our own preferences and biases as teachers, the modes in which we respond, and the broader institutional and sociocultural contexts that inform the entire response construct. Constructivist educational theory emphasizes the learner's central role in shaping knowledge, and in this sense research on self-assessment (Boud 1995; Falchikov 2005; Yancey 1998b) and transfer (Anson and Moore 2016; Moore and Bass 2017; Yancey et al. 2014) integrates with a constructivist approach to response—and is integrated into my heuristic. In answering each of the questions of the heuristic, I found that the literature on response and the results of my national study of response point to the value of shifting the focus of response from teachers to students and from final drafts of discrete assignments to student self-assessment, metacognition, and growth.

https://doi.org/10.7330/9781646423682.c006

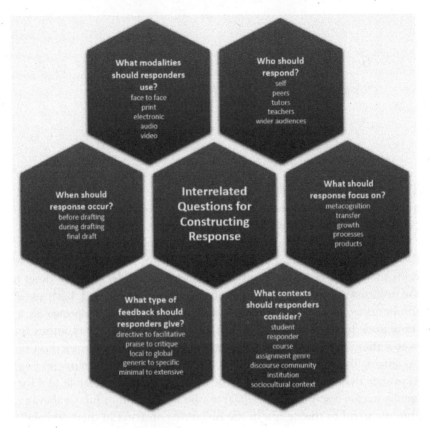

Figure 6.1. A constructivist heuristic for response.

In this chapter, I summarize my findings and consider the implications of the shift in response focus I am arguing for. These implications have relevance for first-year writing teachers, teachers across disciplines, writing center tutors, writing program administrators, and upper-level college administrators.

MOVING BEYOND THE STUDENT/TEACHER DYAD

The empirical research on response, and the findings of my large-scale study of response, indicate that college teachers too often focus their labor on response that has little lasting impact. To be sure, some of the teacher response in my corpus does align with what the research defines as best practices in response: balancing praise with constructive criticism, avoiding overly directive or vague comments, considering genre and discourse community conventions when giving feedback, and responding to drafts and not just final products. However, throughout chapter 3, I reflected on the numerous teacher comments from my corpus that are a questionable use of the labor of response: comments that are angry and sarcastic; comments that could be rubber-stamped from one essay to the next; comments that overwhelm students by their sheer amount; comments that focus almost exclusively on local, sentence-level concerns; comments on final drafts that appear to be written mainly to justify a grade. Even though student self-reflection essays and self-assessment process memos are ubiquitous in the ePortfolios in my corpus, most teacher response in my study exists in a bubble, with no dialogue between teacher and student, no connection between teacher feedback and peer feedback, and no indication of how students could apply comments to future writing contexts beyond the course.

In their self-reflective artifacts in the ePortfolios that make up my corpus, students often report feeling overwhelmed or confused or disheartened by teacher comments, and they long for more content-focused comments and for feedback they can apply to future writing. Students focus on their growth as writers in their own self-assessments, but teachers rarely comment on growth, despite the fact that most of the teachers in my corpus implement a portfolio pedagogy that integrates drafts and asks students to write process memos reflecting on their revisions. Many teachers in my study focus their response on the student/teacher dyad, but students reject this dyad structure, seeking out feedback from friends and family. Students also seek out feedback from their campus writing center and report being highly satisfied with the feedback they receive from tutors. Students especially appreciate that writing center tutors are focused on the content of their writing, even though teachers often send students to the writing center merely to work on sentence-level concerns. My study adds further evidence to the growing body of research that shows that students who work with writing center tutors make substantial revisions. These students also receive better grades, although I argue that teachers and tutors should turn students' attention as far away from grades as possible.

GRADING UNDERMINES RESPONDING

There is an acknowledgment in the response literature that grading has a negative impact on the response construct. Research has found that teachers' comments often focus on justifying grades rather than on student growth (Brannon and Knoblauch 1982; Orrell 2006), that many students care about feedback only as it relates to improving their grade

(Brown 2007; Burkland and Grimm 1986; Cunningham 2019; Hoon Lee et al. 2017), that grading often dictates how much time a student decides to spend on a paper (Carroll 2002; Dohrer 1991), that because of grading many students become obsessed with correctness (Bitchener and Ferris 2012; McMartin-Miller 2014; Richardson 2000), that grading has the effect of reducing self-efficacy and decreasing motivation to learn (Bowden 2018; Lipnevich and Smith 2009), and that grading is racist when it relies on a single, dominant white European standard (Inoue 2019; S. Wood 2020). By no means has response research ignored the impacts of grading on teacher response and students' uptake of our feedback, but my research leads me to believe that more needs to be made of the harm that grading does to learning and to transfer. In their self-reflections, students in my study consistently frame feedback as a means to figure out what the teacher wants and revising as a process of trying to meet the teacher's grading demands, which typically appear idiosyncratic to students. The students in my study reinforce Anne Beaufort's (2007) argument that "writing a paper is perceived by students as an activity to earn a grade rather than to communicate to an audience of readers in a given discourse community" (10). When teachers in my research write comments on final, graded drafts, there is often a sense of missed opportunities: if only the students had done this or that, it could have all ended differently. Responding to final, graded drafts is responding too late, and with little impact on student learning.

Most teachers work in institutions that require final grades, but there are a variety of strategies for deemphasizing grades. The portfolio assessment pedagogy that I focus on in my corpus postpones grading until students have had a chance to engage in cycles of feedback from peers and the teacher. Contract grading (Elbow and Danielewicz 2009; Inoue 2019) is an excellent fit for a constructivist response pedagogy. Contract grading focuses less on the teacher's criteria for final drafts and more on the processes and labor students engage in, as well as students' reflection on that labor and on their growth as writers. Of course, not all grading contracts truly fulfill the shift to student self-assessment and the deemphasizing of final products that I am arguing for, but Inoue's (2019) labor-emphasis model provides one example (see chapter 16 of *Engaging Ideas* [Bean and Melzer 2021], "Alternatives to Traditional Grading," for my own take on labor-emphasis contract grading). Another point of leverage for deemphasizing grades that is an option at most institutions of higher education is the "credit/no credit" course grading structure. I have had the good fortune of teaching a number of courses that were offered as "credit/no credit," and in these courses

I experienced a noticeable improvement in student attitude and in my relationship with students. What was not noticeable in these credit/no credit courses was any reduction in student effort or quality of writing. I created high expectations for what counted as credit, and students met those expectations—just as most students complete the rigorous labor required to make an A in my labor-based grading contract.

PEER RESPONSE AS MORE THAN A
COMPLEMENT TO TEACHER RESPONSE

The literature on peer response is definitive: when teachers implement peer response with training, accountability, and a carefully designed script, and students receive feedback from more than one peer, most students like peer response and make substantial revisions based on their peers' feedback (Allen and Mills 2016; Leijen 2017; Mendonca and Johnson 1994; Paulus 1999; Price et al. 2007; Villamil and de Guerrero 1996, 2020). Research shows that peer response generates feedback that is similar to—and often even more useful than—teacher feedback (Beason 1993; Caulk 1994; Devenney 1989; N. Diab 2011; McGroarty and Zhu 1997; Patchan et al. 2009; Patton 2012; Tannacito and Tuzi 2002; Yang et al. 2006; Zhu 1994). Even if students do not receive helpful feedback from their peers during peer response, research shows that students improve as writers from reading their peers' responses to the assignment and applying lessons from what their peers have written to their own writing (Ballantyne et al. 2002; Lundstrom and Baker 2009; Nicol et al. 2014; Purchase 2000). In their reflections on peer response, students in my research frequently comment on how helpful their peers' feedback was, and how it led them to make substantial revisions to their writing—a claim that is supported by comparisons of their drafts before and after peer response.

One of the strongest patterns in my research is the frequency of student testimony that reading their peers' writing helped them improve their own drafts and also helped them improve as writers. Even students in my study who expressed initial skepticism about peer response begrudgingly admitted that it helped them. Perhaps the greatest impediment to students being willing to trust their peers' advice is the looming threat of the teacher as judge and jury hanging over the peer response endeavor—a constant reminder to students that in the end the teacher will be the one to dictate their fate. Teachers across disciplines would do well to decrease their own response load by putting more of their effort into designing and implementing peer response. Given that the research indicates there is no significant difference between the quality and impact of peer response conducted in class or outside of class via synchronous or asynchronous tools, teachers in the disciplines should not think of peer response as something that necessitates taking away time spent on other types of course content.

To create a more collaborative response construct and further validate and support peer response, teachers should remain in dialogue with peers' responses. Before a teacher responds to a student, they should know what kind of feedback the student received from their peers, and how that feedback influenced the student's revisions. Of course, class sizes can constrain teachers' ability to engage in dialogue with peer response. However, this kind of dialogue can be achieved quite easily by assigning a process memo to be submitted with drafts. In their own response, teachers can both amplify peers' suggestions and add additional insight from the perspective of a discourse community expert. Teachers will always have a mentoring role to play in the response construct, but peer response can function as more than just a compliment to teacher response. The same is true for student self-assessment.

THE STUDENT AS THE CENTER OF RESPONSE AND ASSESSMENT

In shifting response and assessment away from teachers and toward students, the ultimate goal is to empower students to have the self-efficacy as writers to be able to monitor their own writing processes and learn to better assess their own strengths and challenges as writers. The literature emphasizes that metacognition is critical to growth and transfer (Beaufort 2007; Dively and Nelms 2007; Downs and Wardle 2007; Mikulecky et al. 1994; Yancey et al. 2014). In designing the response construct, teachers should ask students to set goals for themselves as writers, assess their strengths and challenges, and reflect on both their literacy histories and their future writing contexts. With guidance and practice, students in my study are adept at assessing their strengths and challenges, reflecting on their writing processes and how those processes developed over the course of the semester, and considering how what they learned about writing might transfer to future contexts. Admittedly, in their final portfolio reflection essays some students in my research reflect on their learning in shallow or vague ways or present a pat narrative of suddenly "seeing the light" that feels contrived and meant to please the teacher. But in the courses in my study that fully integrate self-assessment and provide guidance for students about how to reflect with depth and focus, students' self-assessments were similar to their teachers' assessments. An additional step teachers can take to discourage students from writing pat "narratives of progress" (Emmons 2003) and to promote critical self-reflection is to build into their prompts for reflective assignments space for students to question hegemonic discourse norms and to reflect on sociocultural and sociopolitical contexts for entering and communicating within academic disciplines. In addition to considering issues of race, class, and gender, when students reflect on their literacy histories and processes, they may share valuable information for teachers regarding documented or undocumented learning differences. Wood and Madden (2013) found that students wanted more opportunities to openly discuss their disabilities with teachers, and self-assessment provides this opportunity.

Self-assessment and critical self-reflection on writing processes and habits should happen throughout the course and throughout writing processes. Especially in courses where writing is the focus, my research indicates that teachers should devote less of their response labor to the discrete academic genres they assign and devote more of their response labor to student artifacts of self-reflection, such as literacy inventories, literacy narratives, theories of writing essays, process memos, revision plans, field notes, learning logs, and portfolio reflection essays. Responding to student metacognition will make it easier to respond with greater impact: to respond for transfer.

RESPONDING FOR TRANSFER

Of the 635 pieces of writing in my corpus that teachers responded to, and the thousands of teacher comments I analyzed, there are only a dozen comments that focus on transfer of learning. The type of response that the research shows is most impactful is the type of response that is the rarest in my study. And this despite the fact that most of the teachers in my research use a portfolio pedagogy that includes student self-assessment, peer response, teacher response to drafts in progress, and a culminating portfolio reflection essay. Certainly it is likely that teachers made transfer-focused comments during response I was unable to analyze due to the limitations of my research, such as one-on-one conferences or final portfolio feedback. But it is notable that only twelve written comments in my corpus mention transfer. Just as Writing Studies scholars have focused on designing writing and reading assignments for transfer (Adler-Kassner et al. 2012; Anson and Moore 2016; Beaufort 2007; Carillo 2014; Downs and Robertson 2015;

Moore and Bass 2017; Wardle 2009; Yancey et al. 2014; Yancey et al. 2018), we need to more carefully consider responding for transfer. The concept of *feedforward* is a central concern in international literature on response (Carless 2006; Duncan 2007; Martini and DiBattista 2014; Orsmond and Merry 2011; Pokorny and Pickford 2010; Vardi 2012), but even feedforward is typically focused on transfer from one assignment to the next within a course, as opposed to more far-reaching transfer and more vertical design of response curriculum across departments and the entire institution.

In order to respond for transfer, teachers should place student self-assessment at the center of the response construct. Unfortunately, most college students are used to response and assessment as a one-way transmission from the teacher, and few students have significant experience with self-assessment. To scaffold self-assessment, students should be prompted to think about growth and transfer throughout their writing processes. At the beginning of the course, students could be asked to fill out a literacy inventory, reflect on their writing strengths and challenges in a needs assessment, compose a literacy narrative reflecting on prior experiences with reading and writing, or share what they already know and believe about the writing of the particular discipline of the course. Later in the course students could be asked to write process memos for peer response and teacher response drafts and complete a midterm reflection that includes self-assessment of their writing progress. A culminating reflection could include explicit questions about how what students have learned about writing might transfer to future writing contexts. In lecture/exam format courses, a final and extended reflection on what students have learned and how that could transfer to future contexts would surely be more useful and impactful on student learning than a final exam that only asks of students rote memorization and regurgitation.

In a responding for transfer approach, teachers would place more emphasis on responding to students' self-assessments and less emphasis on responding to the content of rough and final drafts of discrete assignments. This requires a great deal of dialogue, which may include teachers interacting with student process memos, revision plans, midterm reflections, and final reflection essays (to the extent possible, given the class size). When teachers do comment on student writing, they would do well to focus most of their comments on growth and transfer. In addition, teachers should consider developing assignments that ask students to write to audiences outside of the classroom, either real or hypothetical, and then respond in the role of the target audience. This would help encourage teachers to make comments that transfer to contexts beyond the course.

Responding for transfer focuses teachers' attention beyond their individual courses when designing the response construct and encourages faculty to think of response in terms of programs, departments, and the entire institution. Just as faculty map outcomes and assignments in courses, departments, and institutions and intentionally sequence writing courses and assignments for a vertical design, faculty should consider response in terms of vertical curriculum design. Constructing response for a vertical transfer design in departments and across institutions might mean developing shared language for responding; creating shared rubrics; making connections for students among what is taught in the courses in our department when we respond to students' writing; creating sequences of self-reflective assignments across a curriculum that build to a culminating reflective moment such as a portfolio reflection essay; and promoting pedagogies of response that can be implemented across a department, program, or institution, such as peer response, portfolio assessment, and contract grading.

In the opening of this book, I described my frustrations with the results of the narrow and teacher-centered ways I constructed response earlier in my teaching career. In my current teaching experiences, I have found that by deploying a constructivist approach, response in my courses has become richer and more useful. I ask students to complete a literacy inventory the first week of class and share their experiences and attitudes about reading and writing in class discussions and reading journal responses so that I get to know them as writers before I begin to respond to their writing. Cycles of response in my courses focus on student self-reflection and peer response, and when I do respond in one-on-one conferences (admittedly an affordance of small class sizes and a reasonable teaching load), I ask students to begin our conferences by discussing their self-assessment and the revisions they made based on peer feedback. This has allowed me to focus on affirming students' own assessment and their peers' assessments of their writing, and to narrow my feedback to filling in gaps as a disciplinary expert. I focus my final response on students' portfolio reflection essays rather than going through with a fine-toothed comb and commenting on every paragraph they have written. In my comments on the final portfolio, I look to affirm what students have articulated regarding the writing knowledge and habits they have gained that they can apply to future writing contexts, as well as highlight one or two areas they might focus on as they look to grow as writers. I let students choose genres and discourse community audiences for their writing projects, and when I do respond to aspects of student writing such as organization or development or style or integration of sources, I role-play whatever audience students are writing to in order to lessen the focus on my own role as the teacher as grader. Because I use labor-based contract grading and focus the majority of my responding on drafts in progress, I am able to mostly divorce grades from response. Although there is not a vertical response curriculum at my institution, I know that through programmatic faculty development and shared artifacts and pedagogies of response such as peer response, portfolio assessment, and contract grading, students across sections of the first-year composition program I direct are receiving consistent response experiences that are informed by empirical research.

FUTURE RESEARCH ON RESPONSE ACROSS DISCIPLINES

Research on response has evolved from a focus on teacher comments to an increasing concern with the social contexts that make up the response construct, with a call from current researchers to focus especially on student uptake of peer and teacher feedback (Anson 2012; Edgington 2004; Formo and Stallings 2014; Lee 2014; Zigmond 2012). Digital methods of collecting data have made large-scale studies of response more manageable, although recent large-scale studies of teacher or peer response focus on linguistic analysis of comments and, given the corpus sizes, understandably do not include contextual factors or students' perspectives (I. Anson and C. Anson 2017; Dixon and Moxley 2013; Lang 2018; Wärnsby et al. 2018). While my research does not include classroom observations or interviews with teachers or students, I hope it represents a happy medium between smaller-scale but context-rich studies that cannot provide a broad view of college response and larger-scale studies that present valuable big data but lack context. In *Reconstructing Response to Student Writing*, I have made it a point to focus on student perspectives on teacher and peer response, as well as students' self-assessments of their writing. I have also considered the ways that students' rough and final drafts are impacted by response, and the ways their drafts reflect (or sometimes fail to reflect) the claims students make in their self-assessments of their revision processes.

My constructivist heuristic and my argument to place students at the center of the response construct builds a case for focusing more future response research on metacognition and transfer. What is especially lacking in the response literature is research on the ways that response and self-assessment intersect with students' longitudinal development as writers and their ability to transfer what they learned about writing in college to their careers and their personal and public writing after college. My corpus includes a handful of career portfolios, and career portfolios may be valuable artifacts for exploring the issue of vertical transfer and response. Just as Writing Studies scholars have devoted considerable recent attention to the design of curriculum for vertical transfer, we should investigate what kinds of curriculum aid in the vertical transfer of response.

Some of the limitations of my own research point to areas in which we need additional research in response. A constructivist framework encourages us to consider contextual factors in response such as race, class, gender, and disability in regard to both students and teachers. Although I mention places in my research where students reflect on their linguistic backgrounds, my data does not lend itself to considering issues of race, class, gender, and response. For the sake of equity and racial justice, we would do well to focus more of our response research on issues such as white privilege, stereotype threat, translingualism, and antiracist writing assessment and response. My research also lacks reflections from students with disabilities, and the intersections of response and disability is an area sorely needing more research in Writing Studies.

Another contextual factor that has been understudied in response is the role of audience. How is student writing and student uptake of response impacted when we ask students to write to and receive feedback from wider audiences outside of the class—for example, for internships or service-learning projects or writing circulated on the Internet or via social media? In my research there are precious few examples of writing for wider audiences beyond the teacher, either real or hypothetical. The ways teacher response interacts with the classroom culture, the assessment ecology of the department, and the assessment culture of the institution as a whole are also areas that need more attention in response research—areas that I was unable to explore in any depth due to the limitations of my data.

Although my data on response certainly has substantial limitations, taken together with my earlier large-scale research on writing assignments across disciplines, *Assignments across the Curriculum* (2014), I believe it represents a panoramic view of college writing and responding in the United States that future researchers may build on. In the postscript, I offer reflections on two decades of conducting large-scale research on college writing and responding.

POSTSCRIPT
Reflections on Two Decades of Researching
College Writing and Responding

Over the last twenty years, I have focused as a researcher on investigating college writing and responding across the curriculum in the United States on a national scale. My research began with a dissertation analyzing seven hundred writing assignments from courses across the curriculum, which I expanded on in *Assignments across the Curriculum* to include over two thousand writing assignments from courses across disciplines at one hundred institutions of higher education. In *Reconstructing Response to Student Writing*, I have investigated responses from teachers and peers to over 1,000 pieces of student writing at seventy institutions, as well as student self-assessment in 128 portfolio reflection essays. If my research into college writing and responding is taken as a two-stage project, I have examined over 3,000 artifacts of college writing and tens of thousands of comments from teachers and peers from a total of 170 institutions of higher education in the United States. In these research projects, I have tried to take a bird's eye view of college writing and focus not on individual students or teachers or courses but on the most prominent patterns across college writing and responding in the United States.

Case studies of individual students and teachers have been invaluable to WAC research on assigning and responding, as have more extensive longitudinal studies of students' development as writers over their college careers (Beaufort 2007; Carroll 2002; Fishman et al. 2005; Gere 2019; Sommers and Saltz 2004; Sternglass 1997; Walvoord and McCarthy 1991). Along with the other recent big data studies of responding I cited in the previous chapter, my hope is that my research provides a complement to ethnographic studies that are of greater depth but smaller scale than my research. I cannot generalize to all of college writing and responding from my research, but the most prominent patterns in my two-part research project point to specific issues about the way college writing is taught and responded to that are worth considering as possible indications of more widespread strengths to build on and concerns to address.

https://doi.org/10.7330/9781646423682.c007

As I reflect on the writing assignments and responses to student writing I collected in *Assignments across the Curriculum* and *Reconstructing Response to Student Writing*, my most lasting impression is empathy for the challenges college students in my research face from their first year to graduation. Regardless of what kind of institutions the students in my research attended, and regardless of their majors, they were more likely to be asked by their teachers to use writing to regurgitate information from reading and lectures in the form of timed exams or to write generic essays that resembled a five-paragraph theme than to be asked to compose in authentic disciplinary genres that required critical and creative thinking. The criteria teachers used to assess this writing, as spelled out in their assignments and rubrics, was often idiosyncratic, confusing, or contradictory. When students in my research received response to their writing, teacher comments were often focused obsessively on lower-order editing concerns. Teacher feedback was sometimes vague, and when it was specific, often overwhelming. Students rarely received feedback focused on growth and transfer, despite their desire to grow as writers in college and transfer what they are learning to future writing contexts.

The students in my research, however, were also likely to come across teachers who design assignments in authentic genres, use writing to learn, teach writing as a social process and integrate peer response, and provide feedback that is both constructive and encouraging. This was especially true of students who were lucky enough to be attending institutions that are intentional about writing pedagogy and have implemented sequences of lower-division writing coordinated by Writing Studies and multilingual writing specialists, general education courses that include writing requirements, designated writing-intensive or writing-enriched courses/departments, an institutional career portfolio requirement, and well-funded and expansive WAC programs and writing centers.

Although I critique the writing pedagogy of many of the teachers in my research, I sympathize with them just as I sympathize with the students. College professors rarely complete their degrees with any training in writing pedagogy, and at most institutions faculty development for the teaching of writing—if it exists at all—is underfunded and considered something to be done as an "add on" for busy faculty. It is no wonder that most faculty replicate the writing pedagogies that were inflicted upon them as undergraduates—namely, lectures followed by timed exams. It is also no wonder that faculty respond to students the way they were responded to by their teachers. Only a series of robust university writing requirements combined with an expansive WAC faculty development program can break this cycle on a scale that transforms an institution's culture of writing. And only WAC as a movement can break this cycle on a national scale.

Some institutions have built a vertical writing curriculum that ensures that students receive the sequenced writing instruction they need to develop as college writers and that faculty across disciplines receive the training in teaching writing and providing feedback that they most likely did not get in their graduate coursework. However, most institutions simply leave it to the luck of the draw. Given some of the hurdles the students who took the courses in my research faced regarding writing assignments and teacher response, it is no wonder that many college students attempt to avoid courses with substantial writing requirements. My research reveals that a large portion of college writing involves a system set up to reward making an A grade through pleasing the whims of individual teachers. Given the system we ask them to operate under, it is no surprise that many of the students in my research associate writing with sniffing out the rules of the game, following those rules blindly, and obtaining that A, self-efficacy be damned. Writing as critical and creative thinking, writing as discovery, writing as a mode of learning, and writing as communicating to an audience is not as common in most colleges as writing to regurgitate information under timed conditions in a formulaic structure to a teacher playing the role of examiner.

In my research into college writing and responding, I have expressed concern for how we teach college writing across disciplines and argued for a variety of shifts in our thinking. I have argued for a shift from exams to more sophisticated disciplinary and professional research projects, and I have argued for us to shift our focus away from the teacher as grader. I have argued for less focus on written products and more focus on process, growth, and transfer. I have encouraged teachers to connect their assignments—and now their responding—to the broader contexts of disciplinary and professional genres and discourse communities, as well as discourse communities that students are already a part of. And in *Reconstructing Response to Student Writing*, I have argued that students should occupy the very center of the response construct, shifting our emphasis from teacher response and assessment to peer response and student self-assessment.

In the twenty years I have spent researching college writing, I have worked in a variety of writing program administrator roles: as a WAC program coordinator, a writing center coordinator, and a first-year writing program director. I have taught diverse student populations at multiple institutions, from community colleges to state comprehensive universities to R1 institutions. I have taught in an English department and an independent writing program and led a faculty development program that was connected to a center for teaching and learning. I have been able to consider what I have learned from my research in the context of my own experiences working with faculty across disciplines on their assignments and their response to student writing; helping students with their writing in courses across disciplines as a tutor; and teaching first-year and advanced composition. I draw on my research, my experiences as a teacher, and my work as a writing program administrator to provide some final reflections on the implications of my two decades of research into college writing and responding in the United States. I believe these implications are of interest to all of the various stakeholders involved in teaching students to write in college: first-year writing teachers, faculty in the disciplines, writing center tutors, writing program administrators, and upper-level administrators.

BARRIERS AND OPPORTUNITIES IN THE TEACHING OF COLLEGE WRITING

In both *Assignments across the Curriculum* and *Reconstructing Response to Student Writing*, I note significant patterns that point to some of the most sizeable barriers for student writing development in college:

- A focus on grading over learning
- A focus on grammar and correctness over content
- The teacher-as-examiner as the primary audience for most writing
- The dominance of a reductive view of academic discourse (the expository essay, the five-paragraph theme) and rigid "rules" about academic discourse features (theses, introductions, conclusions, the use of "I")
- A lack of writing in authentic disciplinary, professional, personal, and public genres
- A lack of explicit discourse community contexts in assignments and in response
- Idiosyncratic teacher expectations and assessment criteria, even within the same discipline or subdiscipline

Despite these barriers that are predominant in my research, in both stages of my research into college writing I found emerging use of WAC pedagogies across disciplines:

- Writing to learn in the form of reading journals
- Peer response
- Teachers responding to drafts in progress
- Sophisticated disciplinary research genres in courses designated as writing intensive

- Guided self-assessment in the form of process memos, revision plans, and reflection essays
- Implementation of WAC pedagogies in courses using portfolio assessment

Given both the affordances and constraints of college writing and responding as reflected in my research, I believe it is both possible and critical for all institutions of higher education to design a vertical transfer curriculum for writing and responding. I conclude this book with advice for designing a vertical transfer writing and responding curriculum across an institution.

Focus writing assignments and response to writing on transfer.

The WAC movement has encouraged teachers across disciplines to shift their focus from products to processes. My research indicates that this impact has been felt in college writing in the United States, both in terms of teachers responding to works in progress and integrating peer response in their courses across disciplines. I argue that the next step in the WAC movement is to shift our focus in assigning and responding to writing, to emphasize not just process and growth but transfer. When teachers design an assignment, they should consider how the task will apply to students' future disciplinary, professional, public, and personal literacy contexts. When teachers respond to student writing, they should think about how their comments could help students apply what they are learning to future assignments within the course and future writing contexts beyond the course. Teachers should focus more of their labor on responding to artifacts of student metacognition rather than getting bogged down in paragraphs and sentences in discrete final drafts of particular genres. No doubt there are some courses in which a focus on the conventions of discrete genres is appropriate—for example, a capstone business writing course in which students learn to write a resume and a memo and a business plan. But even when the conventions of discrete genres are emphasized as much as students' critical self-reflection on their writing processes and knowledge, teachers should connect their writing assignments to wider discourse community expectations.

Shift the focus of the response construct from teacher response to peer response and student self-assessment.

The teacher as grader looms menacingly over every aspect of college literacy in both *Assignments across the Curriculum* and *Reconstructing*

Response to Student Writing, whether it is the predominance of exam writing; the strange mutt genres many teachers have created that have little connection to authentic disciplinary and professional writing; the often idiosyncratic writing rubrics teachers include with their assignments; the wrestling of control of students' texts in response; the obsession with correctness as defined by white, middle-class, Eurocentric norms; or students' admission that they have surrendered their agency as writers in order to give their teachers what they want in order to chase after an A. The response construct should not be conceived of as a teacher/student dyad, but rather student self-assessment should be at the center. The next rung in the response construct should be peer response, with teacher response occurring only after students have assessed themselves and received feedback from peers. Every course in every discipline should integrate student self-assessment early in the course, peer response throughout the course, and metacognitive tasks during writing processes such as process memos, revision plans, and culminating reflection essays. Portfolio pedagogy lends itself to this approach, and it is past time that portfolio assessment becomes the norm in higher education and traditional grading becomes the outlier—or even better, disappears from the college assessment scene altogether.

End the practice of grading discrete writing assignments.

Most teachers have to assign a reductive one-dimensional grade to students at the end of the semester, but there is no reason teachers need to grade each writing assignment or subject students to the rote memorization and reductive writing requirements of a mid-term and final exam. Portfolio assessment allows teachers to assess a collection of student work, including drafts. This collection can include multiple, authentic disciplinary, professional, personal, or public genres. When teachers ask students to write an extended reflection essay as part of their portfolios, they can focus more of their attention on the quality of students' self-assessments when they consider the final grade and let students' self-assessment guide teacher response. Not grading discrete assignments will make it far more likely students will carefully read teachers' comments and apply them to future tasks.

An even more powerful tool than portfolio assessment in helping turn students' attention away from grades and toward growth is contract grading (see Elbow and Danielewicz 2009; Inoue 2019; and the 2020 *Journal of Writing Assessment* special issue on contract grading edited by

Inoue). A grading contract that encourages students to complete the rigorous processes of researching, drafting, revising, and editing that experienced writers engage in will result in quality of student work that reflects just as much effort and growth as student writing that is submitted in a traditional grading framework, but with far less emphasis on writing to merely please the teacher and get an A. I have found in my research on response that grading is such an impediment to writing development that I believe that whenever possible writing-focused courses should be graded credit/no credit. There are a number of universities that do not assign grades in any course, and those gradeless universities can be looked upon as the ideal model for encouraging writing development in college. The less grading, the more writing development. A college that truly values student learning, growth, and self-efficacy would abolish grades altogether.

Make research writing the focus of college writing.

Writing across the curriculum program directors take note: it appears that there is no greater leverage point for moving faculty away from the lecture/exam model, and for challenging students to grow as writers, than research writing. In my studies of college writing and response, the assignments that students find most engaging, that result in the most growth for student writers, that focus the most on critical and creative thinking, and that connect most explicitly to authentic disciplinary and professional genres are research writing projects. Teachers who assign research writing often have a built-in assignment sequence to shape their courses and emphasize feedforward: from proposals to annotated bibliographies to literature reviews to research articles to presentations of research results. This is a writing and researching sequence that replicates what college teachers do in their own research writing processes and what many professional writers engage in on the job. Research writing should be a central component of first-year writing, and a requirement of writing-intensive courses. Each department should have a capstone course that focuses on a research project, and universities should integrate service learning and internship requirements that ask students to conduct authentic research written to wider audiences beyond teachers. Most institutions have undergraduate research conferences, and WAC efforts should make connections to these events—or should create such an event if one does not exist. Classic WAC pedagogies such as freewriting and journals and microthemes are all important tools to share with faculty across disciplines, and by no means am I arguing against continuing to make these pedagogies central elements of WAC programs. I am also not arguing against the value of narrative writing. I have found that my students' research projects are more memorable and impactful for them and for their readers when students integrate their own stories or the stories of primary research participants into their research. But I am arguing that there is much leverage to be found in conceptualizing WAC primarily as "research writing across the curriculum."

Design an intentional, coordinated, vertical sequence of writing and responding experiences from initial writing placement to lower-division coursework to writing in the majors.

Teachers, writing program administrators, and upper-level administrators have a responsibility to ensure that students get vertical writing and responding support from the moment they enter college until they graduate. This takes a great deal of intentional design and requires colleges to overcome turf battles and think more collaboratively than is often the case in siloed, competitive, masculinist university structures. What might vertical transfer writing and response structures look like? For starters, they do not begin with a timed placement exam. The reductive, formulaic composing called for in one-shot timed exams from ACCUPLACER to the SAT has a negative transfer with the kind of curriculum found in the first-year writing and writing-intensive courses in my research, which emphasize writing as a complex and recursive social process. Placement tools such as Directed Self-Placement or portfolios encourage self-reflection, rhetorical awareness, and transfer. Any institution that relies on a timed writing exam for placement is undermining transfer from the moment students start their college writing careers.

Many institutions think of a single semester of first-year writing as the norm and label students who need more support prior to first-year writing as, at best, "underprepared" or at worst "remedial." Even more misguided, most colleges allow a percentage of students to skip first-year writing entirely using scores on reductive AP, IB, or SAT tests (all of which have negative transfer with college first-year writing curriculum). As the students in my research attest in their reflections on making the transition from high school to college writing, colleges cannot expect students to come to us prepared to make this difficult transition smoothly. At a minimum, colleges should offer a two-course or stretch course lower division writing sequence for all students, and should also provide the option of additional support—for example, via writing center tutoring or small-group studio workshops or sheltered supplemental instruction options for language learners. First-year writing courses should focus on transfer, and this means focusing not on any particular modes of discourse or genres or nonwriting-related themes (e.g., "the environment" or "vampires" or "enduring issues") but on writing as the subject—just as introduction to biology focuses on biology and introduction to psychology focuses on psychology. The Writing about Writing (WAW) approach emphasizes the kinds of metacognition, rhetorical awareness, teacher response to student self-reflection, and far-reaching transfer that is crucial for the first steps in a vertical transfer writing curriculum (Downs and Wardle 2007). Not enough has been made of the fact that a WAW curriculum lends itself to responding for transfer.

Institutions cannot expect student writers to be "complete" in their development once they have taken a few first-year or sophomore writing courses (if they have even taken a single writing course). Vertical transfer demands shared general education writing requirements and robust oversight to ensure those requirements are being attended to. In regard to response, a shared general education writing rubric can aid in transfer, as can shared WAC pedagogies across general education courses, such as peer response or writing to learn or portfolio assessment. Writing is the primary mode of thinking, meaning-making, and communicating in most disciplines, and departments need to work collaboratively—and with the consultation of a WAC expert or experts—to design vertical transfer writing and responding curriculum in their majors. This requires curriculum mapping and backward design. Courses that students take early in the major should introduce them to disciplinary ways of thinking through writing, and capstone courses should ask students to produce the kind of research writing that is valued by disciplinary professionals as well as help students transfer what they have learned in their major to their future professional writing contexts. Aiding in vertical transfer writing and responding curriculum in the majors are features such as shared rubrics, shared learning outcomes, writing in the major guides for students, major ePortfolios, internship courses, service learning courses, and disciplinary student writing journals and conferences.

At the broader level of the institution, there are a variety of activities and programs that can help reinforce the essential structures of a vertical transfer writing and responding design: undergraduate research conferences, campus writing awards, a campus student writing journal, a campus writing rubric, a campus student writing guide, a career ePortfolio. The last item is important enough that I highlight it separately.

Implement career ePortfolios.

Career ePortfolios are becoming more common at institutions of higher education across the United States, and I believe they should be a central component of a vertical transfer writing and responding curriculum. The vertical transfer benefits of career ePortfolios are numerous. They encourage metacognition, and if designed thoughtfully they require students to end their career on a note of extended critical self-reflection. Career ePortfolios encourage students to see connections in the writing required at different points in their academic career. They help make curriculum transparent to students, teachers, administrators, and parents—and may make visible weaknesses in an institution's vertical curriculum design that can be improved upon. They can serve as a placement tool to provide targeted support as students enter their majors. Finally, ePortfolios can be used as a tool to support writing transfer to students' next steps beyond college.

Make writing a focus of academic governance structures.

Universal writing requirements and/or writing-enriched curriculum are crucial to a vertical transfer writing and response curriculum design. To develop these requirements and ensure their continued oversight, writing needs to be a part of academic governance systems. This might mean the creation of an academic senate writing committee or a writing subcommittee of an academic senate curriculum committee. An informal campus writing board or a writing committee formed by a provost can be helpful, but I believe it is best to form a writing-focused committee that is connected directly to the primary policy-making body of the institution. The charge of this committee should be not solely faculty development, or solely approving and reviewing writing-intensive courses or Writing Enriched Curriculum (WEC) departments, but also strategic planning for a vertical transfer writing and responding curriculum. Developing this curriculum requires a broad vision, solid connections to the campus policy-making body, and a committee that includes stakeholders from across the campus networks and a leader or leaders with expertise in WAC and the political protection of tenure status.

Make writing centers and Writing across the Curriculum faculty development programs central hubs of student and faculty support.

Based on my research into writing assignments and response across the curriculum, faculty are in dire need of more training in and support for the teaching of writing and responding to writing, and students are in dire need of more individualized support for their writing. Most institutions have a writing center, and most writing centers have moved out of a closet of an English department to a more central and expansive location. However, there are still far too many writing centers that are mere appendages of an English department. There are still far too many writing centers that lack the space and staffing and budget to truly serve the entire student body—in the way, for example, that massive football programs or shiny new student recreation centers or luxury dorm suites are amply funded by administrators and viewed as a central feature of the institution. Too often colleges view writing centers as locations of "remediation" that are funded—or rather underfunded—accordingly. If colleges begin to think of writing centers as playing a central role in the response construct of all student writers in every course, their perceived place in the institution would be elevated from a support unit for struggling writers to a central part of the college response construct.

WAC programs often fare worse than writing centers in regard to academic budgeting priorities. If a campus has a faculty development program for writing at all, it is often run by someone on a shoestring budget and a fraction of the course release time required to develop a sustainable campus-wide initiative. Often WAC programs (like many writing centers) are merely an appendage of an English department—a node within a node of the institutional network and lacking the campus-wide presence of, say, a center for teaching and learning. All of the stakeholders involved in college writing seem to agree that writing is a high impact practice, that writing is one of the central ways that all disciplines create new knowledge and communicate that knowledge, and that many students struggle to learn the new genres and discourse community expectations of college writing. There is less agreement among college administrators, however, as to how this consensus about the importance of writing should translate to actual financial support for the teaching of writing.

Ideally, a WAC program should be run by a tenure-line or tenured WAC specialist or team, with a centrally funded line-item budget appropriate for a campus-wide initiative that is focused on one of the most critical and high-impact aspects of student learning. WAC should be located in a centralized location as a campus hub or connected to a campus hub (for example, a writing center or a center for teaching and learning). Here I am revisiting arguments Michelle Crow (formerly Cox), Jeffrey Galin, and I make in *Sustainable WAC* (2018), but I do so with an eye toward vertical transfer writing and responding design. A vertical transfer writing and responding curriculum will have trouble getting off the ground and will be impossible to develop and sustain without the institution taking seriously its responsibilities to support all students as writers in the form of a well-funded writing center and to support all faculty as writing teachers in the form of an extensive WAC program.

There are innumerable barriers to the vertical transfer writing and responding curriculum I have outlined above—decades of shrinking funding for higher education from state governments; increasing turf battles among departments and programs as resources become more scarce; a dearth of grants for WAC initiatives; administrative bloat occurring at the same time tenure-line positions are being replaced by contingent positions; university priorities shifting from learning to leisure in the form of expensive recreation centers, luxury dorms, fancy eateries, and new state-of-the-art football stadiums and basketball arenas. In my own efforts to facilitate vertical transfer writing and response curriculum, I have come across hurdles such as skeptical or even hostile English department colleagues who felt any expansion to the writing program would mean a concurrent shrinking of the literature program, deans and provosts who talked a mean game about the importance of writing until it came time to dole out release time and operating budgets, and some disciplinary faculty who felt vehemently that the responsibility for teaching college writing begins and ends with a single first-year writing course.

However, there are examples of numerous institutions that have been successful in thinking vertically in regard to writing and responding. There have been successful efforts at North Carolina State University and the University of Minnesota—among other institutions—to ensure a vertical writing curriculum in every department through Writing Enriched Curriculum efforts led by experienced WAC experts and a well-supported WAC program. There are institutions with carefully sequenced multiple course writing-intensive requirements, such as Iowa State University, the University of Missouri-Columbia, George Mason, and Appalachian State University. There are institutions that have made career ePortfolios central to students' literacy experiences, such as LaGuardia Community College, Auburn University, and Stonybrook. Often thanks in part to a generous alumni donation, there are universities that have developed centralized and independent student and faculty writing support hubs that are a far cry from a writing center in the closet of an English department, such as the University of Michigan's Sweetland Writing Center, the University of Miami, Ohio's Howe Center for Writing Excellence, and Elon University's Center for Writing Excellence.

Teaching writing and responding to student writing is a central concern for every college discipline, and writing is not only a high-impact practice but the primary way that most disciplines create and communicate knowledge. But students' development as college writers is undermined when institutions fail to sequence and support teaching writing and responding to student writing as vertical transfer. Teachers need the support of WAC faculty development specialists to help them move beyond exams as their primary writing assignments and to help them see responding as more than correcting errors or justifying a grade on a final draft. Students need the support of writing centers and teachers with training in the teaching of writing (and not just the teaching of literary criticism) to help them make the difficult transition from high school to college writing expectations, and to guide them in the challenging task of moving from novice to expert in the complex disciplinary and professional genres they will be asked to write in within their majors. Institutions need robust and carefully sequenced writing requirements, from initial writing placement to first-year and sophomore writing courses to writing and responding integrated throughout general education to writing and responding experiences planned vertically in each major. The teaching of college writing should not be isolated in a single first-year writing course or a single course in the disciplines designated as writing-intensive.

The growth of campus writing centers, the rise of Writing Studies as a discipline, the development of independent writing programs, and the impact of fifty years of the Writing across the Curriculum movement has moved the teaching of college writing from the margins toward the center and has put writing and responding on the radar of faculty across disciplines, deans and department chairs, provosts and presidents. I believe the next steps in the evolution of college writing are to ensure that teaching writing and responding to student writing are at the very center of student learning, integrated into every course and carefully sequenced from first year to graduation, supported by independent writing departments and well-funded campus writing hubs of student tutoring and faculty development support. In most cases this requires transforming institutional cultures of literacy, and based on my research it requires dramatically changing the way we teach and respond to writing in the United States. Reform at this level requires that everyone who cares about students' development as college writers has a responsibility to join the movement that can and should continue to work toward transforming college writing on a national scale: Writing across the Curriculum.

APPENDIX

Alverno College
Alvin Community College
Arizona State University
Bloomsburg University
Boise State University
Boston University
Brigham Young University
California State University–Fullerton
California State University–Long Beach
California State University–Northridge
College of Southern Idaho
College of Southern Maryland
Colorado State University
Dartmouth
DePaul University
Elizabethtown College
Fairfield University
Ferris State University
Fresno State University
Grand Canyon University
Iowa State University
Kingsborough Community College
Lewis and Clark College
Manhattanville College
Mercy College (NY)
Miami University
Mississippi State University
Mount Mary University
North Carolina State University
Northeastern University
Norwalk Community College
Ohio State University
Oregon State University
Otis College of Art and Design

Penn State University
Rowan Cabarrus Community College
Rutgers
Sacramento State University
Salem State University
Salt Lake Community College
Santa Clara University
Seton Hall University
Skidmore College
South Piedmont Community College
Southern Illinois University-Carbondale
St. John's University
Texas Tech University
Texas Wesleyan University
University at Buffalo SUNY
University of California–Irvine
University of California–Los Angeles
University of California–Merced
University of California–Santa Barbara
University of Central Florida
University of Hawaii at Manoa
University of Kentucky
University of North Carolina–Chapel Hill
University of North Carolina–Charlotte
University of Rhode Island
University of Richmond
University of South Florida Polytechnic
University of Tennessee-Martin
University of Virginia
University of Washington
University of Wisconsin–Stevens Point
Utah State University
Wake Forest
Weber State University
West Valley College
York County Community College

REFERENCES

Ackerman, David S., and Barbara L. Gross. 2010. "Teacher Feedback: How Much Do Students Really Want?" *Journal of Marketing Education* 18: 172–81. https://doi.org/10.1177/0273475309360159.

Adler-Kassner, Linda, John Majewski, and Damian Koshnick. 2012. "The Value of Troublesome Knowledge: Transfer and Threshold Concepts in Writing and History." *Composition Forum* 26. https://compositionforum.com/issue/26/troublesome-knowledge-thres hold.php.

Ahern-Dodson, Jennifer, and Deborah Reisinger. 2017. "Moving beyond Corrective Feedback: (Re) Engaging with Student Writing in L2 through Audio Response." *Journal of Response to Writing* 3(1): 129–52. https://journalrw.org/article-71/.

Allen, David, and Amy Mills. 2016. "The Impact of Second Language Proficiency in Dyadic Peer Feedback." *Language Teaching Research* 20(4): 498–513. https://doi.org/10.1177/1362168814561902.

Amores, María. 1997. "A New Perspective on Peer Editing." *Foreign Language Annals* 30(4): 513–23. https://doi.org/10.1111/j.1944-9720.1997.tb00858.x.

Anderson, Rebecca S. 1998. "Why Talk about Different Ways to Grade? The Shift from Traditional Assessment to Alternative Assessment." In *Changing the Way We Grade Student Performance: Classroom Assessment and the New Learning Paradigm*, edited by Rebecca S. Anderson and Bruce W. Speck, 5–16. San Francisco: Jossey-Bass.

Andrade, Maureen Snow, and Norman W. Evans. 2013. *Principles and Practices for Response in Second Language Writing*. New York: Routledge.

Anson, Chris M. 1989. "Response Styles and Ways of Knowing." In *Writing and Response: Theory, Practice, and Research*, edited by Chris Anson, 333–66. Urbana: IL: NCTE.

Anson, Chris M. 2000. "Talking about Writing: A Classroom-Based Study of Students' Reflections on Their Drafts." In *Self-Assessment and Development in Writing: A Collaborative Inquiry*, edited by Jane Bowman Smith and Kathleen B. Yancey, 59–74. Cresskill, NJ: Hampton Press.

Anson, Chris M. 2012. "What Good Is It? The Effects of Teacher Response on Students' Development." In *Writing Assessment in the Twenty-First Century: Essays in Honor of Edward M. White*, edited by Norbert Elliot and Les Perelman, 187–202. New York, NY: Hampton Press.

Anson, Chris M. 2016. "Students' Perceptions of Oral Screencast Responses to Their Writing: Exploring Digitally Mediated Identities." *Journal of Business and Technical Communication* 30(3): 378–411. https://doi.org/10.1177/1050651916636424.

Anson, Chris M. 2017. "'She Really Took the Time': Students' Opinions of Screen-capture Response to Their Writing in Online Courses." In *Writing in Online Courses: How the Online Environment Shapes Writing Practices*, edited by Christopher Weaver and Phoebe Jackson, 21–45. Norwood, NJ: Hampton Press.

Anson, Chris M., and Jessie L. Moore, eds. 2016. *Critical Transitions: Writing and the Question of Transfer*. Boulder, CO: University Press of Colorado.

Anson, Ian, and Chris M. Anson. 2017. "Assessing Peer and Teacher Response to Writing: A Corpus Analysis from an Expert Survey." *Assessing Writing* 33: 12–24. https://doi.org/10.1016/j.asw.2017.03.001.

https://doi.org/10.7330/9781646423682.c009

Arndt, Valerie. 1993. "Response to Writing: Using Feedback to Inform the Writing Process." In *Teaching Composition around the Pacific Rim: Politics and Pedagogy*, edited by Mary N. Brock and Larry Walters, 90–116. Clevedon, UK: Multilingual Matters.

Askew, Susan, and Caroline Lodge. 2000. "Gifts, Ping-Pong and Loops: Linking Feedback and Learning," In *Feedback for Learning*, edited by Susan Askew, 1–17. London: Routledge.

Bailey, Richard, and Mark Garner. 2010. "Is the Feedback in Higher Education Assessment Worth the Paper It Is Written On? Teachers' Reflections on Their Practices." *Teaching in Higher Education* 15(2): 187–98. https://doi.org/10.1080/13562511003620019.

Baker, Wendy, and Rachel Hansen Bricker. 2006. "The Effects of Direct and Indirect Speech Acts on Native English and ESL Speakers' Perception of Teacher Written Feedback." *System* 38: 75–84. https://doi.org/10.1016/j.system.2009.12.007.

Ballantyne, Roy, Karen Hughes, and Aliisa Mylonas. 2002. "Developing Procedures for Implementing Peer Assessment in Large Classes Using an Action Research Process." *Assessment and Evaluation in Higher Education* 27(5): 427–41. https://doi.org/10.1080/0260293022000009302.

Barnes, Linda L. 1990. "Gender Bias in Teacher's Written Comments." In *Gender in the Classroom: Power and Pedagogy*, edited by Susan Laine and Isaiah Gabriel. Urbana, IL: University of Illinois Press.

Bauer, Sara. 2011. "When I Stopped Writing on Their Papers: Accommodating the Needs of Student Writers with Audio Comments." *English Journal* 101(2): 64–67.

Bean, John C., and Melzer, Dan. 2021. *Engaging Ideas: The Professor's Guide to Integrating Writing, Critical Thinking, and Active Learning in the Classroom*, 3rd ed. Hoboken, NJ: Jossey-Bass.

Beason, Larry. 1993. "Feedback and Revision in Writing across the Curriculum Classes." *Research in the Teaching of English* 27(4): 395–422.

Beaufort, Anne. 2007. *College Writing and Beyond: A New Framework for University Writing Instruction*. Logan: Utah State University Press.

Beaumont, Chris, Michelle O'Doherty, and Lee Shannon. 2011. "Reconceptualising Assessment Feedback: A Key to Improving Student Learning?" *Studies in Higher Education* 36: 671–87. https://doi.org/10.1080/03075071003731135.

Bell, James H. 2000. "When Hard Questions Are Asked: Evaluating Writing Centers." *Writing Center Journal* 21(1): 7–28.

Berg, E. Catherine. 1999. "The Effects of Trained Peer Response on ESL Students' Revision Types and Writing Quality." *Journal of Second Language Writing* 8(3): 215–41. https://doi.org/10.1016/S1060-3743(99)80115-5.

Berger, Virginia. 1990. "The Effect of Peer and Self-Feedback." *CATESOL Journal* 3: 21–35.

Bevan, Ruth, Joanne Badge, Alan Cann, Chris Willmott, and Jon Scott. 2008. "Seeing Eye-to-Eye? Staff and Students' Views on Feedback." *Bioscience Education* 12(1): 1–15. https://doi.org/10.3108/beej.12.1.

Biber, Douglas, Tatiana Nekrasova, and Brad Horn. 2011. "The Effectiveness of Feedback for L1-English and L2-Writing Development: A Meta-Analysis." *TOEFL iBT Research Report-14.*

Bitchener, John, and Dana Ferris. 2012. *Written Corrective Feedback in Second Language Acquisition and Writing*. New York: Routledge.

Boud, David. 1991. *Implementing Student Self-Assessment*. Sydney: Higher Education Research and Development Society of Australia.

Boud, David. 1995. *Enhancing Learning through Self-Assessment*. London: Kogan Page.

Bourgault, Annette M., Cynthia Mundy, and Thomas Joshua. 2013. "Comparison of Audio vs. Written Feedback on Clinical Assignments of Nursing Students." *Nursing Education Perspectives* 34(1): 43–46. https://doi.org/10.5480/1536-5026-34.1.43.

Bouzidi, L'hadi, and Alain Jaillet. 2009. "Can Online Peer Assessment Be Trusted?" *Educational Technology and Society* 12(4): 257–68.

Bowden, Darsie. 2018. "Comments on Student Papers: Student Perspectives." *Journal of Writing Assessment* 11(1). http://journalofwritingassessment.org/article.php?article=121.

Bower, Laurel L. 2003. "Student Reflection and Critical Thinking: A Rhetorical Analysis of 88 Portfolio Cover Letters." *Journal of Basic Writing* 22(2): 47–66. https://wac.colostate.edu/docs/jbw/v22n2/bower.pdf.

Brammer, Charlotte, and Mary Rees. 2007. "Peer Review from the Students' Perspective: Invaluable or Invalid?" *Composition Studies* 35(2): 71–85.

Brannon, Lil, and C. H. Knoblauch. 1982. "On Students' Rights to Their Own Texts: A Model of Teacher Response." *College Composition and Communication* 33(2): 157–66. https://doi.org/10.2307/357623.

Breuch, Lee-Ann K. 2004. *Virtual Peer Review: Teaching and Learning about Writing in Online Environments.* Albany, NY: State University of New York Press.

Brew, Angela. 1999. "Towards Autonomous Assessment: Using Self-Assessment and Peer Assessment." In *Assessment Matters in Higher Education: Choosing and Using Diverse Approaches,* edited by Sally Brown and Angela Glasner, 159–71. Buckingham and Philadelphia: SRHE and Open University Press.

Bromley, Pam, Eliana Schonberg, and Kara Northway. 2018. "L2 Student Satisfaction in the Writing Center: A Cross-Institutional Study of L1 and L2 Students." *Praxis: A Writing Center Journal* 16(1): 20–31.

Brown, James. 2007. "Feedback: The Student Perspective." *Research in Post-Compulsory Education* 12(1): 33–51. https://doi.org/10.1080/13596740601155363.

Burkland, Jill, and Nancy Grimm. 1986. "Motivating through Responding." *Journal of Teaching Writing* 5: 237–47.

Calfee, Robert, and Pamela Perfumo, eds. 1996. *Writing Portfolios in the Classroom: Policy and Practice, Promise and Peril.* Mahwah, NJ: Lawrence Erlbaum.

Calhoon-Dillahunt, Carolyn, and Dodie Forrest. 2013. "Conversing in Marginal Spaces: Developmental Writers' Responses to Teacher Comments." *Teaching English in the Two-Year College* 40(3): 230–47.

Carillo, Ellen C. 2014. *Securing a Place for Reading in Composition: The Importance of Teaching for Transfer.* Logan: Utah State University Press.

Carino, Peter, and Enders, Doug. 2001. "Does Frequency of Visits to the Writing Center Increase Student Satisfaction? A Correlational Study—or Story." *Writing Center Journal* 22(1): 83–103.

Carless, David. 2006. "Differing Perceptions in the Feedback Process." *Studies in Higher Education* 21(2): 219–33. https://doi.org/10.1080/03075070600572132.

Carroll, Lee Ann. 2002. *Rehearsing New Roles: How College Students Develop as Writers.* Carbondale: Southern Illinois University Press.

Carson, Joan G., and Gayle L. Nelson. 1994. "Writing Groups: Cross-Cultural Issues." *Journal of Second Language Writing* 3(1): 17–30. https://doi.org/10.1016/1060-3743(94)90003-5.

Carson, Joan G., and Gayle Nelson. 1996. "Chinese Students' Perceptions of ESL Peer Response Group Interaction." *Journal of Second Language Writing* 5(1): 1–19. https://doi.org/10.1016/S1060-3743(96)90012-0.

Caswell, Nicole I. 2018. "Affective Tensions in Response." *Journal of Response to Writing* 4(2): 70–98. https://scholarsarchive.byu.edu/journalrw/vol4/iss2/4/.

Caulk, Nat. 1994. "Comparing Teacher and Student Responses to Written Work." *TESOL Quarterly* 28(1): 181–88. https://doi.org/10.2307/3587209.

Chang, Carrie Yea-huey. 2016. "Two Decades of Research in L2 Peer Review." *Journal of Writing Research* 8(1): 81–117. https://doi.org/10.17239/jowr-2016.08.01.03.

Chang, Ching-Fen. 2009. "Peer Review through Synchronous and Asynchronous CMC Modes: A Case Study in a Taiwanese College English Writing Course." *JALT CALL Journal* 5(1): 45–64.

Chaudron, Craig. 1984. "The Effects of Feedback on Students' Composition Revisions." *RELC Journal* 15: 1–14. https://doi.org/10.1177/003368828401500201.

Cho, Kwangsu, and Charles MacArthur. 2010. "Student Revision with Peer and Expert Reviewing." *Learning and Instruction* 20(4): 328–38. https://doi.org/10.1016/j.learninstruc.2009.08.006.

Choi, Jaeho. 2013. "Does Peer Feedback Affect L2 Writers' L2 Learning, Composition Skills, Metacognitive Knowledge, and L2 Writing Anxiety?" *English Teaching* 68(3): 187–213. https://doi.org/10.15858/engtea.68.3.201309.187.

Choi, Jessie. 2014. "Online Peer Discourse in a Writing Classroom." *International Journal of Teaching and Learning in Higher Education* 26(2): 217–31.

Cohen, Andrew D. 1987. "Student Processing of Feedback on Their Compositions." In *Learner Strategies in Language Learning*, edited by Anita L. Wenden and Joan Rubin, 57–70. Englewood Cliffs, NJ: Prentice Hall.

Cohen, Andrew D., and Marilda C. Cavalcanti. 1990. "Feedback on Written Compositions: Teacher and Student Verbal Reports." In *Second Language Writing: Research Insights for the Classroom*, edited by Barbara Kroll, 155–77. Cambridge: Cambridge University Press.

Coleman, Lerita M., Lee Jussim, and Jerry L. Isaac. 1991. "Black Students' Reactions to Feedback Conveyed by White and Black Teachers." *Journal of Applied Social Psychology* 21(6): 460–81. https://doi.org/10.1111/j.1559-1816.1991.tb00531.x.

Condon, Frankie, and Vershawn Ashanti Young, eds. 2017. *Performing Antiracist Pedagogy.* Boulder: University Press of Colorado.

Connor, Ulla, and Karen Asenavage. 1994. "Peer Response Groups in ESL Writing Classes: How Much Impact on Revision?" *Journal of Second Language Writing* 3: 257–76. https://doi.org/10.1016/1060-3743(94)90019-1.

Connors, Robert J., and Andrea Lunsford. 1988. "Frequency of Formal Errors in Current College Writing, or, Ma and Pa Kettle Do Research." *College Composition and Communication* 39(4): 395–409. https://doi.org/10.2307/357695.

Connors, Robert J., and Andrea Lunsford. 1993. "Teachers' Rhetorical Comments on Student Papers." *College Composition and Communication* 44(2): 200–233. June 24, 2016. https://doi.org/10.2307/358839.

Cooper, Steve. 2008. "Delivering Student Feedback in Higher Education: The Role of Podcasting." *Journal of Music, Technology and Education* 1(2–3): 153–65. https://doi.org/10.1386/jmte.1.2and3.153_1.

Coté, Robert A. 2014. "Peer Feedback in Anonymous Peer Review in an EFL Writing Class in Spain." *Gist Education and Learning Research Journal* 9: 67–87. https://doi.org/10.24071/llt.v23i2.2799.

Covill, Amy E. 2010. "Comparing Peer Review and Self-Review as Ways to Improve College Students' Writing." *Journal of Literacy Research* 42(1): 199–226. https://doi.org/10.1080/10862961003796207.

Cox, Michelle, Jeffrey R. Galin, and Dan Melzer. 2018. *Sustainable WAC: A Whole Systems Approach to Launching and Developing WAC Programs.* Urbana, IL: NCTE.

Creswell, John W. 2009. *Research Design: Qualitative, Quantitative, and Mixed Methods Approaches*, 3rd ed. Los Angeles: SAGE Publications.

Creswell, John W. 2013. *Qualitative Inquiry and Research Design: Choosing among Five Approaches*, 4th ed. Los Angeles: SAGE Publications.

Crook, Stephanie. 2022. "A Social-Constructionist Review of Feedback and Revision Research: How Perception of Written Feedback Might Influence Understandings of Revision Processes." *College Composition and Communication* 73(3): 593–614.

Cunningham, Jennifer M. 2019. "Composition Students' Opinion of and Attention to Teacher Feedback." *Journal of Response to Student Writing* 5(1): 4–38. https://scholarsarchive.byu.edu/cgi/viewcontent.cgi?article=1029&context=journalrw.

Daiker, Donald. 1989. "Learning to Praise." In *Writing and Response: Theory, Practice, and Research*, edited by Chris Anson, 103–13. Urbana, IL: NCTE.

Davis, Kevin. 1988. "Improving Students' Writing Attitudes: The Effects of a Writing Center." *Writing Lab Newsletter* 12(10): 3–6.

Devenney, Raymond. 1989. "How ESL Teachers and Peers Evaluate and Respond to Student Writing." *RELC Journal* 20(1): 77–90. https://doi.org/10.1177/003368882890200106.

Devet, Bonnie. 2015. "The Writing Center and Transfer of Learning: A Primer for Directors." *Writing Center Journal* 35(1): 119–50.

Devet, Bonnie, and Dana Lynn Driscoll. 2020. "Transfer of Learning in the Writing Center." *Writing Lab Newsletter*. https://wlnjournal.org/digitaleditedcollection2/.

Diab, Nuwar Mawlawi. 2010. "Effects of Peer- Versus Self-Editing on Students' Revision of Language Errors in Revised Drafts." *System* 38(1): 85–95. https://doi.org/10.1016/j.system.2009.12.008.

Diab, Nuwar Mawlawi. 2011. "Assessing the Relationship between Different Types of Student Feedback and the Quality of Revised Writing." *Assessing Writing* 16(4): 274–92. https://doi.org/10.1016/J.ASW.2011.08.001.

Diab, Rula L. 2005. "EFL University Students' Preferences for Error Correction and Teacher Feedback on Writing." *TESL Reporter* 38(1): 27–51.

Dively, Ronda Leathers, and Gerald Nelms. 2007. "Perceived Roadblocks to Transferring Knowledge from First-Year Writing to Writing-Intensive Major Courses: A Pilot Study." *Writing Program Administration* 31(1–2): 214–40.

Dixon, Zachary, and Joe Moxley. 2013. "Everything Is Illuminated: What Big Data Can Tell Us about Teacher Commentary." *Assessing Writing* 18(4): 241–56. https://doi.org/10.106/j.asw.2103.08.002.

Dohrer, Gary. 1991. "Do Teachers' Comments on Students' Papers Help?" *College Composition and Communication* 39(2): 48–54. https://doi.org/10.1080/87567555.1991.9925485.

Donovan, Pam. 2014. "Closing the Feedback Loop: Physics Undergraduates' Use of Feedback Comments on Laboratory Coursework." *Assessment and Evaluation in Higher Education* 39(8): 1017–29. https://doi.org/10.1080/02602938.2014.881979.

Dowden, Tony, Sharon Pittaway, Helen Yost, and Robyn McCarthy. 2013. "Students' Perceptions of Written Feedback in Teacher Education: Ideally Feedback Is a Continuing Two-Way Communication That Encourages Progress." *Assessment and Evaluation in Higher Education* 38(3): 349–62. https://doi.org/10.1080/02602938.2011.632676.

Downs, Doug, and Liane Robertson. 2015. "Threshold Concepts in First-Year Composition." In *Naming What We Know: Threshold Concepts of Writing Studies*, edited by Linda Adler-Kassner and Elizabeth Wardle, 105–21. Logan: Utah State University Press.

Downs, Doug, and Elizabeth Wardle. 2007. "Teaching about Writing, Writing Misconceptions: (Re)Envisioning 'First-Year Writing' as 'Introduction to Writing Studies.'" *College Composition and Communication* 58(4): 552–84.

Dragga, Sam. 1988. "The Effects of Praiseworthy Grading on Students and Teachers." *Journal of Teaching Writing* 7: 41–50.

Duncan, Neil. 2007. "'Feedforward': Improving Students' Use of Tutors' Comments." *Assessment and Evaluation in Higher Education* 32(3): 271–83. https://doi.org/10.1080/02602930600896498.

Edgington, Anthony. 2004. "Encouraging Collaborating with Students on Teacher Response." *Teaching English in the Two-Year College* 31(3): 287–96.

Edgington, Anthony. 2005. "'What Are You Thinking?' Understanding Teacher Reading and Response through a Protocol Analysis Study." *Journal of Writing Assessment* 2(2): 125–48.

Elbow, Peter. 1997. "High Stakes and Low Stakes in Assigning and Responding to Writing." In *Writing to Learn: Strategies for Assigning and Responding to Writing across the Disciplines*, edited by Peter Elbow and Mary Deane Sorcinelli, 5–13. San Francisco: Jossey-Bass.

Elbow, Peter, and Jane Danielewicz. 2009. "A Unilateral Grading Contract to Improve Learning and Teaching." *College Composition and Communication* 61(2): 244–68.

Ellis, Gwen. 2001. "Looking at Ourselves—Self-Assessment and Peer Assessment: Practice Examples from New Zealand." *Reflective Practice* 2(3): 289–302. https://doi.org/10.1080/1462394012010303.

Elola, Idoia, and Ana Oskoz. 2016. "Supporting Second Language Writing Using Multi-modal Feedback." *Foreign Language Annals* 49(1): 58–74. https://doi.org/10.1111/flan.12183.

Emmons, Kimberly. 2003. "Rethinking Genres of Reflection: Student Portfolio Cover Letters and the Narrative of Progress." *Composition Studies* 31(1): 43–62.

Enginarlar, Hüsnü. 1993. "Student Response to Teacher Feedback in EFL Writing." *System* 21(2): 193–204. https://doi.org/10.1016/0346-251X(93)90041-E.

Evans, Carol. 2011. "The Feedback Landscape." In *Facilitating Transitions to Masters-Level Learning: Improving Formative Assessment and Feedback Processes*, edited by David Scott, Carol Evans, Gwenyth Hughes, Penny Jane Burke, David Watson, Catherine Walter, Mary Stiasny, Mandy Bentham, and Sharon Huttly, 56. London: Institute of Education.

Evans, Carol. 2013. "Making Sense of Assessment Feedback in Higher Education." *Review of Educational Research* 83(1): 70–120. https://doi.org/10.3102/0034654312474350.

Falchikov, Nancy. 2005. *Improving Assessment through Student Involvement.* London: Routledge-Falmer.

Fathman, Ann K., and Elizabeth Whalley. 1990. "Teacher Response to Student Writing." In *Second Language Writing: Research Insights for the Classroom*, edited by Barbara Kroll, 178–90. Cambridge: Cambridge University Press.

Ferris, Dana R. 1995. "Student Reactions to Teacher Response in Multiple-Draft Composition Classes." *TESOL Quarterly* 29(1): 33–53. https://doi.org/10.2307/3587804.

Ferris, Dana R. 1997. "The Influence of Teacher Commentary." *TESOL Quarterly* 31(2): 315–39. https://doi.org/10.2307/3588049.

Ferris, Dana R. 2003. *Response to Student Writing: Implications for Second Language Students.* Mahwah, NJ: Lawrence Erlbaum Associates.

Ferris, Dana R. 2004. "The 'Grammar Correction' Debate in L2 Writing: Where Are We, and Where Do We Go from Here? (and What Do We Do in the Meantime . . . ?)." *Journal of Second Language Writing* 13(1): 49–62. https://doi.org/10.1016/j.jslw.2004.04.005.

Ferris, Dana R. 2006. "Does Error Feedback Help Student Writers? New Evidence on the Short and Long-Term Effects of Written Error Correction." In *Feedback in Second Language Writing*, edited by Ken Hyland and Fiona Hyland, 81–104. Cambridge: Cambridge University Press.

Ferris, Dana R. 2011. *Treatment of Error in Second Language Student Writing.* Ann Arbor: University of Michigan Press.

Ferris, Dana R. 2014. "Responding to Student Writing: Teachers' Philosophies and Practices." *Assessing Writing* 19: 6–23. https://doi.org/10.1016/j.asw.2013.09.004.

Ferris, Dana R., Jeffrey Brown, Hsiang Liu, Maria Eugenia, and Arnaudo Stine. 2011. "Responding to L2 Students in College Writing Classes: Teacher Perspectives." *TESOL Quarterly* 45(2): 207–34. https://doi.org/10.5054/tq.2011.247706.

Ferris, Dana R., and John S. Hedgcock. 1998. *Teaching ESL Composition: Purpose, Process, and Practice.* Mahwah, NJ: Lawrence Erlbaum.

Fife, Jane Mathison, and Peggy O'Neill. 2001. "Moving beyond the Written Comment: Narrowing the Gap between Response Practice and Research." *College Composition and Communication* 53(2): 300–320. https://doi.org/10.2307/359079.

Fishman, Jenn, Andrea Lunsford, Beth McGregor, and Mark Otuteye. 2005. "Performing Writing, Performing Literacy." *College Composition and Communication* 57(2): 224–52.

Formo, Dawn M., and Lynne M. Stallings. 2014. "Where's the Writer in Response Research? Examining the Role of Writer as Solicitor of Feedback in (Peer) Response." In *Peer Pressure, Peer Power: Theory and Practice in Peer Review and Response for the Writing Classroom*, edited by Steven J. Corbett, Michelle LaFrance, and Teagan E. Decker, 43–60. Southlake, TX: Fountainhead Press.

Frankenberg-Garcia, Ana. 1999. "Providing Student Writers with Pre-Text Feedback." *ELT Journal* 53(2): 100–106. https://doi.org/10.1093/elt/53.2.100.

Freestone, Nicholas. 2009. "Drafting and Acting on Feedback Supports Student Learning When Writing Essay Assignments." *Advances in Physiology Education* 33: 98–102. https://doi.org/10.1152/advan.90127.2008.

Garner, Joe, and Oliver Hadingham. 2019. "Anonymizing the Peer Response Process: An Effective Way to Increase Proposed Revisions?" *Journal of Response to Writing* 5(1): 102–16. https://scholarsarchive.byu.edu/cgi/viewcontent.cgi?article=1030&context=journalrw.

Gere, Anne Ruggles, ed. 2019. *Developing Writers in Higher Education: A Longitudinal Study.* Ann Arbor: University of Michigan Press. https://www.fulcrum.org/epubs/x059c8342?locale=en#/6/8[Gere-0004]!/4/2[bk]/2/2[piii]/1:0.

Glover, Chris, and Evelyn Brown. 2006. "Written Feedback for Students: Too Much, Too Detailed or Too Incomprehensible to Be Effective?" *Bioscience Education* 7(1): 1–16. https://doi.org/10.3108/beej.2006.07000004.

Goldstein, Lynn M. 2005. *Teacher Written Commentary in Second Language Writing Classrooms.* Ann Arbor: University of Michigan Press.

Grigoryan, Anna. 2017. "Audiovisual Commentary as a Way to Reduce Transactional Distance and Increase Teaching Presence in Online Writing Instruction: Student Perceptions and Preferences." *Journal of Response to Writing* 3(1): 83–128. https://scholarsarchive.byu.edu/journalrw/vol3/iss1/5/.

Grimm, Nancy Maloney. 1999. *Good Intentions: Writing Center Work for Postmodern Times.* Portsmouth, NH: Heinemann.

Grouling, Jennifer. 2018. "The Genre of Teacher Comments from Hard Copy to iPad." *Journal of Response to Writing* 4(1): 70–99. https://scholarsarchive.byu.edu/cgi/viewcontent.cgi?article=1092&context=journalrw.

Guardado, Martin, and Ling Shi. 2007. "ESL Students' Experiences of Online Peer Feedback." *Computers and Composition* 24: 443–61. https://doi.org/10.1016/j.compcom.2007.03.002.

Guénette, Danielle. 2007. "Is Feedback Pedagogically Correct?: Research Design Issues in Studies of Feedback on Writing." *Journal of Second Language Writing* 16: 40–53. https://doi.org/10.1016/j.jslw.2007.01.001.

Guilford, William H. 2001. "Teaching Peer Review and the Process of Scientific Writing." *Advances in Physiology Education* 25(3): 167–75. https://doi.org/10.1152/advances.2001.25.3.167.

Hamer, John, Helen Purchase, Andrew Luxton-Reilly, and Paul Denny. 2015. "A Comparison of Peer and Tutor Feedback." *Assessment and Evaluation in Higher Education* 40(1): 151–64. https://doi.org/10.1080/02602.938.2014.893418.

Hase, Stewart, and Helen Saenger. 1997. "Videomail—a Personalised Approach to Providing Feedback on Assessment to Distance Learners." *Distance Education* 18: 362–70. https://doi.org/10.1080/0158791970180211.

Hattie, John, and Helen Timperley. 2007. "The Power of Feedback." *Review of Educational Research* 77(1): 81–112. https://doi.org/10.3102/003465430298487.

Hayes, Mary F., and Donald Daiker. 1984. "Using Protocol Analysis in Evaluating Responses to Student Writing." *Freshman English News* 13(2): 1–4.

Hedgcock, John, and Natalie Lefkowitz. 1996. "Some Input on Input: Two Analyses of Student Response to Expert Feedback on L2 Writing." *Modern Language Journal* 80(3): 287–308.

Hennessy, Claire, and Gillian Forester. 2014. "Developing a Framework for Effective Audio Feedback: A Case Study." *Assessment and Evaluation in Higher Education* 39(7): 777–89. doi.org/10.1080/02602938.2013.870530.

Henson, Roberta, and Sharon Stephenson. 2009. "Writing Consultations Can Affect Quantifiable Change: One Institution's Assessment." *Writing Lab Newsletter* 33: 1–5.

Hester, Vicki. 2007. "When Pragmatics Precede Pedagogy: Post-Process Theories of Assessment and Response to Student Writing." *Journal of Writing Assessment* 3(2): 123–44.

Hilgers, Thomas L., Edna L. Hussey, and Monica Stitt-Bergh. 2000. "The Case for Prompted Self-Assessment in the Writing Classroom." In *Self-Assessment and Development in Writing: A Collaborative Inquiry*, edited by Jane Bowman Smith and Kathleen B. Yancey, 1–24. New York: Hampton Press.

Ho, Mei-ching. 2015. "The Effects of Face-to-Face and Computer-Mediated Peer Review on EFL Writers' Comments and Revisions." *Australasian Journal of Educational Technology* 31(1): 1–15. https://doi.org/10.14742/ajet.495.

Ho, Mei-ching, and Sandra J. Savignon. 2007. "Face-to-Face and Computer-Mediated Peer Review in EFL Writing." *CALICO Journal* 24(2): 270–90. https://doi.org/10.1558/cj.v24i2.269-290.

Hoon Lee, Hwee, Alvin Ping Leon, and Geraldine Song. 2017. "Investigating Teacher Perceptions of Feedback." *ELT Journal*, 71(1): 60–68. https://doi.org/10.1093/elt/ccw047.

Honeycutt, Lee. 2001. "Comparing E-Mail and Synchronous Conferencing in Online Peer Response." *Written Communication* 18(1): 26–60. https://doi.org/10.1177/0741088301018001002.

Howard, Craig D., Andrew F. Barrett, and Theodore W. Frick. 2010. "Anonymity to Promote Peer Feedback: Pre-Service Teachers' Comments in Asynchronous Computer-Mediated Communication." *Journal of Educational Computing Research* 43(1): 89–112. https://doi.org/10.2190/EC.43.1.f.

Hu, Guangwei. 2005. "Training Chinese ESL Student Writers for Effective Peer Review." *Asian Englishes* 8(2): 64–77. https://doi.org/10.1080/13488678.2005.10801167.

Huot, Brian. 2002. *(Re)Articulating Writing Assessment for Teaching and Learning*. Logan: Utah State University Press.

Hyland, Fiona. 1998. "The Impact of Teacher-Written Feedback on Individual Writers." *Journal of Second Language Writing* 7(3): 255–86. https://doi.org/10.1016/S1060-3743(98)90017-0.

Hyland, Fiona. 2003. "Focusing on Form: Student Engagement with Teacher Feedback." *System* 31(2): 217–30. https://doi.org/10.1016/S0346-251X(03)00021-6.

Hyland, Ken, and Fiona Hyland. 2006. "Feedback on Second Language Students' Writing." *Language Teaching* 39: 77–95. https://doi.org/10.1017/S0261444806003399.

Hyland, Ken, and Fiona Hyland. 2019. *Feedback in Second Language Writing: Contexts and Issues*. New York: Cambridge University Press.

Inoue, Asao. 2019. *Labor-Based Grading Contracts: Building Equity and Inclusion in the Compassionate Writing Classroom*. Boulder: University Press of Colorado.

Inoue, Asao, ed. 2020. Special Issue on Contract Grading. *Journal of Writing Assessment* 13(2).

Inoue, Asao, and Tyler Richmond. 2016. "Theorizing the Reflection Practices of Female Hmong College Students: Is Reflection a Racialized Discourse?" In *A Rhetoric of Reflection*, edited by Kathleen B. Yancey, 125–45. Logan: Utah State University Press.

Irons, Alastair. 2008. *Enhancing Learning through Formative Assessment and Feedback*. Abingdon, UK: Routledge.

Jeffery, Francie, and Bonita Selting. 1999. "Reading the Invisible Ink: Assessing the Responses of Non-Composition Faculty." *Assessing Writing* 6(2): 179–97. https://doi.org/10.1016/S1075-2935(00)00007-6.

Jin, Li, and Wei Zhu. 2010. "Dynamic Motives in ESL Computer-Mediated Peer Response." *Computers and Composition* 27: 284–303. https://doi.org/10.1016/j.compcom.2010.09.001.

Jones, Harriet, Laura Hoppitt, Helen James, John Prendergast, Stephen Rutherford, Kay Yeoman, and Mark Young. 2012. "Exploring Students' Initial Reactions to the Feedback They Receive on Coursework." *Bioscience Education* 20(1): 3–21. https://doi.org/10.11120/beej.2012.20000004.

Junqueira, Luciana, and Caroline Payant. 2015. "'I Just Want to Do It Right, but It's So Hard': A Novice Teacher's Written Feedback Beliefs and Practices." *Journal of Second Language Writing* 27: 19–36. https://doi.org/10.1016/j.jslw.2014.11.001.

Juwah, Charles, Debra MacFarlane-Dick, Bob Matthew, David Nicol, David Ross, and Brenda Smith. 2004. *Enhancing Student Learning through Effective Formative Feedback.* York, UK: Higher Education Academy Generic Centre.

Kamimura, Taeko. 2006. "Effects of Peer Feedback on EFL Student Writers at Different Levels of English Proficiency: A Japanese Context." *TESL Canada Journal* 23: 12–39. https://doi.org/10.18806/tesl.v23i2.53.

Kauffman, Julia H., and Christian D. Schunn. 2011. "Students' Perceptions about Peer Assessment for Writing: Their Origin and Impact on Revision Work." *Instructional Science* 39(3): 387–406. https://doi.org/10.1007/s11251-010-9133-6.

King, Dave, Stuart McGugan, and Nick Bunyan. 2008. "Does It Make a Difference? Replacing Text with Audio Feedback." *Practice and Evidence of Scholarship of Teaching and Learning in Higher Education* 3(2): 145–63.

Kirschner, Paul A., Henk van den Brink, and Marthie Meester. 1991. "Audiotape Feedback for Essays in Distance Education." *Innovative Higher Education* 15(2): 185–95. https://doi.org/10.1007/BF00898030.

Knauf, Helen. 2016. "Reading, Listening, and Feeling: Audio Feedback as a Component of an Inclusive Learning Culture at Universities." *Assessment and Evaluation in Higher Education* 41(3): 442–49. https://doi.org/10.1080/02602938.2015.1021664.

Knoblauch, C. H., and Lil Brannon. 1981. "Teacher Commentary on Student Writing: The State of the Art." *Freshman English News* 10(2): 1–4.

Knoblauch, C. H., and Lil Brannon. 2006. "Introduction: The Emperor (Still) Has No Clothes: Revisiting the Myth of Improvement." In *Key Works on Teacher Response*, edited by Richard Straub, 1–15. Portsmouth, NH: Heinemann/Boynton-Cook.

Kryger, Kathleen, and Griffin X. Zimmerman. 2020. "Neurodivergence and Intersectionality in Labor-Based Contracts." *Journal of Writing Assessment* 13(2). https://escholarship.org/uc/item/0934x4rm.

Kynard, Carmen. 2006. "'Y'all Are Killin Me Up in Here': Response Theory from a Newjack Composition Teacher/Sistahgurl Meeting Her Students on the Page." *Teaching English in the Two-Year College* 33: 361–85.

Lang, Susan. 2018. "Evolution of Teacher Response? Analysis of Five Years of Feedback to Students." *Journal of Writing Analytics* 2: 1–33. https://wac.colostate.edu/docs/jwa/vol2/lang.pdf.

Latta, Susan, and Janice Lauer. 2000. "Student Self-Assessment: Some Issues and Concerns from Postmodernist and Feminist Perspectives." In *Self-Assessment and Development in Writing: A Collaborative Inquiry*, edited by Jane Bowman Smith and Kathleen B. Yancey, 25–33. Cresskill, NJ: Hampton Press.

Lee, Given, and Diane L. Schallert. 2008. "Meeting in the Margins: Effect of the Teacher-Student Relationship on Revision Processes of EFL College Students Taking a Composition Course." *Journal of Second Language Writing* 17: 165–82. https://doi.org/10.1016/j.jslw.2007.11.002.

Lee, Icy. 2009. "Ten Mismatches between Teachers' Beliefs and Written Feedback Practice." *ELT Journal,* 63(1): 13–22. https://doi.org/10.1093/elt/ccn010.

Lee, Icy. 2014. "Feedback in Writing: Issues and Challenges." *Assessing Writing* 19(1): 1–5. https://doi.org/10.1016/j.asw.2013.11.009.

Lee, Joseph J., Farzaneh Vahabi, and Dawn Bikowski. 2018. "Second Language Teachers' Written Response Practices: An In-house Inquiry and Response." *Journal of Response to Writing* 4(1): 34–70. https://scholarsarchive.byu.edu/journalrw/vol4/iss1/3/.

Leijen, Djuddah A. J. 2017. "A Novel Approach to Examine the Impact of Web-Based Peer Review on the Revisions of L2 Writers." *Computers and Composition* 34: 35–54. https://doi.org/10.1016/j.compcom.2016.11.005.

Leijen, Djuddah A. J., and Anna Leontjeva. 2012. "Linguistic and Review Features of Peer Feedback and Their Effect on the Implementation of Changes in Academic Writing:

A Corpus Based Investigation." *Journal of Writing Research* 4(2): 177–202. https://doi .org/10.17239/jowr-2012.04.02.4.

Leki, Ilona. 1990. "Coaching from the Margins: Issues in Written Response." In *Second Language Writing: Research Insights for the Classroom*, edited by Barbara Kroll, 57–68. New York: Cambridge University Press.

Leki, Ilona. 1991. "The Preferences of ESL Students for Error Correction in College-Level Writing Classes." *Foreign Language Annals* 24(3): 203–18. https://doi.org/10.1111/j.1944 -9720.1991.tb00464.x.

Li, Lan, Allen L. Steckelberg, and Sribhagyam Srinivasan. 2008. "Utilizing Peer Interactions to Promote Learning through a Computer-Assisted Peer Assessment System." *Canadian Journal of Learning and Technology* 34(2): 133–48. https://doi.org/10.21432 /T21C7R.

Liang, Jyh-Chong, and Chin-Chung Tsai. 2010. "Learning through Science Writing Via Online Peer Assessment in a College Biology Course." *The Internet and Higher Education* 13(4): 242–47. https://doi.org/10.1016/j.iheduc.2010.04.004.

Lin, S. J. Sunny, E. Z. F. Liu, and Shyan-Ming Yuan. 2001. "Web-Based Peer Assessment: Does Attitude Influence Achievement?" *IEEE Transactions on Education* 44(2): 211. https://doi.org/10.1109/13.925865.

Lipnevich, Anastasiya A., and Jeffrey K. Smith. 2009. "'I Really Need Feedback to Learn': Students' Perspectives on the Effectiveness of the Differential Feedback Messages." *Educational Assessment, Evaluation and Accountability* 21: 347–67. https://doi.org/10.1007/s11 092-009-9082-2.

Lizzio, Alf, and Keithia Wilson. 2008. "Feedback on Assessment: Students' Perceptions of Quality and Effectiveness." *Assessment and Evaluation in Higher Education* 33(3): 263–75. https://doi.org/10.1080/02602930701292548.

Lo, Ya-Fen. 2010. "Assessing Critical Reflection in Asian EFL Students' Portfolios: An Exploratory Study." *Asia-Pacific Education Researcher* 19(2): 347–55. https://doi.org/10.3860 /taper.v19i2.1602.

Lu, Ruiling, and Linda Bol. 2007. "A Comparison of Anonymous Versus Identifiable e-Peer Review on College Students' Writing Performance and the Extent of Critical Feedback." *Journal of Interactive Online Learning* 6(2): 100–15.

Lundstrom, Kristi, and Wendy Baker. 2009. "To Give Is Better Than to Receive: The Benefits of Peer Review to the Reviewer's Own Writing." *Journal of Second Language Writing* 18: 30–43. https://doi.org/10.1016/j.jslw.2008.06.002.

Lunt, Tom, and John Curran. 2010. "'Are You Listening Please?' The Advantages of Electronic Audio Feedback Compared to Written Feedback." *Assessment and Evaluation in Higher Education* 35(7): 759–70. https://doi.org/10.1080/02602930902977772.

Mabrito, Mark. 1991. "Electronic Mail as a Vehicle for Peer Response: Conversations of High- and Low-Apprehensive Writers." *Written Communication* 8(4): 509–32. https://doi .org/10.1177/0741088391008004004.

Macgregor, George, Alex Spiers, and Chris Taylor. 2011. "Exploratory Evaluation of Audio Email Technology in Formative Assessment Feedback." *Research in Learning Technology* 19(1): 39–59. https://doi.org/10.1080/09687769.2010.547930.

Mahfoodh, Omer Hassan Ali. 2017. "'I Feel Disappointed': EFL University Students' Emotional Responses to Teacher Written Feedback." *Assessing Writing* 31: 53–72. https://doi.org/10.1016/j.asw.2016.07.001.

Mahfoodh, Omer Hassan Ali, and Ambigapathy Pandian. 2011. "A Qualitative Case Study of EFL Students' Affective Reactions to and Perceptions of Their Teachers' Written Feedback." *English Language Teaching* 4(2): 14–25. https://doi.org/10.1016/j.asw.2016 .07.001.

Mangelsdorf, Kate. 1992. "Peer Reviews in the ESL Composition Classroom: What Do Students Think?" *ELT Journal* 46(3): 274–84.

Mangelsdorf, Kate, and Ann Schlumberger. 1992. "ESL Student Response Stances in a Peer-Review Task." *Journal of Second Language Writing* 1(3): 235–54. https://doi.org/10.1093/ELT/46.2.274.

Martini, Tanya, and David DiBattista. 2014. "The Transfer of Learning Associated with Audio Feedback on Written Work." *Canadian Journal for the Scholarship of Teaching and Learning* 5(1): 1–7. https://doi.org/10.5206/cjsotl-rcacea.2014.1.8.

Matsumura, Shoichi, and George Hann. 2004. "Computer Anxiety and Students' Preferred Feedback Methods in EFL Writing." *Modern Language Journal* 88(3): 403–15. https://doi.org/10.1111/j.0026-7902.2004.00237.x.

McAlexander, Patricia J. 2000. "Developmental Classroom Personality and Response to Peer Review." *Research and Teaching in Developmental Education* 17: 4–12.

McGroarty, Mary E., and Wei Zhu. 1997. "Triangulation in Classroom Research: A Study of Peer Revision." *Language Learning* 47(1): 1–43. https://doi.org/10.1111/0023-8333.11997001.

McMahon, Tim. 2010. "Peer Feedback in an Undergraduate Programme: Using Action Research to Overcome Students' Reluctance to Criticise." *Educational Action Research* 18(2): 273–87. https://doi.org/10.1080/09650791003741814.

McMartin-Miller, Cristine. 2014. "How Much Feedback Is Enough?: Teacher Practices and Student Attitudes toward Error Treatment in Second Language Writing." *Assessing Writing* 19: 24–35. https://doi.org/10.1016/j.asw.2013.11.003.

Melzer, Dan. 2014. *Assignments across the Curriculum: A National Study of College Writing.* Logan: Utah State University Press.

Mendonca, Cássia O., and Karen E. Johnson. 1994. "Peer Review Negotiations: Revision Activities in ESL Writing Instruction." *TESOL Quarterly* 28(4): 745–70. https://doi.org/10.2307/3587558.

Mikulecky, Larry J., Peggy Albers, and Michele Peers. 1994. *Literacy Transfer: A Review of the Literature.* Philadelphia: National Center of Adult Literacy.

Min, Hui-Tzu. 2006. "The Effects of Trained Peer Review on EFL Students' Revision Types and Writing Quality." *Journal of Second Language Writing* 15: 118–41. https://doi.org/10.1016/j.jslw.2006.01.003.

Min, Hui-Tzu. 2007. "Writer Perceptions of Reviewer Stances: A Qualitative Study." *English Teaching and Learning* 31(3): 29–61. https://doi.org/10.6330/ETL.2007.31.3.02.

Molloy, Elizabeth, and David Boud. 2014. "Feedback Models for Learning, Teaching, and Performance." In *Handbook of Research on Educational Communications and Technology*, edited by J. Michael Spector, M. David Merrill, Jan Elen, and M. J. Bishop, 412–24. Berlin: Springer.

Montgomery, Julie L., and Wendy Baker. 2007. "Teacher-Written Feedback: Student Perceptions, Teacher Self-Assessment, and Actual Teacher Performance." *Journal of Second Language Writing* 16: 82–99. https://doi.org/10.1016/j.jslw.2007.04.002.

Moore, Jessie L., and Randall Bass. 2017. *Understanding Writing Transfer: Implications for Transformative Student Learning in Higher Education.* Sterling, VA: Stylus Publishing.

Munroe, Wendy, and Linda Hollingworth. 2014. "Audio Feedback to Physiotherapy Students for Viva Voce: How Effective Is the 'Living Voice'?" *Assessment and Evaluation in Higher Education* 39(7): 865–78.

Murphy, Carole, and Jo Cornell. 2010. "Student Perceptions of Feedback: Seeking a Coherent Flow." *Practitioner Research in Higher Education* 4(1): 41–51. https://doi.org/10.1080/02602930903197883.

Neal, Michael. 2016. "The Perils of Standing Alone: Reflective Writing in Relation to Other Texts." In *A Rhetoric of Reflection*, edited by Kathleen B. Yancey, 64–83. Logan: Utah State University Press.

Nelson, Gayle L. 1997. "How Cultural Differences Affect Written and Oral Communication: The Case of Peer Response Groups." *New Directions for Teaching and Learning* 70: 77–84. https://doi.org/10.1002/TL.7009.

Nelson, Gayle L., and Joan G. Carson. 1995. "Social Dimensions of Second-Language Writing Instruction: Peer Response Groups as Cultural Context." In *Composing Social Identity in Written Communication*, edited by Donald L. Rubin, 89–109. Hillsdale, NJ: Lawrence Erlbaum.

Nelson, Gayle L., and John M. Murphy. 1992. "An L2 Writing Group: Task and Social Dimensions." *Journal of Second Language Writing* 1(3): 171–93. https://doi.org/10.1016/1060-3743(92)90002-7.

Newkirk, Thomas. 1984. "Direction and Misdirection in Peer Response." *College Composition and Communication* 35(3): 301–11. https://doi.org/10.2307/357458.

Nicol, David J., and Dera Macfarlane-Dick. 2006. "Formative Assessment and Self-Regulated Learning: A Model and Seven Principles of Good Feedback Practice." *Studies in Higher Education* 31(2): 199–218. https://doi.org/10.1080/03075070600572090.

Nicol, David, Avril Thomson, and Caroline Breslin. 2014. "Rethinking Feedback Practices in Higher Education: A Peer Review Perspective." *Assessment and Evaluation in Higher Education* 39(1): 102–22. https://doi.org/10.1080/02602938.2013.795518.

Office for Human Research Protections. 2018. 45 CFR 46. United States Department of Health and Human Services. https://www.hhs.gov/ohrp/regulations-and-policy/regulations/45-cfr-46/index.html#46.102.

Olesova, Larisa A., Jennifer C. Richardson, Donald Weasenforth, and Christine Meloni. 2011. "Using Asynchronous Instructional Audio Feedback in Online Environments: A Mixed Methods Study." *Journal of Online Learning and Teaching* 7(1): 30–42.

O'Neill, Peggy, and Jane Mathison-Fife. 1999. "Listening to Students: Contextualizing Response to Student Writing." *Composition Studies* 27(2): 39–51.

Orrell, Janice. 2006. "Feedback on Learning Achievement: Rhetoric and Reality." *Teaching in Higher Education* 11(4): 441–56. https://doi.org/10.1080/13562510600874235.

Orsmond, Paul, and Stephen Merry. 2011. "Feedback Alignment: Effective and Ineffective Links between Tutors' and Students' Understanding of Course Feedback." *Assessment and Evaluation in Higher Education* 36(2): 125–36. https://doi.org/10.1080/02602930903201651.

Patchan, Melissa M., David Charney, and Christian D. Schunn. 2009. "A Validation Study of Students' End Comments: Comparing Comments by Students, a Writing Teacher, and a Content Teacher." *Journal of Writing Research* 1(2): 124–52. https://doi.org/10.17239/jowr-2009.01.02.2.

Patton, Chloe. 2012. "'Some Kind of Weird, Evil Experiment': Student Perceptions of Peer Assessment." *Assessment and Evaluation in Higher Education* 37(6): 719–31. https://doi.org/10.1080/02602938.2011.563281.

Patton, Martha Davis, and Summer Smith Taylor. 2013. "Re-evaluating Directive Commentary in an Engineering Activity System." *Across the Disciplines* 10. https://wac.colostate.edu/atd/articles/patton_taylor2013.cfm.

Paulus, Trena M. 1999. "The Effect of Peer and Teacher Feedback on Student Writing." *Journal of Second Language Writing* 8: 265–89. https://doi.org/10.1016/S1060-3743(99)80117-9.

Pearce, C. Glenn, and R. Jon Ackley. 1995. "Audiotaped Feedback in Business Writing: An Exploratory Study." *Business Communication Quarterly* 58(3): 31–34. https://doi.org/10.1177/108056999505800306.

Phelps, Louise Wetherbee. 2000. "Cyrano's Nose: Variations on the Theme of Response." *Assessing Writing* 7: 91–110. https://doi.org/10.1016/S1075-2935(00)00018-0.

Pitts, Stephanie E. 2005. "'Testing, Testing . . .': How Do Students Use Written Feedback?" *Active Learning in Higher Education* 6(3): 218–29. https://doi.org/10.1177/1469787405057663.

Pokorny, Helen, and Pamela Pickford. 2010. "Complexity, Cues and Relationships: Student Perceptions of Feedback." *Active Learning in Higher Education* 11(1): 21–30. https://doi.org/10.1177/1469787409355872.

Polio, Charlene. 2012. "The Relevance of Second Language Acquisition Theory to the Written Error Correction Debate." *Journal of Second Language Writing* 21: 375–89. https://doi.org/10.1016/j.jslw.2012.09.004.

Pond, Keith, Rehan Ul-Haq, and Winnie Wade. 1995. "Peer Review: A Precursor to Peer Assessment." *Innovations in Education and Training International* 32(3): 314–23. https://doi.org/10.1080/1355800950320403.

Pope, Nigel K. L. 2005. "The Impact of Stress in Self and Peer Assessment." *Assessment and Evaluation in Higher Education* 30(1): 51–63. https://doi.org/10.1080/0260293042003243896.

Poulos, Ann, and Mary Jane Mahony. 2008. "Effectiveness of Feedback: The Students' Perspective." *Assessment and Evaluation in Higher Education* 33(2): 143–54. https://doi.org/10.1080/02602930601127869.

Price, Margaret, Karen Handley, Jill Millar, and Berry O'Donovan. 2010. "Feedback: All That Effort but What Is the Effect?" *Assessment and Evaluation in Higher Education* 35(3): 277–89. https://doi.org/10.1080/02602930903541007.

Price, Margaret, and Berry O'Donovan. 2006. "Improving Performance through Enhancing Understanding of Criteria and Feedback." In *Innovative Assessment in Higher Education*, edited by Cordelia Bryan and Karen Clegg, 100–109. New York: Routledge.

Price, Margaret, Berry O'Donovan, and Chris Rust. 2007. "Putting a Social-Constructivist Assessment Process Model into Practice: Building the Feedback Loop into the Assessment Process through Peer Review." *Innovations in Education and Teaching International* 44(2): 143–52. https://doi.org/10.1080/14703290701241059.

Prior, Paul. 1998. "Contextualizing Teachers' Responses to Writing in the College Classroom." In *The Reading-Writing Connection*, edited by Robert C. Calfee and Nancy Nelson, 153–77. Chicago: National Society for Studies of Education.

Probst, Robert E. 1989. "Transactional Theory and Response to Student Writing." In *Writing and Response: Theory, Practice, and Research*, edited by Chris Anson, 68–79. Urbana, IL: NCTE.

Purchase, Helen C. 2000. "Learning about Interface Design through Peer Assessment." *Assessment and Evaluation in Higher Education* 25(4): 341–52. https://doi.org/10.1080/02602930044245.

Radecki, Patricia M., and John M. Swales. 1988. "ESL Student Reaction to Written Comments on Their Written Work." *System* 16(3): 355–65. https://doi.org/10.1016/0346-251X(88)90784.

Rae, Agnes M., and Davis K. Cochrane. 2008. "Listening to Students: How to Make Written Assessment Feedback Useful." *Active Learning in Higher Education* 9(3): 217–30. https://doi.org/10.1177/1469787408095847.

Rahimi, Mohammad. 2013. "Is Training Student Reviewers Worth Its While? A Study of How Training Influences the Quality of Students' Feedback and Writing." *Language Teaching Research* 17(1): 67–89. https://doi.org/10.1177/1362168812459151.

Read, Barbara, Becky Francis, and Jocelyn Robson. 2005. "Gender, 'Bias,' Assessment and Feedback: Analyzing the Written Assessment of Undergraduate Student Essays." *Assessment and Evaluation in Higher Education* 30(3): 241–60. https://doi.org/10.1080/02602930500063827.

Reddy, Maureen T., and Bonnie TuSmith, eds. 2002. *Race in the College Classroom: Pedagogy and Politics*. New Brunswick, NJ: Rutgers University Press.

Reid, Joy. 1994. "Responding to ESL Students' Texts: The Myths of Appropriation." *TESOL Quarterly* 28(2): 273–92. https://doi.org/10.2307/3587434.

Rhind, Susan M., Graham W. Pettigrew, Jo Spiller, and Geoff T. Pearson. 2013. "Experiences with Audio Feedback in a Veterinary Curriculum." *Journal of Veterinary Medical Education* 40(1): 12–18. https://doi.org/10.3138/jvme.0912-081R.

Richardson, S. 2000. "Students' Conditioned Response to Teachers' Response: Portfolio Proponents, Take Note!" *Assessing Writing* 7(2): 117–41. https://doi.org/10.1016/S1075 -2935(00)00021-0.

Robinson, Sarita, Debbie Pope, and Lynda Holyoak. 2013. "Can We Meet Their Expectations?" *Assessment and Evaluation in Higher Education* 38(3): 260–72.

Rodway, Claire Louise. 2017. "Encouraging Active Participation in Dialogic Feedback through Assessment as Learning." *Journal of Response to Writing* 3(2): 74–92. https:// scholarsarchive.byu.edu/cgi/viewcontent.cgi?article=1086&context=journalrw.

Rodway-Dyer, Sue, Jasper Knight, and Elizabeth Dunne. 2011. "A Case Study on Audio Feedback with Geography Undergraduates." *Journal of Geography in Higher Education* 35(2): 217–31. https://doi.org/10.1080/03098265.2010.524197.

Ruegg, Rachael. 2015. "The Relative Effects of Peer and Teacher Feedback on Improvement in EFL Students' Writing Ability." *Linguistics and Education* 29: 73–82. https://doi .org/10.1016/j.linged.2014.12.001.

Ruegg, Rachael. 2018. "The Effect of Peer and Teacher Feedback on Changes in EFL Students' Writing Self-Efficacy." *Language Learning Journal* 46(2): 87–102. https://doi .org/10.1080/09571736.2014.958190.

Ruecker, Todd. 2014. "Analyzing and Addressing the Effects of Native Speakerism on Linguistically Diverse Peer Review." In *Peer Pressure, Peer Power: Theory and Practice in Peer Review and Response for the Writing Classroom,* edited by Steven J. Corbett, Michelle LaFrance, and Teagan E. Decker, 91–105. Southlake, TX: Fountainhead Press.

Rutz, Carol. 2004. "Marvelous Cartographers." In *Classroom Spaces and Writing Instruction,* edited by Ed Nagelhout and Carol Rutz, 117–32. Cresskill, NJ: Hampton Press.

Rysdam, Sheri, and Lisa Johnson-Shull. 2016. "Introducing Feedforward: Renaming and Reframing Our Repertoire for Written Response." *JAEP* 21: 70–85.

Saito, Hiroko. 1994. "Teachers' Practices and Students' Preferences for Feedback on Second Language Writing: A Case Study of Adult ESL Learners." *TESL Canada Journal* 11(2): 46–70. https://doi.org/10.18806/tesl.v11i2.633.

Schwegler, Robert A. 1991. "The Politics of Reading Student Papers." In *The Politics of Writing Instruction: Postsecondary,* edited by Richard H. Bullock and John Trimbur, 203–26. Portsmouth: Boynton/Cook.

Scrocco, Diana Lin Awad. 2012. "Do You Care to Add Something? Articulating the Student Interlocutor's Voice in Writing Response Dialogue." *Teaching English in the Two-Year College* 39(3): 274–92.

Seker, Meral, and Ayca Dincer. 2014. "An Insight to Students' Perceptions on Teacher Feedback in Second Language Writing Classes." *English Language Teaching* 7(2): 73–83. https://doi.org/10.5539/elt.v7n2p73.

Séror, Jérémie. 2009. "Institutional Forces and L2 Writing Feedback in Higher Education." *Canadian Modern Language Review* 66(2): 203–32.

Séror, Jérémie. 2011. "Alternative Sources of Feedback and Second Language Writing Development in University Content Courses." *Canadian Journal of Applied Linguistics* 14(1): 118–43.

Siczek, Megan M. 2020. "L2 Writers' Experience with Peer Review in Mainstream First-Year Writing: Socioacademic Dimensions." *Journal of Response to Writing* 6(2): 102–28. https://scholarsarchive.byu.edu/journalrw/vol6/iss2/5/.

Silva, Mary Lourdes. 2012. "Camtasia in the Classroom: Student Attitudes and Preference for Video Commentary or Microsoft." *Computers and Composition* 29(1): 1–22. https://doi.org/10.1016/j.compcom.2011.12.001.

Sinclair, Hazel K., and Jennifer A. Cleland. 2007. "Undergraduate Medical Students: Who Seeks Formative Feedback?" *Medical Education* 41: 580–82. https://doi.org/10.1111/j .1365-2923.2007.02768.x.

Sipple, Susan. 2007. "Ideas in Practice: Developmental Writers' Attitudes toward Audio and Written Feedback." *Journal of Developmental Education* 30(2): 22–31.

Sitko, Barbara M. 1993. "Exploring Feedback: Writers Meet Readers." In *Hearing Ourselves Think: Cognitive Research in the College Writing Classroom,* edited by Ann M. Penrose and Barbara M. Sitko, 278–94. New York: Oxford University Press.

Sluijsmans, Dominique M. J., Saskia Brand-Gruwel, and Jeroen J. G. van Merriënboer. 2002. "Peer Assessment Training in Teacher Education: Effects on Performance and Perceptions." *Assessment and Evaluation in Higher Education* 27(5): 443–54. https://doi .org/10.1080/0260293022000009311.

Small, Felicity, and Kath Attree. 2015. "Undergraduate Student Responses to Feedback: Expectations and Experiences." *Studies in Higher Education* 41(11): 2078–94. https://doi.org /10.1080/03075079.2015.1007944.

Snymanski, Erika Amethyst. 2014. "Instructor Feedback in Upper-Division Biology Courses: Moving from Spelling and Syntax to Scientific Discourse." *Across the Disciplines* 11(2): 1–13. https://wac.colostate.edu/atd/articles/szymanski2014.cfm.

Sommers, Jeffrey. 1989. "The Effects of Tape-Recorded Commentary on Student Revision: A Case Study." *Journal of Teaching Writing* 8: 49–75.

Sommers, Jeffrey. 2012. "Response Rethought . . . Again: Exploring Recorded Comments and the Teacher-Student Bond." *Journal of Writing Assessment* 5(1). http:// journalofwritingassessment.org/article.php?article=59.

Sommers, Jeffrey. 2016. "Problematizing Reflection: Conflicted Motives in the Writer's Memo." In *A Rhetoric of Reflection,* edited by Kathleen B. Yancey, 271–87. Logan: Utah State University Press.

Sommers, Nancy. 1982. "Responding to Student Writing." *College Composition and Communication* 33(2): 148–56. https://doi.org/10.2307/357622.

Sommers, Nancy. 2006. "Across the Drafts." *College Composition and Communication* 58(2): 248–57.

Sommers, Nancy, and Laura Saltz. 2004. "The Novice as Expert: Writing the Freshman Year." *College Composition and Communication* 56(1): 124–49.

Spencer, Brenda. 1998. "Responding to Students' Writing: The Students' Perspective." *Southern African Journal of Applied Language Studies* 6(1): 27–42. https://doi.org/10 .1080/10189203.1998.9724674.

Spencer, Liz, Jane Ritchie, Rachel Ormston, William O'Connor, and Matt Barnard. 2014. "Analysis: Principles and Processes." In *Qualitative Research Practice: A Guide for Social Science Students and Researchers,* edited by Jane Ritchie, Jane Lewis, Carol McNaughton Nicholls, and Rachel Ormston, 269–93. London: SAGE Publications.

Stern, Lesa A., and Amanda Solomon. 2006. "Effective Faculty Feedback: The Road Less Traveled." *Assessing Writing* 11: 22–41. https://doi.org/10.1016/j.asw.2005.12.001.

Sternglass, Marilyn. 1997. *Time to Know Them: A Longitudinal Study of Writing and Learning at the College Level.* Mahwah, NJ: Lawrence Erlbaum Associates.

Still, Brian, and Amy Koerber. 2010. "Listening to Students: A Usability Evaluation of Teacher Commentary." *Journal of Business and Technical Communication* 24(2): 206–33. https://doi.org/10.1177/1050651909353304.

Straub, Richard. 1996. "The Concept of Control in Teacher Response: Defining the Varieties of 'Directive' and 'Facilitative' Commentary." *College Composition and Communication* 47: 223–51. https://doi.org/10.2307/358794.

Straub, Richard. 1997. "Students' Reactions to Teacher Comments." *Research in the Teaching of English* 31(1): 91–119.

Straub, Richard. 2002. "Reading and Responding to Student Writing: A Heuristic for Reflective Practice." *Composition Studies* 3(1): 15–60.

Straub, Richard, ed. 2006. *Key Works on Teacher Response.* Portsmouth, NH: Heinemann/ Boynton-Cook.

Straub, Richard, and Ronald F. Lunsford. 1995. *Twelve Readers Reading: Responding to College Student Writing.* Cresskill, NJ: Hampton Press.

Strijbos, Jan-Willem, Theresa Ochoa, Dominique Sluijsmans, Mien R. Segers, and Harm H. Tillema. 2009. "Fostering Interactivity through Formative Peer Assessment in (Web-Based) Collaborative Learning Environments." In *Cognitive and Emotional Processes in Web-Based Education: Integrating Human Factors and Personalization,* edited by Constantinos Mourlas, Nikos Tsianos, and Panagiotas Germanakos, 375–95. Hershey, PA: IGI Global.

Sugita, Yoshishito. 2006. "The Impact of Teachers' Comment Types on Students' Revision." *ELT Journal* 60(1): 34–41. https://doi.org/10.1093/elt/ccio79.

Sutton, Paul, and Wendy Gill. 2010. "Engaging Feedback: Meaning, Identity and Power." *Practitioner Research in Higher Education* 4(1): 3–13. https://doi.org/10.1093/elt/ccio79.

Tannacito, Terry, and Frank Tuzi. 2002. "A Comparison of E-Response: Two Experiences, One Conclusion." *Kairos* 7(3). https://kairos.technorhetoric.net/7.3/coverweb/tannacito/E-Response-Tannacito-Tuzi.pdf.

Tao, Jian, Qing Shao, and Xuesong Gao. 2017. "Ethics-Related Practices in Internet-Based Applied Linguistic Research." *Applied Linguistics Review* 8(4): 1–25. https://doi.org/10.1515/applirev-2016-2024.

Taylor, Summer Smith, and Martha D. Patton. 2006. "Ten Engineers Reading: Disjunctions between Preference and Practice in Civil Engineering Faculty Responses." *Journal of Technical Writing and Communication* 36: 253–71. https://doi.org/10.2190/07LL-2K2M-27KH-CX1W.

Thompson, Graham, Alan Pilgrim, and Kristy Oliver. 2005. "Self-Assessment and Reflective Learning for First-Year University Geography Students: A Simple Guide or Simply Misguided?" *Journal of Geography in Higher Education* 29(3): 403–20. https://doi.org/10.1080/03098260500290959.

Thompson, Isabelle, Alyson Whyte, David Shannon, Amanda Muse, Kristen Miller, Milla Chappell, and Abby Whigham. 2009. "Examining Our Lore: A Survey of Students' and Tutors' Satisfaction with Writing Center Conferences." *The Writing Center Journal* 29(1): 78–105.

Thompson, Riki, and Meredith J. Lee. 2012. "Talking with Students through Screencasting: Experimentations with Video Feedback to Improve Student Learning." *The Journal of Interactive Technology and Pedagogy* 1. https://jitp.commons.gc.cuny.edu/talking-with-students-through-screencasting-experimentations-with-video-feedback-to-improve-student-learning/.

Thorpe, Mary. 2000. "Encouraging Students to Reflect as Part of the Assignment Process." *Active Learning in Higher Education* 1(1): 79–92. https://doi.org/10.1177/1469787400001001006.

Tiruchittampalam, Shanthi, Alistair Ross, Elizabeth Whitehouse, and Tom Nicholson. 2018. "Measuring the Effectiveness of Writing Center Consultations on L2 Writers' Essay Writing Skills." *Languages* 3(14): 4. https://www.mdpi.com/2226-471X/3/1/4.

Tobin, Lad. 2004. *Reading Student Writing: Confessions, Meditations, and Rants.* Portsmouth, NH: Boynton/Cook.

Tolar Collins, Vicki. 2000. "Freewriting in the Middle: Self-Help for College Writers across the Curriculum." In *Self-Assessment and Development in Writing: A Collaborative Inquiry,* edited by Jane Bowman Smith and Kathleen B. Yancey, 105–24. Cresskill, NJ: Hampton Press.

Truscott, John. 1999. "The Case for 'The Case against Grammar Correction in L2 Writing Classes': A Response to Ferris." *Journal of Second Language Writing* 8(2): 111–22. https://doi.org/10.1016/S1060-3743(99)80124-6.

Tsui, Amy B. M., and Maria Ng. 2000. "Do Secondary L2 Writers Benefit from Peer Comments?" *Journal of Second Language Writing* 9:147–70. https://doi.org/10.1016/S1060-3743(00)0022-9.

Tuck, Jackie. 2012. "Feedback-Giving as Social Practice: Teachers' Perspectives on Feedback as Institutional Requirement, Work and Dialogue." *Teaching in Higher Education* 17(2): 209–21. https://doi.org/10.1080/13562517.2011.611870.

Tuzi, Frank. 2004. "The Impact of E-Feedback on the Revisions of L2 Writers in an Academic Writing Course." *Computers and Composition* 21: 217–35. https://doi.org/10.1016/j.compcom.2004.02.003.

Van den Berg, Ineke, Wilfried Admiraal, and Albert Pilot. 2006. "Design Principles and Outcomes of Peer Assessment in Higher Education." *Studies in Higher Education* 31(3): 341–56. https://doi.org/10.1080/03075070600680836.

Van Steendam, Elke, Gert Rijlaarsdam, Lies Sercu, and Huub Van den Bergh. 2010. "The Effect of Instruction Type and Dyadic or Individual Emulation on the Quality of Higher-Order Peer Feedback in EFL." *Learning and Instruction* 20(4): 316–27. https://doi.org/10.1016/j.learninstruc.2009.08.009.

Vann, Roberta J., Frederick O. Lorenz, and Daisey E. Meyer. 1991. "Error Gravity: Faculty Response to Errors in the Written Discourse of Nonnative Speakers of English." In *Assessing Second Language Writing in Academic Contexts*, edited by Liz Hamp-Lyons, 181–95. Norwood, NJ: Ablex.

Vardi, Iris. 2009. "The Relationship between Feedback and Change in Tertiary Student Writing in the Disciplines." *International Journal of Teaching and Learning in Higher Education* 20(3): 350–61.

Vardi, Iris. 2012. "Effectively Feeding Forward from One Written Assignment Task to the Next." *Assessment and Evaluation in Higher Education* 39(5): 599–610. https://doi.org/10.1080/02602938.2012.670197.

Villamil, Olga S., and Maria C. M. de Guerrero. 1996. "Peer Revision in the L2 Classroom: Social-Cognitive Activities, Mediating Strategies, and Aspects of Social Behavior." *Journal of Second Language Writing* 5(1): 51–76. https://doi.org/10.1016/S1060-3743(96)90015-6.

Villamil, Olga S., and Maria C. M. de Guerrero. 2020. "Sociocultural Theory: A Framework for Understanding the Social-Cognitive Dimensions of Peer Feedback." In *Feedback in Second Language Writing: Contexts and Issues*, edited by Ken Hyland and Fiona Hyland, 23–44. New York: Cambridge University Press.

Vincelette, Elizabeth Jackson, and Timothy Bostic. 2013. "Show and Tell: Student and Teacher Perceptions of Screencast Assessment." *Assessing Writing* 18(4): 257–77. https://doi.org/10.1016/j.asw.2013.08.001.

Walker, Mirabelle. 2013. "Feedback and Feedforward: Student Responses and Their Implication." In *Reconceptualising Feedback in Higher Education: Developing Dialogue with Students*, edited by Stephen Merry, Margaret Price, David Carless, and Maddelena Taras, 103–12. London: Routledge.

Walvoord, Barbara, and Lucille McCarthy. 1991. *Thinking and Writing in College: A Naturalistic Study of Students in Four Disciplines*. Urbana, IL: NCTE.

Wang, Weiqiang. 2014. "Students' Perceptions of Rubric-Referenced Peer Feedback on EFL Writing: A Longitudinal Inquiry." *Assessing Writing: An International Journal* 19(1): 80–96. https://doi.org/10.1016/j.asw.2013.11.008.

Wardle, Elizabeth. 2009. "'Mutt Genres' and the Goal of FYC: Can We Help Students Write the Genres of the University?" *College Composition and Communication* 60(4): 765–89.

Ware, Paige D., and Mark Warschauer. 2006. "Electronic Feedback and Second Language Writing." In *Feedback in Second Language Writing: Contexts and Issues*, edited by Ken Hyland and Fiona Hyland, 118–22. New York: Cambridge University Press.

Wärnsby, Anna, Asko Kauppinen, Laura Aull, Djuddah Leijen, and Joe Moxley. 2018. "Affective Language in Student Peer Reviews: Exploring Data from Three Institutional Contexts." *Journal of Academic Writing* 8(1): 28–53. https://doi.org/10.18552/JOAW.V8I1.429.

Weaver, Melanie R. 2006. "Do Students Value Feedback? Student Perceptions of Tutors' Written Responses." *Assessment and Evaluation in Higher Education* 31(3): 379–94. https://doi.org/10.1080/02602930500353061.

Wilson, Emily, and Justine Post. 2019. "Toward Critical Engagement: Affect and Action in Student Interactions with Teacher Feedback." In *Developing Writers in Higher Education: A Longitudinal Study*, edited by Anne Ruggles Gere. Ann Arbor: University of Michigan Press. https://www.fulcrum.org/concern/monographs/ww72bc25j.

Wingard, Joel, and Angela Geosits. 2014. "Effective Comments and Revisions in Student Writing in WAC Courses." *Across the Disciplines* 11(1): 1–16. https://wac.colostate.edu/atd/articles/wingard_geosits2014.cfm.

Wingate, Ursula. 2010. "The Impact of Formative Feedback on the Development of Academic Writing." *Assessment and Evaluation in Higher Education* 35(5): 519–33. https://doi.org/10.1080/02602930903512909.

Wood, Shane. 2020. "Engaging in Resistant Genres as Antiracist Teacher Response." *The Journal of Writing Assessment* 13(2). http://journalofwritingassessment.org/article.php?article=157.

Wood, Tara. 2017. "Cripping Time in the College Composition Classroom." *College Composition and Communication* 69(2): 260–86.

Wood, Tara, and Shannon Madden. 2013. "Suggested Practices for Syllabus Accessibility Statements." *Kairos: A Journal of Rhetoric, Technology, and Pedagogy* 18(1). https://praxis.technorhetoric.net/tiki-index.php?page=Suggested_Practices_for_Syllabus_Accessibility_Statements.

Yancey, Kathleen B., ed. 1992. *Portfolios in the Writing Classroom: An Introduction.* Urbana, IL: NCTE.

Yancey, Kathleen B. 1996. "Dialogue, Interplay, and Discovery: Mapping the Role and the Rhetoric of Reflection in Portfolio Assessment." In *Writing Portfolios in the Classroom: Policy and Practice, Promise and Peril*, edited by Robert Calfee and Pamela Perfumo, 83–102. Mahwah, NJ: Lawrence Erlbaum.

Yancey, Kathleen B. 1998a. "Getting beyond Exhaustion: Reflection, Self-Assessment, and Learning." *Clearing House* 72(1): 13–17. https://doi.org/10.1080/00098659809599378.

Yancey, Kathleen B. 1998b. *Reflection in the Writing Classroom.* Logan: Utah State University Press.

Yancey, Kathleen B. 2009. "Reflection and Electronic Portfolios: Inventing the Self and Reinventing the University." In *Electronic Portfolios 2.0: Emergent Research on Implementation and Impact*, edited by Darren Cambridge, Barbara Cambridge, and Kathleen B. Yancey, 5–16. Sterling, VA: Stylus Publishing.

Yancey, Kathleen B., ed. 2016. "Introduction: Contextualizing Reflection." *A Rhetoric of Reflection.* Logan: Utah State University Press.

Yancey, Kathleen B., Matthew Davis, Liane Roberston, Kara Taczak, and Erin Workman. 2018. "Writing across College: Key Terms and Multiple Contexts as Factors Promoting Students' Transfer of Writing Knowledge and Practice." *WAC Journal* 29: 42–63. https://doi.org/10.37514/WAC-J.2018.29.1.02.

Yancey, Kathleen B., Matthew Davis, Liane Roberston, Kara Taczak, and Erin Workman. 2019. "The Teaching for Transfer Curriculum: The Role of Concurrent Transfer and Inside- and Outside-School Contexts in Supporting Students' Writing Development." *College Composition and Communication* 71(2): 268–95.

Yancey, Kathleen B., Liane Robertson, and Kara Taczak. 2014. *Writing across Contexts: Transfer, Composition, and Sites of Writing.* Logan: Utah State University Press.

Yancey, Kathleen B., and Irwin Weiser, eds. 1997. *Situating Portfolios: Four Perspectives.* Logan: Utah State University Press.

Yang, Miao, Richard Badger, and Zhen Yu. 2006. "A Comparative Study of Peer and Teacher Feedback in a Chinese EFL Writing Class." *Journal of Second Language Writing* 15: 179–200. https://doi.org/10.1016/j.jslw.2006.09.004.

Young, Beth Rapp, and Barbara A. Fritzsche. 2002. "Writing Center Users Procrastinate Less: The Relationship between Individual Differences in Procrastination, Peer Feedback, and Student Writing Success." *Writing Center Journal* 23(1): 45–58.

Zamel, Vivian. 1985. "Responding to Student Writing." *TESOL Quarterly* 19(1): 79–102. https://doi.org/10.2307/3586773.

Zhang, Shuqiang. 1995. "Reexamining the Affective Advantage of Peer Feedback in the ESL Writing Class." *Journal of Second Language Writing* 4: 209–22. https://doi.org/10.1016/1060-3743(95)90010-1.

Zhao, Yong. 1998. "The Effects of Anonymity on Computer-Mediated Peer Review." *International Journal of Educational Telecommunications* 4(4): 311–45.

Zhu, Wei. 1994. "Effects of Training for Peer Response on Students' Comments and Interactions." *Written Communication* 12(4): 492–528. https://doi.org/10.1177/0741088395012004004.

Ziegler, Nicholas A., and Aleidine J. Moeller. 2012. "Increasing Self-Regulated Learning through the LinguaFolio." *Foreign Language Annals* 45(3): 330–48. https://doi.org/10.111/j.1944-9720.2012.01205.x.

Zigmond, Rosalyn H. 2012. "Students' Perceptions of Comments on Their Papers." *Journal of Teaching Writing* 27(1): 111–38.

Ziv, Nina D. 1984. "The Effect of Teacher Comments on the Writing of Four College Freshmen." In *New Directions in Composition Research*, edited by Richard Beach and Lillian S. Bridwell, 362–80. New York: Guilford.

INDEX

ableism, 38, 39
academic disciplines, 122, 135
academic governance systems, writing requirements, 149
accessibility, online research sites, 11–12
administration, writing programs, 143, 147, 150, 151
affirmation, teacher response to student self-assessment, 113, 125, 126, 128, 137
age of student, 37
Allen, David, 48
Andrade, Maureen Snow, 22, 33
anonymous review, 27–28, 53
Anson, Chris, 14–15, 16, 40, 41, 45
Anson, Ian, 16
antiracist writing assessments, 38, 139
apprehension, writing, 43, 51, 66, 98
assessment rubrics: audience, 69; citation style, 4; grading, 3, 56, 143, 145–46; grammar, 30, 66, 74, 106–7, 141; peer response, 64, 142; praise/critique, 73; scaffolding, 25, 26, 48, 110, 125, 136; self-reflection essays, 144–45; shared, 127, 148; writing development, 141
assessment. *See* ePortfolios; self-assessments
assigning, research, 140
Assignments across the Curriculum, 4, 5, 9, 15, 16, 19, 32, 54, 57, 66, 69, 73, 74, 88
assignment genres: context, *8, 130*; conventions, 67; creative/critical thinking, 141, 142, 146; design, 144; disciplines, 88–89, 142–45; discourse communities, 121–22, 142, 144; feedback, 4–7, 40; grading, 142, 145; prompts, 111; response constructs, *8,* 21, 22, 40, *130,* 133; sequence, 146; social construct, 6, 88–89
asynchronous response, 50, 51, 110, 134
attitudes toward writing, 29, 37, 120, 133, 137
audience: discourse community, 69, 70, 121, 132, 137–38; drafts in progress, 109, 110; external, 136; feedback, 55–58; response model, 22, 32–33, 36–39, 88, 99; role-play, 122, 138, 139; target, 45, 55, 114; teacher-reader, 3, 31; writing development, 122, 142

audio response, *8,* 22, 49, 51, 86–87, 110, *130*
authentic disciplinary genre, 67, 88–89, 141, 143, 145–47

backward course design, 126, 148
backward-looking, self-assessment, *126*
Bailey, Richard, 40
Baker, Wendy, 26
Ballantyne, Roy, 26
Barnes, Linda L., 39
Beason, Larry, 25, 44
Beaufort, Ann, 132
before drafting, response, *8,* 22, 32, 37, 48, *130,* 134
Bell, James H., 29
Berg, E. Catherine, 27
best practices, teacher response, 89–91, 130
Bevan, Ruth, 31–32
bias: class, 122, 135, 139; disabilities, students with, 39, 41, 139; gender, 38, 39, 41, 122, 135, 139; grading, 31, 129, 132; implicit, 3–4, 38–39; personal, 65; race, 38–39, 41, 122, 135, 139
Biber, Douglas, 20, 30
big data, response constructs research, 5, 138, 139
Boud, David, 7, 23, 60–61
Bower, Laurel L., 128
Brannon, Lil, 12, 21, 29, 30
Breuch, Lee-Ann K., 49–50, 87
Brew, Angela, 23
Bromley, Pam, 28
Brown, Evelyn, 45
budgets, higher education, 40, 41, 150, 151
business writing, 45, 63, 118, 122, 125–26

campus policies, curriculum, 40–41, 149, 151
campus writing centers: constructivist approach, 21; ESL/EFL, 29; feedback, 57–59, 131; funding, 150, 151; future writing context, 58–59; high school to college transition, 148; response constructs, 22, 28–29, 150; staffing, 141, 142, 143; tutors, 37–38

praise/critique feedback, *8,* 43–44, 72–74, 100–2, *103,* 104, *130*
pre-draft feedback, 22
preference, teacher, 129
Price, Margaret, 48
print response, *8,* 22, *130*
Prior, Paul, 36
Probst, Robert E., 23
process memos, 144; drafts in progress, 113, 125, 134; ePortfolios, 18, 63; first-year writing students, 113; peer response, 95–98; self-assessments, 125–28; writing development, 61, 125, 131, 145
processes, response constructs, *8,* 22, 35–36, *130*
products, response constructs, *8,* 22, 35–36, *130*
professional genre, 88–89, 143–47
proficiency level of student, 37
program coordinators/directors, 142, 143
public genres, 88–89, 143, 145
Purchase, Helen, 26

qualitative data/quantitative data. *See* data analysis/data collection
Quinn, DJ, 13, 74

racial bias, 31, 38–39, 41, 128, 132, 135, 139
Rahimi, Mohammad, 27
reading journals, 143
Reading Student Writing, 38
(Re)Articulating Writing Assessment for Teaching and Learning, 8
reductive view in academic discourse, 143
reflection essays, 144; artifacts, 15; business writing, 45, 63, 118, 122, 125–26; course activities, 16, 120–21; drafts in progress, 116, 117; ePortfolios, 10, 11, 125, 137, 149; first-year writing students, 113, 120, 123–24; genre writing 45; goal setting, 23; growth and transfer, 13, 24, 36, 63–64, 117; midterm, 116, 117; models, 90, 128; narrative of progress, 117; peer response, 18, 93–94, 119–20, 125, 133–34; research, 6; revisions, 23, 117; rhetorical strategies, 121; scripts, 90, 128; self-assessment, 23, 36; sequencing, 137; sociopolitical factors, 24; students of color, 128; teacher response, 117, 134, *127,* Writing About Writing (WAW), 148; writing as a process, 118–19, 145
requirements. *See* general education requirements
research: anonymity, 53; bias, 139; campus policies, 40–41; classroom dynamics, 40; constructivist heuristic, 6–7, *8,* 14, 21, 24, 27, 53, 129, *130,* 132; cross-disciplinary writing, 140; culture, influence of, 41–42; data collection/analysis, 9–11, 12–15, 138; empirical research on response, 12, 20, 21, 40, 45, 48, 52, 130; ethnographic studies, 140; evolution, 14, 52, 138; findings validation, 13; human rights subject status, 12; Institutional Review Board (IRB), 12; institutions, influence on, 40–41; international, 7–9, 12–13, 17, 20, 22, 25, 32, 34, 44, 136; L1/L2 literature, 40; limitations, 15–17; linguistic analysis, 138; participants, 154–55; results, 20–21; snowballing, 20–21; student-centered, 14–15, 18–19, 22, 138; topic sensitivity, 12. *See also* data analysis/data collection
response constructs, 8, 22, 130; asynchronous, 50, 51, 110, 134; audiences, 22, 32–33, 99; campus student writing guide, 148; collaboration, 134; contextual factors, 139; course design, 129, 146–47; digital, 87; disciplinary genres, 88–89, 142, 143, 144, 145, 148; face-to-face conferences, 7, 8, 22, 27, 32, 49, 50, 130; faculty development, 150; first-year writing program, 138; grading system, 18, 131–32; peer response, 21–22, 24–28, 111, 142, 144–45; processes and products, *8,* 22, *130;* self-assessment, 7, 21–24; service-learning courses, 148; shared rubrics, 137, 148; sociocultural context, 22; student literary history, 37, 120; student-centered, 5–6, 17, 20, 22, 28, 37, 52, 128, 136, 142; teacher-centered, 3–4, 6, 21, 89, 144–45; transfer, 7, *8,* 22, 34–35, 89, *130,* 136, 137, 147; tutors, 22, 28–32
"Responding to Student Writing," 43, 70
revisions: drafts in progress, 21, 76–78, 80–82, 105; ESL/EFL, 49; final drafts, 49, 77–78, 119–20, 125, 144; future writing, 82–83; genre conventions, 67–68; grading, 48, 119–20, 132; NNES, 48–49; peer response, 48, 64, 104, 106, 109, 118–20, 125, 137; portfolios, 18; self-assessments, 23, 117, 119–20, 123, 125, 136; teacher feedback, 32, 119–20, 124; writing center tutors, 58; writing process, 117–18, 145
rewriting teacher response, 54, *55*
rhetorical situation, 24, 36, 121–22, 147–48
Richmond, Tyler, 128
Robinson, Sarita, 35